RENAISSANCE SOCIETY OF AMERICA REPRINT TEXTS 8

THE SOCIETY OF RENAISSANCE FLORENCE:

A Documentary Study

Edited by Gene Brucker

Published by University of Toronto Press
Toronto Buffalo London
in association with the Renaissance Society of America

The edition is reprinted from the 1971 Harper & Row edition by
arrangement with Gene A. Brucker.

Printed on acid-free paper

Canadian Cataloguing in Publication Data

Main entry under title:

The society of Renaissance Florence : a documentary study

(Renaissance Society of America reprint texts ; 8)
Includes bibliographical references.
ISBN 0-8020-8079-0
1. Renaissance – Italy – Florence – Sources.
2. Florence (Italy) – Social conditions – Sources. 3. Florence (Italy) –
Economic conditions – Sources. 4. Florence (Italy) – Moral conditions –
Sources.   I. Brucker, Gene A.   II. Renaissance Society of America.
III. Series.

HN488.F56B77 1998   306'.0945'5109024   C97-932012-7

University of Toronto Press acknowledges the financial
assistance to its publishing program of the Canada Council
for the Arts and the Ontario Arts Council.

University of Toronto Press acknowledges the financial
support for its publishing activities of the Government of Canada
through the Book Publishing Industry Development Program (BPIDP).

CONTENTS

Preface   xiii

PART ONE: THE ECONOMIC STRUCTURE   I

I. A PRIMITIVE TAX ASSESSMENT
   1. The Levy of a Forced Loan, Quarter of
      S. Maria Novella, April 1378   4

II. THE *Catasto* OF 1427
   2. The Declaration of Conte di Giovanni
      Compagni   6
   3. The Declaration of Francesco di Messer
      Giovanni Milanese   8
   4. The Declaration of Lorenzo Ghiberti,
      sculptor   10
   5. The Declaration of Agnolo di Jacopo, weaver   12
   6. The Declaration of Biagio di Niccolò, wool
      carder   13

III. ECONOMIC FORTUNE AND SOCIAL MOBILITY
   7. The Mercantile Career of Paolo Morelli,
      d. 1374   14
   8. The Fortunes of Gregorio Dati, d. 1435   15
   9. From Laborer to Entrepreneur, 1399   17
  10. Business Losses and Confiscatory Taxation,
      1442   18
  11. Misfortunes of a Political Exile, 1382   21
  12. The Wreck of a Business Venture, 1408   22

IV. ATTITUDES TOWARD WEALTH

    13. A Cautious Merchant, c. 1400   23

    14. A Rich Patrician, c. 1460   24

    15. Lorenzo de' Medici, the Magnificent   27

PART TWO: THE FAMILY   28

  I. MARRIAGE

    16. The Marriages of Gregorio Dati   29

    17. Two Marriages in the Valori Family, 1452 and 1476   31

    18. Marriage Negotiations: the Del Bene, 1381   32

    19. Marriage Negotiations: the Strozzi, 1464–65   37

    20. Illegitimacy and Marriage, 1355   40

  II. DEATH

    21. Deaths in the Sassetti Family, 1383   42

    22. Deaths in the Panzano Family, 1423–46   44

    23. A Pestilence Victim, 1374   46

    24. The Death of a Son, 1459   47

  III. PROPERTY AND INHERITANCE

    25. The Testament of Fetto Ubertini, 1348   49

    26. The Testament of Michele di Vanni Castellani, c. 1370   52

    27. The Testament of Andrea di Feo, stonemason, 1380   56

    28. Two Petitions for Legitimization, 1388-89   59

    29. The Diminution of an Orphan's Estate, 1397   60

  IV. FAMILY ENMITIES

    30. Father and Son, 1380   62

    31. Son and Father, 1405   64

    32. Disputes Among Heirs, 1385   67

    33. A Broken Marriage, 1377   69

    34. The Murder of a Brother, 1393   70

PART THREE: COLLECTIVITIES 74

I. CORPORATIONS AND COMMUNITY
  35. An Occasion of Solidarity 75
  36. A Community in Disorder 78

II. THE COMMUNE
  37. Civic Spirit 81
  38. A Patriotic Appeal 82
  39. The Dissolution of the Confraternities, 1419 83

III. THE PARTE GUELFA
  40. A Guelf Association, c. 1350 84
  41. Guelfs and Ghibellines, 1347 86
  42. The Decline of the Parte Guelfa, 1413 88

IV. THE GUILDS
  43. The Corporation of Wine Merchants 90
  44. A Charitable Enterprise, 1421 92
  45. Guild Rivalry, 1425 93

PART FOUR: VIOLENCE AND ITS CONTROL 95

I. PATTERNS OF VIOLENCE
  46. A Soldier's Crimes, 1379 97
  47. A Private Quarrel, 1396 98
  48. The Exploits of a Highwayman, 1391 99
  49. The Depredations of a Magnate, 1404 101
  50. An Escapade in the Apennines, 1400 104

II. THE VENDETTA
  51. The Medieval Inheritance 106
  52. The Strozzi and the Lenzi, 1387–92 111
  53. The Revenge of Luca da Panzano, 1420 116
  54. The Decline of the Vendetta, 1420 119

III. *Prepotenza*
  55. A Despoiler of Property, 1377 120
  56. An Assault Upon a Peasant Family, 1381 122

57. The Terror of the Countryside, 1381　　123
58. A Powerful Family: the Strozzi　　125
59. A Career of Violence: Simone Guicciardini,
　　c. 1395　　127

IV. AUTHORITY AND ITS ABUSE

60. The Offenses of a Magistrate, 1382　　130
61. The Maladministration of the *Contado*　　131
62. An Official Reprimand, 1418　　132
63. The Misdeeds of a Rector, 1461　　133
64. The Abuse of Clerical Authority, 1415　　137

PART FIVE: CRIME AND PUNISHMENT　　139

I. CRIMES OF GRAVITY

65. Greed and Uxoricide　　140
66. Passion and Uxoricide　　142
67. Infanticide　　146
68. Forgery and Homicide　　147
69. Incest and Sacrilege　　150
70. The Career of a Professional Criminal　　153

II. CRIMES OF SUBTLETY

71. An Artful Swindler　　156
72. The Alchemist　　157
73. Extortion　　159
74. A Forger　　162

III. PRISON

75. Inmates of the Stinche　　166

IV. DIMINISHED RESPONSIBILITY: INSANITY

76. A Demented Woman　　168
77. A Plea of Insanity　　170
78. A Sacrilegious Act　　172

V. MERCY AND ITS RATIONALE

79. Religious Enthusiasm and the Release of Prisoners   174
80. The Plea of an Adulteress   175
81. The Excuse of Poverty   176
82. A Juvenile Delinquent   177

PART SIX: PUBLIC MORES   179

I. SUMPTUARY LEGISLATION

83. The Fiscal Rationale, 1373   179
84. The Social Rationale, 1433   180
85. Prosecutions and Penalties, 1378–97   181

II. GAMBLING

86. The Clientele   183
87. A Compulsive Gambler   186

III. PROSTITUTION

88. The Establishment of Communal Brothels, 1415   190
89. Profits of Prostitution   190
90. Prostitutes and the Courts, 1398–1400   191
91. The Recruitment of Prostitutes, 1379   196
92. A Panderer's Career   199

IV. SODOMY

93. Civic Opinion, 1415   201
94. Legislation Against the Vice, 1418   202
95. Establishment of a Magistracy to Extirpate Sodomy, 1432   203
96. Convictions and Penalties   204

V. THE SURVEILLANCE OF THE CONVENTS

97. Civic Responsibility for Conventual Purity   206
98. A Delinquent Priest   207

99. A Foreign Intruder   208
100. Temptation   209
101. A Penitent   211

PART SEVEN: THE *Popolo Minuto*   213

  I. TRIBULATIONS OF THE POOR
    102. Harassment of Workers in the Cloth In-
         dustry   214
    103. An Imprisoned Pauper   216
    104. A Marginal Subsistence   217
    105. The Story of the Servant Girl Nencia   218

  II. SERVITUDE
    106. Slavery Legalized, 1364   222
    107. The Search for Slaves   223
    108. Christians Forced into Servitude   223
    109. The Tribulations of a Slave Girl   224

  III. SUCCOR FOR THE INDIGENT
    110. Pensions for Retired Employees   229
    111. Plague, Famine, and Civic Disorder   229
    112. The Distribution of Alms   231

  IV. VOICES OF THE POOR
    113. Appeal for Tax Relief   233
    114. Justice for the Poor   234
    115. The Condemnation of a Labor Organizer,
         1345   235
    116. The Demands of the Ciompi, 1378   236

PART EIGHT: ABERRANTS AND OUTGROUPS   240

  I. THE JEWS
    117. Early Communal Legislation on the Jews   240
    118. Regulation of the Jewish Community, 1463   241
    119. The Condemnation of a Jewish Physician   243
    120. The Transgressions of a Seditious Jew, 1434   245

121. Extortion and Betrayal, 1435   246
122. Anti-Semitism and the Commune, 1488–93   248

II. HERETICS
123. Legislation Against the Fraticelli, 1382   250
124. Fraticelli Sympathizers and the Inquisition,
         1383   252
125. The Execution of Fra Michele of Calci, 1389   253
126. The Unorthodox Views of a Priest, 1418   257
127. The Prosecution of Giovanni Cani, 1450   258

III. SORCERERS
128. The Enchantress   260
129. The Professional Sorcerer   261
130. A Sorcerer *Manqué*   266
131. A Sorcerer and His Clientele   268
132. A Witch's Career   270
Select Bibliography   275

PREFACE

The origins of this documentary collection go back to my first visit to the Florentine *Archivio di Stato* in the early 1950s. Like all students who work for extended periods in the *Archivio,* I soon became aware of the magnitude of its resources, and the broad range of historical problems which could be explored there. In searching for material on my dissertation subject, political conflict in Florence before and after the Black Death, I came across documents which were not germane to my thesis, but which provided fascinating insights into the social world of fourteenth-century Florence. Private letters and diaries constituted a particularly fruitful category of source materials; but public documents, particularly the records of the criminal courts, also yielded their quota of enlightening information: the trial record of an accused sorcerer, the petition of a tax delinquent, the anonymous denunciation of a magnate by his maltreated victim. Initially, I copied the references to these documents in a desultory and haphazard fashion; later, my investigation of the sources of Florentine social history became more rational and systematic. Five years ago, I began to organize this material into coherent patterns, and to translate and edit the documents (both printed and archival) which I selected to illustrate aspects of Florentine society in the fourteenth and fifteenth centuries.

Certain assumptions and premises underlie the selection

and organization of this material. I have rarely chosen documents which indicate how Florentines thought about their social order; rather, I have tried to illustrate modes of behavior, and particularly, the tensions between individuals and the community. I have been guided by the counsel of a distinguished Catalan historian, Jaime Vicens Vives: "Neither regulations, nor privileges, nor laws, nor constitutions, bring us close to human reality. These are formulas that establish limits, but nothing more than limits. The expression of life is to be found in the application of the law, statute, decree, or regulation. . . . Instead of the great collections of law, historians should consult archives where law clashes with life—notarial protocols, consular and commercial records, police archives, law-court decisions and so on."* The records of Florence's criminal courts are well represented in this documentary collection, for several reasons. They describe people in trouble, men and women who had violated (or who were charged with violating) society's norms. They indicate the extremes to which they were driven, and often the motives which inspired them. They also reveal the price which society exacted for behavior which it condemned. In describing so many varieties of social problems, these sources instruct us about the general conditions of European life in these years, as well as the distinctive characteristics of Florentine urban existence. They also tell dramatic stories, and I have made a conscious effort to select material which reveals something about the emotions, passions, and temperaments of Renaissance Florentines.

These documents are examples of the raw material with which the historian works, as he attempts to describe social

* *Approaches to the History of Spain,* trans. and ed. by Joan Connelly Ullman (Berkeley and Los Angeles, 1967), p. xvii.

structures, patterns of behavior, and value systems. They should convey some sense of the complexity of this society, and of the formidable task which confronts the student who seeks to generalize about its character. The discerning reader will also become aware of the great range and variety of material which can be exploited to learn about an urban community in these centuries. While it is true that the documentation for Florentine history is exceptionally abundant, probably richer than for any other city in Renaissance Europe, these sources do have their parallels and counterparts in other municipal archives. They can serve as models for the student interested in the problems of urban history in pre-industrial Europe.

While these sources tell us much about the society of Renaissance Florence, they do not reveal the whole story. Some dimensions are missing; others can be perceived only dimly and imperfectly. Most fully described, in this collection and in the archives, is the life style of those Florentines who were affluent, socially prominent, and literate. Such people left private records (letters, diaries, and testaments), some part of which has survived, and they also left their mark in the public records. By contrast, we know very little about the workers and the poor who made up more than one-half of the city's population. Only incidentally do priests, monks, and nuns appear in these documents; their world formed a very distinct enclave in this secular community. There are other, more fundamental limitations to comprehension which derive from the nature of this material. From the initial transcription to the final translation, these documents have passed through a series of filters, each of which may have distorted the original "reality." How accurate, for example, are the accounts of conversations copied by notaries in criminal investigations (no. 66)? How much credence can be placed in the testimony of an accused person who is being tortured (no. 73)? Is there any value in the unverified denunciation of an anonymous citizen who accused a magnate of assault (no. 56)? How much hyperbole is contained in the public statements of citizens who proclaim their devotion to the republic and their willingness to sacrifice their fortunes for its benefit (no. 37)?

It is particularly difficult, in a source collection, to show how people and institutions change over time. A document defines a unique situation, at a particular moment. Rarely can circumstances be duplicated so neatly in a later source that one can discern a significant change in attitude, value, or social pattern. Yet this society was constantly being transformed, as it reacted to demographic and economic imperatives, to political conditions, to changing needs and aspirations. It seems probable, for example, that life and property were more secure in Florence in 1450 than a century earlier, that violence was not as endemic in the Medici period (1434-94) as it had been at the time of the Black Death (1348). The documents printed here do not make this point clearly, although they do suggest how the problem might be confronted and perhaps solved by a careful and systematic analysis of these materials. For example, an exploitation of private and official sources could reveal whether Luca da Panzano's vendetta in 1420 (no. 53) was a common and frequent occurrence in the fifteenth century, or whether the settlement arranged in the same year between Antonio Rustichi and Simone Buonarroti (no. 54) was a more typical response. It is my hope that these documents will raise such questions, even if they do not always provide answers.

Gene Brucker
Berkeley, California, June 1970

The Society of Renaissance Florence

PART ONE

THE ECONOMIC STRUCTURE

The analysis of any human society properly begins with a study of its material foundations. How do the members of a community earn their livelihood? What are the community's resources? How are these exploited and how distributed? Florence has attracted the lively interest of economic historians who have been intrigued by the importance of the city's role in European trade, banking, and industry in the late medieval and Renaissance period, and who have been able to command a wide range of source materials. These sources include the account books of mercantile companies, the private papers of families and individuals, and the records of corporate organizations: guilds, the merchants' court, the Commune, ecclesiastical foundations.

Valuable data on the economic structure of this community of some fifty thousand inhabitants are found in the assessments of taxes and forced loans which were levied by the Commune upon the citizenry in the fourteenth and fifteenth centuries. While these assessments (no. 1) are only rough estimates, they do provide some information about the economic and social configurations of this community. In 1427, the Commune instituted a new method of tax assessment, the *catasto*. Each householder was required to submit to the fiscal authorities a complete record of his property holdings: real estate, communal bonds, cash on hand, investments in businesses, money borrowed and loaned. These tax records have survived almost intact for the fifteenth century, and they constitute a source (nos. 2–6) of unparalleled richness for investigating Florence's demographic and economic structure. Evidence culled from these inventories and from other sources (nos. 7–12) identifies the rich Florentines and the poor, and the many gradations between these extremes. It also provides clues to such complex problems as economic vicissitudes and social mobility, and the attitudes toward wealth which were characteristic of this society.

Some basic information on Florentine money, prices, and wages will assist the reader in interpreting these economic records. The Florentine mint struck both gold and silver coins. The florin contained 3.536 grams of gold, worth approximately $4 at today's price, but worth far more in terms of purchasing power. Independent of the florin was a monetary system based upon the silver pound or lire, a money of account and not a real coin in Florence. The lire was divided into 20 soldi (shillings), each soldo into 12 denari (pence). During the fourteenth and fifteenth centuries, the florin gradually increased in value, in terms of silver money. In 1400, a florin was worth about 75 soldi or 3¾ lire. Unskilled laborers earned 7–10 soldi per day; skilled craftsmen might receive as much as one lire for a day's work. Civil servants in minor administrative posts received an average annual salary of 70 florins, while senior officials in the communal bureaucracy might earn 300 florins annually. The cost of food and housing was low, by our standards. A *staio* (.7 bushel) of wheat cost 15 soldi in times of plenty, but as much as 60 soldi during a famine. A small cottage on the city's outskirts might rent for 1 or 2 florins annually; houses of more ample dimensions in the city center rented for 20–50 florins per year.

Many of the items in this collection are official documents, the deliberations and enactments of agencies of the Communal government. A brief account of that government's structure and function will provide some context for these sources. The chief executive magistracy of the Commune was the priorate or Signoria, composed of nine men selected from lists of eligible citizens for two-month terms of office. In making executive decisions and in formulating legislation to be presented to the councils, the priors were assisted by two collegiate groups, the Sixteen Standard-bearers of the Militia Companies (*gonfalonieri delle compagnie*) and the Twelve Good Men (*dodici buonuomini*). Policy discussions by these collegiate bodies and by other citizens were recorded in the volumes of the *Consulte e Pratiche*. This is a valuable source for civic opinion on social issues (nos. 38, 43, 93). Legislative proposals were submitted by the Signoria to two councils. If a measure obtained a two-thirds vote in both councils, it was enacted into law, and was recorded in the volumes of the *Provvisioni* (nos. 40, 88, 94). Private petitions also required the two-thirds approval of the Signoria and the colleges, and the councils (nos. 11, 12, 28). Executive authority in the Commune did not rest exclusively in the hands of the Signoria. Some was delegated to magistracies with special functions and responsibilities; for example, the officials empowered to revise tax assessments (no. 10), and those responsible for eradicating the vice of sodomy (no. 95).

All dates in these sources are New Style.

I. A Primitive Tax Assessment

1. THE LEVY OF A FORCED LOAN, QUARTER OF S. MARIA NOVELLA; APRIL, 1378*

[Figures are in florins, soldi, denari.]

Luca di Vanni, cobbler	1–11–4
Benedetto di Arrigo Altoviti	0–19–6
Ruggiero di Sandro, messenger	0–11–6
Giovanni di Bartolo, leather dealer	0–10–4
Francesco di Amerigo, leather dealer	1–12–2
Gagliardo di Neri Bonciani	35–16–0
Ser Tegghaio di Ugo Altoviti	7–12–4
Giovanni di Rosso Buondelmonti	14–1–2
Giovanni di Filippo Carducci	4–10–0
Ambrogio di Niccolò, leather merchant	2–3–2
Taddo di Neri, embroiderer	0–19–0
Messer Francesco and Esau di Messer Manente Buondelmonti	68–19–0
Francesco di Arignuoli, leather merchant	2–8–6
Gianni di Giovanni, tailor	0–8–8
Marco and Bartolo di Bartolo Bonciani	32–17–0
Donato di Albizo Acciaiuoli	1–9–0
Lodovico di Adoardo Acciaiuoli	3–9–4
Dardo di Domenico Bonciani	2–1–6
Leone and Michele di Zanobi Acciaiuoli	9–13–4
Alamanno di Messer Alamanno Acciaiuoli	2–15–4

* Source: *Archivio di Stato, Firenze* [*ASF*], *Prestanze,* 334, fols. 8r–10r, 11v.

Giovanni and Michele Naldi, and Arrigo Gucci	6-1-0
Andrea di Tano, messenger	0-10-4
Ser Tommaso Redditi	2-3-10
Naldo and Jacopo di Ser Stefano Casciani	6-18-6
Simone di Messer Tommaso Altoviti	11-8-0
Biagio and Francesco di Messer Giovanni of Milan	58-17-4
Giovanni di Perozzo Altoviti	5-15-0
Antonio di Naldino Altoviti	3-4-6
Domenico di Donato, baker	0-13-10
Filippo di Giunta called Lagrimio	0-8-4
Niccolò di Gherardo, laborer in a furrier shop	0-10-4
Stanietto, servant	0-8-8
Bartolo di Corsello, leather merchant	4-5-4
Filippo Foraboschi, blanket-maker	42-15-5
Ser Viviano di Nero Viviani	3-3-4
Stefano di Salvino, knife-maker	1-0-9
Francesco di Mico, messenger	0-6-2
Sandro di Gentile Altoviti	6-4-6
Leonardo and Bindo di Messer Rainieri Altoviti	2-13-0
Ser Piero di Ser Stefano Casciani	4-10-0
Simone and Stoldo di Messer Bindo Altoviti	37-0-0
Agnolo di Panze, cloth trimmer	0-8-8
Francesco Cavallini	2-8-6
Piero di Fastello and Jacopo di Ubaldino Petriboni	42-14-0
Monna Giovanna di Andrea Cantini	0-17-4
Biagio, cloth-beater	0-10-10
Lodovico di Jacopo Giandonati	5-15-0
Monna Tana and Monna Filippa Giandonati	1-16-0
Giovanni di Piero Giandonati	3-2-6

II. *The Catasto of 1427*

2. THE DECLARATION
OF CONTE DI GIOVANNI COMPAGNI*

[Figures are in florins, soldi, denari.]

Assets of Conte di Giovanni Compagni. . .

A house with furnishings which I inhabit, located in
the parish of S. Trinita on the street of the Lungarno
[not taxable] ⌐ dino Compagni lived there   o

A house in the parish of S. Trinita on the street of
the Lungarno . . . which is rented to Niccolò and
Tommaso Soderini for 24 florins per year, [capitalized]
at 7 percent   342-17-2

A house on the Lungarno in that parish . . . rented
to Giovanni di Simone Vespucci for 24 florins per year,
[capitalized] at 7 percent   342-17-2

A house located in that street . . . rented to Michele
di Piero Dini for 12 florins per year. . . .   171-8-9

Two shops . . . with courtyards and basements for
selling wine, located in the parish of S. Agostino in the
Via de' Terni . . . rented to Daddo di Zanobi, wineseller, for 20 florins per year. . . .   285-14-6

One-half of two-thirds of some shops in the palace of
the Aretti of Pisa. . . . My share [of the rent] is 28
florins per year, more or less. . . .   400-0-0

A farm in the parish of S. Maria a Quarto . . . 238-11-6

A farm in the parish of S. Giorgio in the *contado* of

* Source: *ASF, Catasto*, 75, fols. 214r–216r.

Prato, with laborer's cottage, including several plots of
vineyard and pieces of woodland adjacent to the farm.
. . . Bartolomeo di Filippo cultivates this farm; he has
borrowed 38½ florins [from me] and he keeps a pair
of oxen at his risk. . . . [The farm is valued at]   353-15-2

A small farm in the Valdimarina in the parish of
S. Margherita a Torre with a villa and a laborer's cottage and olive trees and woods [valued at]   139-13-0

A piece of woodland [valued at]   35-14-0

He [Conte] has invested in a shop of the Lana
[woolen cloth manufacturers] guild in the company
of Michele di Benedetto di Ser Michele, the sum of

                                                  2000-0-0

In another account with Michele in that shop, he is
to receive   911-0-0

And in another account, he is to receive   66-0-0

Money which is owed to him by:

    Francesco and Niccolò Tornabuoni   1130-0-0
    Bartolomeo Peruzzi and company   335-5-0
    Lorenzo di Messer Palla Strozzi and
      company   465-0-0
    Michele Dini   75-0-0
    Lorenzo di Messer Palla [Strozzi]
      and company   500-0-0
    Michele di Benedetto di Ser Michele   325-0-0
    Giovanni and Rinaldo Peruzzi and company   17-2-0

[Compagni estimated his holdings in *Monte* shares
(communal bonds) and accrued interest at   4390-3-0

He also estimated that he would collect only 500
florins of some 1,079 florins owed to him by delinquent
debtors.]   500-0-0

Obligations

Money owed to:

Creditors of Gino	39–0–0
Giovanni and Rinaldo di Rinieri Peruzzi	33–0–0
Lorenzo di Messer Palla [Strozzi] and company	118–18–6
Lorenzo di Messer Palla and company	45–11–0
Baldo, my servant	12–0–0
Marco di Bernardo and company, druggists	15–0–0
Monna Guida of the Mugello, my servant	10–0–0
[other obligations]	128–11–6

Personal exemptions:

Conte, aged 61	200–0–0
Monna Nanna, his wife	200–0–0
Ilarione, his son, aged 15	200–0–0
Giovanni, his son, aged 11	200–0–0

[Total estimated value of Conte's taxable assets]	
	13,039–6–3
[Total debts and exemptions]	1,202–1–0
[Net assets subject to taxation]	11,837–5–3

3. THE DECLARATION
OF FRANCESCO DI MESSER GIOVANNI MILANESE*

One-fourth of a cloth factory. . . Bartolomeo Cor-
binelli operated this shop and paid a rent of 42 florins,
but he didn't want to pay that much and he left on
March 6, 1425. Since then, the shop has been closed . . .

    150–0–0

* Source: *ASF, Catasto*, 74, fols. 149v–150v.

One-half of a cottage, which I inhabit, with . . . orchard in the parish of S. Michele a Castello.   o

An adjoining vineyard in the same parish. The vine-yard is cultivated by Fede di Domenico . . .   64-0-0

One house with vineyard in the same parish. . . . I receive a rent of 9 florins   128-11-0

One peasant's cottage in the same parish with vine-yard . . .   163-8-0

In Tunis, I commissioned Piero di Ser Naddo to ar-range for the shipment of 204 bales of wool to Pisa on the ship owned by Giovanni Uzzino. But this wool was never loaded and it remained at the port. It was a total loss, and was valued at 600 florins or more. I have not yet been able to investigate the cause of this loss. . . . Since my return from Tunis, I have been unable to pur-sue this matter on account of the litigation in which I have been involved . . .   o

Also, this Piero di Ser Naddo received 150 florins from Bernardo di Caccione which he was obligated to give me in Tunis but did not. I believe that Bernardo paid him that money without any letter or instruction from me. I have not yet legally demanded the return of that money but have only made an oral request. . . . I don't know how this will end. When this business is settled, I will inform the authorities.   o

Also, Marco di Messer Forese Salviati and company owe me 100 florins or thereabouts, the price of leather which I sent him from Tunis. . . . This debt is not yet settled, but I fear that I will not be repaid, and I don't expect to win a lawsuit against them since they are very influential.   o

[Milanese estimated that his holdings of *Monte* shares amounted to 65 florins.]   65-0-0

Obligations

[Milanese estimated his commercial and personal debts at 115 florins.]   115–0–0

Personal exemptions:

Francesco, aged 56	200–0–0
Monna Ginevra, his wife, aged 50	200–0–0
Antonio, his son, aged 27	200–0–0
Bernardo, his son, aged 24	200–0–0
Michele, his son, aged 21	200–0–0
Gabriello, his son, aged 7	200–0–0
[Total estimated value of Giovanni's taxable assets]	572–7–0
[Total debts and exemptions]	1315–0–0

4. THE DECLARATION
OF LORENZO GHIBERTI,
SCULPTOR*

. . . A house located in the parish of S. Ambrogio in Florence in the Via Borgo Allegri . . . with household furnishings for the use of myself and my family . . .   0

A piece of land in the parish of S. Donato in Franzano . . .   100–0–0

In my shop are two pieces of bronze sculpture which I have made for a baptismal font in Siena. . . . I estimate that they are worth 400 florins or thereabouts, of which sum I have received 290 florins; so the balance is 110 florins.   110–0–0

---

* Source: G. Gaye, *Carteggio inedito d'artisti dei secoli XIV, XV, XVI* (Florence, 1839–40), I, 103–05.

Also in my shop is a bronze casket which I made for Cosimo de' Medici; I value it at approximately 200 florins, of which I have received 135 florins. The balance owed to me is 65 florins.   65-0-0

I have investments in the *Monte* of 714 florins.   714-0-0

I am still owed 10 florins by the Friars of S. Maria Novella for the tomb of the General [of the Dominican Order, Lionardo Dati].

Obligations

Personal exemptions:

Lorenzo di Bartolo, aged 46	200-0-0
Marsilia, my wife, aged 26	200-0-0
Tommaso, my son, aged 10 or thereabouts	200-0-0
Vettorio, my son, aged 7 or thereabouts	200-0-0

I owe money to the following persons:

Antonio di Piero del Vaglente and company, goldsmiths	33-0-0
Nicola di Vieri de' Medici	10-0-0
Domenico di Tano, cutler	9-0-0
Niccolò Carducci and company, retail cloth merchants	7-0-0
Papi d'Andrea, cabinet-maker	16-0-0
Mariano da Gambassi, mason	7-0-0
Papero di Meo of Settignano (my apprentices	
Simone di Nanni of Fiesole in	48-0-0
Cipriano di Bartolo of Pistoia the shop)	
Antonio, called El Maestro, tailor	15-0-0
Domenico di Lippi, cutler	2-0-0
Alessandro Allesandri and company	4-0-0
Duccio Adimari and company, retail cloth merchants	8-0-0

Antonio di Giovanni, stationer	3–0–0
Isau d'Agnolo and company, bankers	50–0–0
Commissioners in charge of maintenance and rebuilding of the church of S. Croce	6–0–0
Lorenzo di Bruciane, kiln operator	3–0–0
Meo of S. Apollinare	45–0–0
Pippo, stocking maker	8–0–0
[Total of Lorenzo's taxable assets]	999–0–0
[Total obligations and exemptions]	1074–0–0

5. THE DECLARATION
OF AGNOLO DI JACOPO,
WEAVER*

He and his mother own a house, in which they live, in the Via Chiara . . .	0
A loom which we operate, valued at	40–0–0
Giano di Masotto owes me	3–5–0
Antonio di Fastello, parish of S. Stefano, owes me	25–0–0
Michele di Piero Serragli owes me	21–0–0
Niccolò di Andrea del Benino owes me	15–8–0

Obligations

Personal exemptions:

Agnolo di Jacopo, aged 30	200–0–0
Mea, his wife, aged 28	200–0–0
Taddea, his mother, aged 72	200–0–0
I owe Giano di Manetto	3–5–0
[Agnolo's taxable assets]	104–13–0
[His obligations and exemptions]	603–5–0

* Source: *ASF, Catasto*, 66, fol. 178r.

6. THE DECLARATION
OF BIAGIO DI NICCOLÒ,
WOOL CARDER*

He owns one-third of a house in the parish of _____;
his father bought it for 30 florins. . . . He lives in it.   o
    One-half of a cottage located in the Via delle Ro-
mite. He receives 3¼ florins of rent annually   46–0–0
    Next to the cottage is a small piece of garden . . .   0–8–8

Obligations

He owes Braccio di Giovanni, cloth manufacturer   20–0–0

Personal exemptions:

    Biagio di Niccolò   200–0–0
    Monna Fiora, his wife   200–0–0
    Gemma, his daughter, aged 9   200–0–0
    Chola, his daughter, aged 5   200–0–0

He pays rent on the two-thirds of his house
    which he does not own . . .   14–5–0

    [Biagio's taxable assets]   65–18–8
    [His obligations and exemptions]   834–5–10

---

* Source: *ASF, Catasto*, 75, fol. 247v.

III. *Economic Fortune and Social Mobility*

7. THE MERCANTILE CAREER OF PAOLO MORELLI, D. 1374*

[Giovanni Morelli describes the business career of his father Paolo (1335-1374).] His brothers all died of the plague in the great epidemic of 1363; they all died within the space of twenty days. . . . Two [brothers] were involved in the woad trade and in dyeing: they had investments of some 15,000 florins [in these enterprises]. . . . The third brother . . . was a usurer and he did little else. He lent money in Florence and in the *contado* [the rural district around the city], to poor laborers and also to great and powerful men. . . .

Paolo, young, inexperienced, and alone . . . frightened by the death of his [brothers] and in fear of his own life, found himself in great confusion as a result of the need to collect credits worth thousands of florins. Many of the creditors and the employees of the company, who had their affairs in their heads, had died. Paolo had to search for these credits in Florence and the *contado*, and beyond, in Arezzo, Borgo [S. Sepulcro], Siena, Pisa, and in other foreign parts. He also had to retrieve merchandise and sell it and take charge of everything. . . . He had to recover capital investments, and the usurious loans made by Calandro in various parts of Florence and the *contado*. Concerning this, he was involved in litigation with the bishop and with prominent citizens of Florence. . . . In addition to this, he was

* Source: The diary of Giovanni Morelli; *Istoria fiorentina di Ricardano Malespini coll'aggiunta di Giachetto e la cronica di Giovanni Morelli* (Florence, 1718), pp. 238–40.

engaged in the manufacture of woolen cloth, as a partner of Tommaso di Guccio and others. He was also involved in *Monte* investments, in exchange and letters of credit, in the importation of French wool, and many other enterprises. . . .

He administered all of his affairs prudently . . . and if it had pleased God to give him another ten years of life, he would have become rich and would have amassed a fortune of 50,000 florins. . . . But just when his affairs were flourishing, he rendered his soul to God, on June 14, 1374. He had been married for ten years and six months. . . . In his testament, he bequeathed property worth 20,000 florins. . . . He was buried with great honors in S. Croce, in the tomb with his father and brothers. . . .

8. The Fortunes of Gregorio Dati, D. 1435*

. . . I was born on April 15, 1362. . . . I began to work in the silk business in 1375. . . . On January 1, 1385 I was made a partner in the business and was supposed to invest 300 florins in it . . . [but] I was already in debt for more than that. . . . In 1388 I got married and received a dowry and was able to pay off the debt that year, as well as furnishing the house decently and keeping almost within my capital. In 1390, my wife Bandecca died and I went to Valencia for the company. I returned in 1392. We had done well during this period, but due to the bad debt that Giovanni Stefani contracted with our company, I found myself rather short of money. In 1393, I married my second

* Source: The diary of Gregorio Dati; *Two Memoirs of Renaissance Florence*, trans. Julia Martines, ed. G. Brucker (New York, 1967), pp. 138–41.

wife. . . . The dowry was substantial but I spent too much In 1394 I was captured and robbed at sea and suffered considerable losses. . . . I went into partnership with Michele [di Ser Parente] in 1396. . . . And I did very well up to the year 1402 . . . When I parted company with Michele, I had about 1,000 florins. . . . I went into partnership with Piero Lana and engaged myself to invest 2,000 florins. . . .

At this point, fortune turned against me. Simone [Dati, Gregorio's brother] had gone into business on his own account in Valencia and was involved in transactions with the King of Castile. I let him have great quantities of merchandise and bills of exchange for large sums of money. I had been against his engaging in this activity, but he was convinced that he was right. He let our company in for trouble, litigation, and losses so that we went deeply into debt and were on the point of going bankrupt. I had to join him in Spain in 1408, and spent almost three years there and in Valencia, recovering only a tiny portion of our losses. . . . Our company lost over 10,000 florins in this affair, which swallowed up all our capital. . . .

After reaching the settlement with Piero Lana's heirs in 1412, I found myself in debt for about 3,000 florins. God came to my aid then with the promotion of my brother [Lionardo] who as Father General [of the Dominican Order], was in a position to help me pay off the debt. . . . The sums he paid out to me and in my name up to the year 1420 amounted to 2,330 florins, and he made me a gift of them. There were still 700 florins to be paid off and, as my living expenses during that time amounted to more than that sum, my total debt was 1,500 florins. . . .

I set up in business again and in 1421 I remarried and my wife brought me 600 florins. In the course of 1421 and 1422 the Father General lent me 1,000 florins. . . . I did well so that when we drew up our third balance sheet on January 1, 1424, my own profit came to 1,100 florins. This profit, together with my wife's dowry and what the Father General had lent me, came to 2,700. When I had subtracted the 500 florins for my debt and further sums for expenses, I had about 900 florins left in hand. . . .

9. From Laborer to Entrepreneur, 1399*

[This petition is presented] on behalf of Braccio di Giovanni Bernardi, of the parish of S. Felice in Piazza of Florence, who from childhood to the present day has always worked in the Lana guild, as is common knowledge, with the masters and manufacturers for more than twenty-five years. Now Braccio wishes to better himself and achieve a more honorable status. Through God's grace, he has learned that several manufacturers . . . would be willing to form a partnership with Braccio. But he cannot do this unless he is matriculated in the guild, which is not possible without your benevolence. . . . He humbly and devotedly petitions your lordships . . . to allow Braccio to exercise freely the profession of cloth manufacturer and to be matriculated in the guild . . . if he pays 10 florins to the treasurer of the guild. . . . [The regular matriculation fee was 25 florins.]

[Petition of Francesco di Berto of the parish of S. Piero Maggiore.] Since boyhood to the present time, Francesco has labored in the Lana guild with its guildsmen and manufacturers, for more than twenty-two years. Now he desires to rise to a superior position and to exercise the profession of cloth manufacturer as master and partner, and to become

* Source: *ASF, Arte della Lana*, 48, fol. 34v.

a member of your guild. However, he cannot afford the fee that is required of those who, for the first time, wish to exercise this trade and matriculate in the guild, since he is an indigent person and not well provided with money. [Francesco requests permission to matriculate in the guild upon payment of 10 florins; the petition is approved.]

10. BUSINESS LOSSES AND CONFISCATORY TAXATION; 1442*

To the most honorable officials of the *popolo* and Commune of Florence, elected to impose the tax distribution upon each citizen. . . . We hereby record and certify all of the property, both real and moveable, owned by Manetto and Niccolò, sons of Jacopo Ammanatini, who live in the Via S. Francesco, and who are inscribed in the tax rolls . . . of the quarter of S. Croce, parish of S. Simone of Florence.

To the magnificent, generous, and benevolent commissioners, assembled in public session to examine the accounts of each citizen appealing to you, I who was born and raised in your city consider myself your servant. I appeal to you with faith and security; pure and sincere motives induce me to write you and inform you of our condition. Although I am certain that you have partial knowledge, I wish to inform you in more detail in a regular manner, as well as I am able, with the help of God. . . . [I am] the procurator for the shares of communal bonds owned by Manetto di Jacopo Ammanatini [Niccolò's brother], who lives in the province of Hungary with his wife Lena and two daughters. Consider his living conditions: there is war and discord among the nobles, and the merciless Turks burn and loot villages and

* Source: *Operette istoriche edite ed inedite di Antonio. Manetti,* ed. G. Milanesi (Florence, 1887), pp. xxv–xxxi.

crops. . . . Whoever lives there must avoid falling into their hands, or be forced to deny [the faith] and to lose in one moment all that he owns. Since the country is so wracked and ruined by conflict, few residents have any possessions. Manetto . . . wished to return home, but he could not travel on account of his family and his lack of funds. When the king died, he lost his pension and since that time, he has had only expense and no income.

In summary, to calculate our property in monetary terms, I have recorded . . . the categories of our assets: houses, farms, and communal bonds. The principal bond investment is in the name of Manetto di Jacopo Ammanatini, 3,821 florins, the interest on which is paid in three installments of 47 florins, 2 lire, 10 soldi per year, the regular bond interest. . . . [Ammanatini then lists other small investments in communal bonds of approximately 500 florins.] Then we have a cottage located in the Via de' Macci (also called the Via S. Francesco). . . . There I live with my wife and four small children . . . and my wife is five months pregnant and ill with fever. Consider in what condition I find myself; for I sleep on straw and have nothing with which to cover myself. God knows that it was a brutal tax which was levied upon us: 8 florins, 5 soldi, 9 denari. This is the cause of my family's poverty: the taxes and the babies which we have every year. My wife has no milk and we must hire a wet nurse, and there are expenses for diapers and swaddling clothes and mattresses and pillows and baby dresses and other items. One thing leads to another and one cannot spend less; the expenses are very heavy, more than we estimated.

And I am old now and do not earn anything. My health is poor and I am shortsighted and have twinges of gout . . . as a result of the heavy labor which I endured as a young man when I was employed by Giovanni di Manetto in Por Santa Maria as a ropemaker. For that work ruined me when I was young, carrying rope from Porta S. Frediano to Porta S. Niccolò and hither and yon. And then at night when I was exhausted, for three hours I had to stretch the straw for the rope, inhaling the dust and chaff. Thus my body was tormented by this labor, and if I complained, I received blows from a slat which he had in his hand for making strainers for the olive oil. Therefore, I recommend myself to you, for I am ill and have been poorly treated. I lost my father when I was seven, and we were in great trouble, with our mother at home and Viviano [his brother] apprenticed, and one miserable farm which produced very little and it entails so many expenses that it is a joke. . . .

I must inform you that my farm is of little value; it is rented for 14 florins a year to Andrea di Oderigho, who makes tools for cloth manufacturing. He is the son-in-law of Niccolò di Ruggiero and he lives in a shop in the Via Maffia, and he has the lease for nine years. I am obligated to give the rent to Rinaldo of S. Miniato, Piero Mellini, and Domenico di Gherardino, bankers in the Mercato Nuovo, for they lent me the money to pay the tax levied by Piero Guicciardini. My assessment was 8 florins, 5 soldi, 9 denari, and if I did not pay it, the penalties would have been even greater, so that this assessment ruined my household.

If you understood my condition and my growing family, you would weep. Look at my poor family, and my wife with tertian fever. May God help me, and may He instill mercy and compassion in the hearts of those who can help me. God will regard this with favor and honor, praise and salvation of the soul will result [from this act]. I have nothing further to report; may Christ be with you always.

11. MISFORTUNES OF A POLITICAL EXILE, 1382*

This petition is presented . . . on behalf of the miserable
and poverty-stricken Ser Piero di Ser Guido di Ser Grifo of
the parish of S. Trinita. . . . On account of the turmoil
which occurred in the city of Florence four years ago [the
Ciompi revolution], Ser Piero . . . was deprived of his
offices in the Florentine Commune, and particularly the
office [of notary] of the magistracy in charge of mercenaries,
which he had held. And since he was regarded with suspicion by those who then ruled, he fled from the city and
traveled in various parts of Italy, supporting himself with
difficulty in those bad times. While enduring this beggarly
existence in Rome, he was recalled to his native city when the
Guelfs were restored to power. Although bearing a safe-
conduct from the iniquitous band of Italian freebooters then
occupying Arezzo, he was betrayed and thrown into prison,
chained by his feet, and robbed of his horse, money, and
baggage, worth 100 florins in all. Moreover, he had to pay a
ransom of 300 florins, which he raised in part from his
possessions, and in part by a usurious loan, so that he could
escape from the hands of those evil soldiers. And even though
he was absent from the city of Florence, he paid the forced
loans of the Florentine Commune, despite the fact that his
assessment was too large for his means. . . . But now his
resources have been reduced to zero and he has contracted
usurious debts, so that he can no longer support these assessments. So he appeals to your benign magnificence that, moved

* Source: *ASF, Provvisioni,* 71, fols. 63v–64r.

by pity, you will assist him in his many difficulties. . . .
He requests that he be granted the office of notary of the
magistracy in charge of mercenaries for six months . . .
[Petition approved.]

12. THE WRECK OF A BUSINESS VENTURE, 1408*

This petition is presented . . . on behalf of Angelo di
Giovenco Bastari who, with his brothers, was quite wealthy
after the death of his father. However, on account of the
communal levies which they willingly paid, a large part of
their estate was consumed. Seeing that he was becoming
impoverished, Angelo decided to make his fortune in trade.
So he took part of his estate and invested it all in cloth and
merchandise and began his journey to distant parts, as is
the custom of merchants. . . . While he was staying in
Ancona, he fell ill, and he committed his merchandise into
the care of others whom he had taken with him. . . . Then,
through adverse fortune, he lost nearly everything that he
possessed when the ship on which his merchandise was carried sank during a storm. Now a pauper, he has returned to
his native city, and, hoping to receive help from your benevolence, he has decided to petition you to concede him that
which has not been denied to others. . . . With humility
and devotion, he appeals to your lordships . . . to authorize his appointment . . . as captain of the citadel of S. Miniato Fiorentino for a period of one year, beginning on
October 1 of this year, with the customary salary, perquisites,
staff, and responsibilities. . . . [Petition approved.]

* Source: *ASF, Provvisioni*, 96, fol. 252r.

IV. Attitudes Toward Wealth

13. A Cautious Merchant,
c. 1400*

Don't advertise the fact that you are rich. Instead, do the contrary: if you gain 1,000 florins, say that you have made 500. If you invest 1,000, say the same, and if you are asked about it, say the money belongs to someone else. Don't let your expenditures be a clue to your wealth. If you are worth 10,000 florins, you should maintain a standard of living as though you possessed 5,000. You should demonstrate this in your speech, the clothes which you and your family wear, your food, your servants and horses. And don't reveal your true worth to anyone: neither relatives nor friends nor partners. You should have a secret place in the *contado*, where no one will be aware of it, and where you store oil and other commodities. Don't reveal your wealth by lavish possessions, but buy only what you need for your subsistence. Don't buy farms that are showplaces, but only those which will yield a good return. You should always complain about your taxes: say that your assessment should be halved, that you have large debts and heavy expenses, that you must pay the obligations in your father's will, that you have incurred business losses, that the harvest from your farms is poor, and that you will have to buy grain, wine, wood, and other staples. Don't make these statements so wild that you will be ridiculed, but tell lies which are close to the truth, so that you will be believed and not considered

* Source: *La cronica di Giovanni Morelli,* pp. 268-70.

a liar. . . . And this is quite legitimate, because you are not
lying to steal from another, but rather so that your property
will not be taken from you unjustly.

Don't be careless with your harvest. If you have reaped
a lot, bring to your house only what you need, and a little
at a time. For if you make a great display of it, your neighbor will observe it and will say that you have a thousand
farms, and that you could sell grain, wine, and oil for six
families. [And he will say]: "He can well afford his taxes,
for he has brought enough food into his house to feed a city,
and throughout the year he sells now one thing and now
another." So in this way, you will be considered wealthy
and you will be given a heavy tax assessment. Keep in your
villa [in the country] whatever you wish to sell, and bring
it into the market if you do not wish to be maligned. . . .
For if the poor man sees that you have grain to sell, and that
you are holding it to obtain a better price, he will curse you
and will rob you and burn your house if he can, and all of
the *popolo minuto* will want to harm you, which is very
dangerous. God guard our city from their government!

14. A RICH PATRICIAN, c. 1460*

Now I shall discuss the best way to invest money: whether
it should be all in cash, or all in real estate and communal
bonds, or some in one and some in the other. Now it is true
that money is very difficult to conserve and to handle; it is
very susceptible to the whims of fortune, and few know how

* Source: Alessandro Perosa, editor, *Giovanni Rucellai ed il suo Zibaldone*,
vol. I, "*Il Zibaldone Quaresimale*" (Studies of the Warburg Institute, vol. 24,
London, 1960), pp. 8–9, 11–13, 28–29. Printed by permission of the Warburg Institute.

to manage it. But whoever possesses a lot of money and knows how to manage it is, as they say, the master of the business community because he is the nerve center of all of the trades and commercial activities. For in every moment of adverse fortune, in times of exile and those disasters which occur in the world, those with money will suffer less than those who are well provided with real estate. . . . I would not wish to deny, however, that real estate is more secure and more durable [than money], although occasionally it has been damaged and even destroyed by war, by enemies with fire and sword. Real estate holdings are particularly useful for minors and for others who have no experience in banking. . . . There is nothing easier to lose, nothing more difficult to conserve, more dangerous to invest, or more troublesome to keep, than money. . . . The prudent family head will consider all of his property, and will guard against having it all in one place or in one chest. If war or other disasters occur here, you might still be secure there; and if you are damaged there, then you may save yourself here. . . .

Let me warn you again that in our city of Florence, wealth is conserved only with the greatest difficulty. This is due to the frequent and almost continual wars of the Commune, which have required the expenditure of great sums, and the Commune's imposition of many taxes and forced loans. I have found no better remedy for defending myself than to take care not to gain enemies, for a single enemy will harm you more than four friends will help. I have always remained on good terms with my relatives and neighbors and the other residents of the district, so that whenever the taxes have been assessed, they have befriended me and taken pity on me. In this business, good friends and relatives are very useful. . . . So guard against making enemies or involving yourself in quarrels or disputes. And if someone with gall and arrogance tries to quarrel with you, you should treat him with courtesy and patience. . . .

With respect to good, honest, and virtuous friends, I again counsel you to serve them and be liberal with them. Lend to them, give to them, trust them. . . . And while being liberal and generous to friends, one should occasionally do the same to strangers, so that one will gain a reputation for not being miserly, and also will acquire new friends.

I have told you, my sons, how I have treated good friends, and also how I have treated the swindlers and beggars who daily petition me. Now I must tell you how to respond when, as happens every day, your close relatives make demands on you. It seems to me that one is obligated to help them, not so much with money, as with blood and sweat and whatever one can, even to sacrificing one's life for the honor of the family. One must know how to spend money and to acquire possessions. He who spends only in eating and dressing, or who does not know how to disburse money for the benefit and honor of his family, is certainly not wise. But in these matters, one must use good judgment, because it makes no sense to destroy one's own fortune in order to save that of a relative. . . .

Of necessity, the rich man must be generous, for generosity is the most noble virtue that he can possess, and to exercise it requires wisdom and moderation. Whoever wishes to be regarded as liberal must spend and give away his wealth, for which trait the rich are much liked. . . . But who gives beyond his means soon dissipates his fortune. But if you wish to acquire a reputation for liberality, consider well your resources, the times, the expenses which you must bear, and the qualities of men. According to your means, give to men who are in need and who are worthy. And whoever does otherwise goes beyond the rule of liberality, and does not acquire praise thereby. Whatever you give to the unworthy is lost, and whoever disburses his wealth beyond measure soon experiences poverty.

15. LORENZO DE' MEDICI, THE MAGNIFICENT*

[1469] To do as others had done, I held a joust in the Piazza S. Croce at great expense and with great pomp. I find we spent about 10,000 ducats. . . . Piero, our father, departed this life on July 2 . . . having been much tormented with gout. He would not make a will, but we drew up an inventory and found we possessed 237,988 scudi [a coin worth approximately a florin]. . . .

I find that from 1434 till now we have spent large sums of money, as appear in a small quarto notebook of the said year to the end of 1471. Incredible are the sums written down. They amount to 663,755 florins for alms, buildings, and taxes, let alone other expenses. But I do not regret this, for though many would consider it better to have a part of that sum in their purse, I consider that it gave great honor to our State, and I think the money was well expended, and am well pleased.

---

* Source: J. Ross, *Lives of the Early Medici* (Boston, 1911), pp. 154–55.

PART TWO

THE FAMILY

In Florentine society, the family was the basic unit and the blood tie the most powerful cohesive agent. The obligations of kinship invariably commanded a higher priority than did the rival claims of state or church. These documents attest to the crucial importance of the blood connection in Florence. Marriages were major family decisions, They involved the transfer of property and the realignment of social rank; they often had political implications. Death, in this age of short life spans, might signify the reallocation of family resources and the forging of new social connections. But the Florentine sense of family had other dimensions, and other rationales, besides the material ones. To belong to an old and respected house like the Strozzi, the Medici, or the Rucellai was a mark of honor and distinction; those family names conferred prestige and status upon their owners. In an age when life was so tenuous and uncertain, the family bond was a source of material and psychic support, a measure of security in a dangerous world. This explains why most Florentines were prepared to pay a heavy price to honor a blood obligation, and why they valued their family's reputation so highly.

I. Marriage

16. THE MARRIAGES OF GREGORIO DATI*

In the name of God and the Virgin Mary, of Blessed Michael the Archangel, of SS. John the Baptist and John the Evangelist, of SS. Peter and Paul, of the holy scholars, SS. Gregory and Jerome, and of St. Mary Magdalene and St. Elisabeth and all the blessed saints in heaven—may they ever intercede for us—I shall record here how I married my second wife, Isabetta, known as Betta, the daughter of Mari di Lorenzo Vilanuzzi and of Monna Veronica, daughter of Pagolo d'Arrigo Guglielmi, and I shall also record the promises which were made to me. May God and his Saints grant by their grace that they be kept.

On March 31, 1393, I was betrothed to her and on Easter Monday, April 7, I gave her a ring. On June 22, a Sunday, I became her husband in the name of God and good fortune. Her first cousins, Giovanni and Lionardo di Domenico Arrighi, promised that she should have a dowry of 900 gold florins and that, apart from the dowry, she should have the income from a farm in S. Fiore a Elsa which had been left her as a legacy by her mother, Monna Veronica. It was not stated at the time how much this amounted to but it was understood that she would receive the accounts. We arranged our match very simply indeed and with scarcely any discussion. God grant that nothing but good may come of it. On the 26th of that same June, I received a payment of 800 gold florins from the bank of Giacomino and Company. This was the dowry. I invested in the shop of

* Source: *Two Memoirs of Renaissance Florence*, ed. Brucker, pp. 113–15, 123, 132–34.

Buonaccorso Berardi and his partners. At the same time I received the trousseau which my wife's cousins valued at 106 florins, in the light of which they deducted 6 florins from another account, leaving me the equivalent of 100 florins. But from what I heard from her, and what I saw myself, they had overestimated it by 30 florins or more. However, from politeness, I said nothing about this. . . . Our Lord God was pleased to call to Himself the blessed soul of . . . Betta, on Monday, October 2 [1402] . . . and the next day, Tuesday, at three in the afternoon she was buried in our grave in S. Spirito. May God receive her soul in his glory. Amen. . . .

I record that on May 8, 1403, I was betrothed to Ginevra, daughter of Antonio di Piero Piuvichese Brancacci, in the church of S. Maria sopra Porta. The dowry was 1,000 florins: 700 in cash and 300 in a farm at Campi. On . . . May 20, we were married, but we held no festivities or wedding celebrations as we were in mourning for Manetto Dati [Gregorio's son], who had died the week before. God grant us a good life together. Ginevra had been married before for four years to Tommaso Brancacci, by whom she had an eight-month-old son. She is now in her twenty-first year.

After that [1411] it was God's will to recall to Himself the blessed soul of my wife Ginevra. She died in childbirth after lengthy suffering, which she bore with remarkable strength and patience. She was perfectly lucid at the time of her death, when she received all the sacraments: confession, communion, extreme unction, and a papal indulgence granting absolution for all her sins. . . . It comforted her greatly, and she returned her soul to her Creator on September 7. . . . On Friday the 8th she was honorably buried and on the 9th, masses were said for her soul.

Memo that on Tuesday, January 28, 1421, I made an
agreement with Niccolò d'Andrea del Benino to take his
niece Caterina for my lawful wife. She is the daughter of
the late Dardano di Niccolò Guicciardini and of Monna Tita,
Andrea del Benino's daughter. We were betrothed on the
morning of Monday, February 3, the Eve of Carnival. I
met Piero and Giovanni di Messer Luigi [Guicciardini] in
the church of S. Maria sopra Porta, and Niccolò d'Andrea
del Benino was our mediator. The dowry promised me was
600 florins, and the notary was Ser Niccolò di Ser Verdiano.
I went to dine with her that evening in Piero's house and
the Saturday after Easter . . . I gave her the ring and
then on Sunday evening, March 30, she came to live in our
house simply and without ceremony. . . .

17. Two Marriages in the Valori Family, 1452 and 1476*

I record this event, that on July 15, 1452, Niccolò di
Piero Capponi sent for me and, after many circumlocutions,
he asked me if I were still in a mood to marry. I told him
that I would not diverge from his judgment in this matter
or in any other, for I had great faith in him and was certain
that his advice would be prudent and honest. Then he told
me that Piero di Messer Andrea de'Pazzi had two nubile
daughters and that he was willing to give me the girl which
I preferred. He was making this offer to me on Piero's behalf. I accepted the bait willingly and asked for two days'
grace to confer with several of my relatives, which I did
extensively, and was advised by them to proceed. After two
days, I returned to Niccolò and told him to ask Piero's

* Source: The diary of Bartolomeo Valori; *Biblioteca Nazionale, Firenze*
[*BNF*], *Fondo Panciatichiano*, 134, fols. 5r, 8v.

consent to marry the eldest whom I knew well, for up to the age of twelve we were practically raised together. [For a dowry, Bartolomeo received 14,000 florins of communal bonds, valued at 2,000 florins. His wife Caterina died on November 20, 1474, leaving two boys and six girls.] . . .

On this day, July 5, 1476, Lorenzo de'Medici [the Magnificent] told me that he wanted to speak to me, and I visited him immediately. He said that Averardo d'Alamanno Salviati had come to see him and told him that he had a daughter of marriageable age that he would willingly give her to my son Filippo, requesting that Lorenzo be the broker. I replied that this pleased me but that I wished first to speak to Filippo to learn his views, which I did that same evening. Finding my son disposed to follow my judgment and my will, on the next day I asked Lorenzo to conclude the business. He sent for Averardo and they agreed on the conditions. On July 7, Lorenzo came to my house and told me that the alliance was sealed, that Alessandra, the daughter of Averardo Salviati, would be the wife of my son Filippo with a dowry of 2,000 florins. And we formally sealed the agreement in the palace of the Signoria, with Lorenzo himself pronouncing the details of the settlement.

18. Marriage Negotiations: the Del Bene, 1381*

[February 20] In the name of God, yesterday I concluded the agreement with Giovanni di Luca [a marriage broker] for the marriage of Caterina [Del Bene, Giovanni's daughter] with Andrea di Castello da Quarata, with a dowry of

---

* Source: Letters from Giovanni d'Amerigo Del Bene in Florence to Francesco di Jacopo Del Bene in the Valdinievole, February, 1381; *ASF, Carte Del Bene,* vol. 51, no pagination.

900 florins. I could not reduce that sum, although I tried hard to persuade Giovanni to adhere to the terms of our previous discussions. But things are very much up in the air, and Giovanni insisted upon it, alleging many reasons. So, to avoid the rupture of negotiations, I surrendered on this point.

Then I requested Giovanni to maintain secrecy about this affair, as we have agreed, and he said that he would give me a reply. Last night he said that it was impossible, because they wanted to discuss the matter with their relatives, who were so numerous that they couldn't keep the affair secret. However, they are very pleased with this match, and they didn't want to displease me on this point. So, after much effort, I persuaded them to keep it secret through Sunday, and then everyone is free to publicize it as he wishes. So, on the same day, our relatives and Amerigo's friends will be informed. . . .

The women of your household to whom I have spoken say that the girl wishes to have a satin gown, which seems too lavish to me. Write me your opinion. On Sunday, I will meet with Giovanni [di Luca] and we will settle this affair in one day, and also the church where the betrothal ceremony will take place. And I will do the same with Lemmo [Balducci] and will explain the reason to Giovanni. And that evening I will relate everything to our women, because Lapa says that Monna Giovanna di Messer Meo has said that Amerigo [Del Bene, Giovanni's son] has a bride and that she informed her son Niccolò.

The marriage chest will be furnished in the customary manner; it will cost between 70 and 75 florins. They will provide the ring, so that everything will be ready at the proper time. In your letter, remind me of anything that, in your opinion, should be done with respect to these marriages.

There is no further news concerning Antonia [Francesco's daughter] except that her mother was very unhappy about that negotiation at Borgo S. Lorenzo. It is my feeling that we shouldn't push this issue and annoy her further, and that we will find some other good prospect for her. You should advise us how we should proceed with the girls; that is, when we should go to see Amerigo's bride, and when the bridegroom should come to see Caterina. I think that Andrea [da Quarata] should come to our house first, and then Caterina, accompanied by our women, should go to see Amerigo's bride. Write me whether you think that Andrea should give the ring that day [of the betrothal ceremony] or not, so that we can arrange the matter beforehand. . . .

[February 21] I wrote you last night and sent the letter off this morning, and so I have little to tell you save that I met Giovanni [di Luca] Mozzi today. We agreed that the betrothal would take place on the first Sunday in Lent, and we may choose the church where it will take place. I don't think that Amerigo's betrothal should be kept secret any longer, so that they won't have any excuse for complaining. I think that on Saturday, Amerigo should go to them [the Balducci] and tell them that we are arranging to marry Caterina, as well as give him a bride. He should tell them everything, and then we can settle that business, and they will learn about it a few days before it becomes public knowledge. Amerigo will write about the deliberations of the women concerning Caterina's trousseau.

I have heard that Dora [Francesco's wife] is somewhat unhappy about this marriage, seeing that Antonia [her daughter] is still unwed. . . . I also think that Antonia may be upset when she sees Caterina's beautiful gown. I urge you to write a comforting letter to Dora, and tell her that we will find a husband for Antonia, if God wills it. Nor should Antonia be unhappy about the new gown, for I think that it will not be long before she too will have one. I shall not be pleased, if I see any discontent in a household where there should be joy.

[February 24] . . . Concerning Caterina, we have concluded the marriage agreement for 900 florins. . . . They wanted to hold the betrothal ceremony on the first Sunday of Lent, and Giovanni [Mozzi] and I agreed on that point, and also that it will take place in [the church of] S. Apollinare. We haven't yet discussed the guest list, but I think that they will want a large assembly. It is my feeling that we should hold the betrothal ceremony before the dinner, so there will be time afterwards to accept and to deliver the contract. I don't know whom they wish to give the ring, but tomorrow I will settle these matters of the guest list and the ring. The women have decided that Caterina's dress will be made of blue silk and that the gown will form part of the dowry; this was a wise decision. Tomorrow everything will be settled.

It is true that Dora, whom I have always considered a sensible woman, has been behaving in a way that redounds neither to her nor to our dignity. She has not wished to join in any part of this affair. Her attitude is so bizarre and so melancholy that she cries all day and says that your daughter [Antonia] will never be married and that you don't care. She says the most shocking things that I have ever heard, and has made your whole family miserable. I am very annoyed by her conduct, and it would please me if you wrote to comfort and correct her, so that she will be content with this affair, and not vexed.

I was with Ser Naddo [di Ser Nepo] on Saturday and

told him about Caterina's marriage, and my opinions on the betrothal of the girl [Amerigo's bride] and of Caterina, and also the question of the church and the guest lists. I also informed him of the penalty [for breaking the betrothal contract] of 2,000 florins, and every other detail concerning this affair. Today Ser Naddo told me that Lemmo is content with everything, except that if Caterina's husband gives her the ring, then he wants Amerigo to give it to his daughter; otherwise not. He also says that the penalty should be no more than 1,000 florins, since the rumors of the dowry which he has provided have ruined him. Concerning the ring, he says that he wants it to be arranged in this way, to do like the others. Concerning the penalty, I told him that you had instructed me in this matter as it was agreed, and that I could not alter it without writing you. . . .

[Letter from Naddo di Ser Nepo to Francesco di Jacopo Dell Bene, February 24, 1381] After you left here, Giovanni d'Amerigo sent for me to inform me of the marriage alliance which, by the grace of God, has been arranged between you and Lemmo. We discussed certain problems, among which was the fact that in the agreement was a clause providing for a penalty of 2,000 florins. After our discussion, I spoke with Lemmo and he agreed to everything except the penalty of 2,000 florins. He argued as follows: "The rumors of this large dowry which I have given are ruining me, with respect to the taxes which I pay to the Commune. And with this matter of a 2,000 florin penalty, everyone will believe that I have given a dowry of that amount, which will destroy me, and surely they [the Del Bene] should not want this to happen. However, this business has been given by Francesco and myself to Messer Bartolomeo [Panciatichi?] for arbitration, and I will abide fully by his decision." On the 24th of this month, I met Giovanni and told him what Lemmo wanted, and that he wanted a penalty of only 1,000 florins, and the reasons for this. Giovanni told me that you had so arranged matters that he could not reply without consulting you.

Speaking with all due reverence and faith, it appears to me that this issue should not disturb or impede this marriage, considering the great friendship which has always existed between you and Lemmo, and which now should be greater than ever. Moreover, you and Amerigo should desire to further his interests, and approve a penalty of 1,000 florins and no more. They entered into this marriage with a positive attitude, and so did you, and therefore I pray you as fervently as I can to be content. I am always ready to carry out your commands.

19. MARRIAGE NEGOTIATIONS: THE STROZZI, 1464–65*

[April 20, 1464] . . . Concerning the matter of a wife [for Filippo], it appears to me that if Francesco di Messer Guglielmino Tanagli wishes to give his daughter, that it would be a fine marriage. . . . Now I will speak with Marco [Parenti, Alessandra's son-in-law], to see if there are other prospects that would be better, and if there are none, then we will learn if he wishes to give her [in marriage]. . . . Francesco Tanagli has a good reputation, and he has held office, not the highest, but still he has been in office. You may ask: "Why should he give her to someone

---

* Source: Letters from Alessandra Strozzi in Florence to her son Filippo in Naples; Alessandra Macinghi Strozzi, *Lettere di una gentildonna fiorentina,* ed. C. Guasti (Florence, 1877), pp. 394–95, 443–45, 458–59, 463–65, 475–76.

in exile?" There are three reasons. First, there aren't many young men of good family who have both virtue and property. Secondly, she has only a small dowry, 1,000 florins, which is the dowry of an artisan. . . . Third, I believe that he will give her away, because he has a large family and he will need help to settle them. . . .

[July 26, 1465] . . . Marco Parenti came to me and told me that for some time, he has been considering how to find a wife for you. . . . There is the daughter of Francesco di Messer Guglielmino Tanagli, and until now there hasn't been anyone who is better suited for you than this girl. It is true that we haven't discussed this at length, for a reason which you understand. However, we have made secret inquiries, and the only people who are willing to make a marriage agreement with exiles have some flaw, either a lack of money or something else. Now money is the least serious drawback, if the other factors are positive. . . . Francesco is a good friend of Marco and he trusts him. On S. Jacopo's day, he spoke to him discreetly and persuasively, saying that for several months he had heard that we were interested in the girl and . . . that when we had made up our minds, she will come to us willingly. [He said that] you were a worthy man, and that his family had always made good marriages, but that he had only a small dowry to give her, and so he would prefer to send her outside of Florence to someone of worth, rather than to give her to someone here, from among those who were available, with little money. . . . He invited Marco to his house and he called the girl down. . . . Marco said that she was attractive and that she appeared to be suitable. We have information that she is affable and competent. She is responsible for a large family (there are twelve children, six boys and six girls), and the mother is always pregnant and isn't very competent. . . .

[August 17, 1465] . . . Sunday morning I went to the first mass at S. Reparata . . . to see the Adimari girl, who customarily goes to that mass, and I found the Tanagli girl there. Not knowing who she was, I stood beside her. . . . She is very attractive, well proportioned, as large or larger than Caterina [Alessandra's daughter]. . . . She has a long face, and her features are not very delicate, but they aren't like a peasant's. From her demeanor, she does not appear to me to be indolent. . . . I walked behind her as we left the church, and thus I realized that she was one of the Tanagli. So I am somewhat enlightened about her. . . .

[August 31, 1465] . . . I have recently received some very favorable information [about the Tanagli girl] from two individuals. . . . They are in agreement that whoever gets her will be content. . . . Concerning her beauty, they told me what I had already seen, that she is attractive and well-proportioned. Her face is long, but I couldn't look directly into her face, since she appeared to be aware that I was examining her . . . and so she turned away from me like the wind. . . . She reads quite well . . . and she can dance and sing. . . . Her father is one of the most respected young men of Florence, very civilized in his manners. He is fond of this girl, and it appears that he has brought her up well.

So yesterday I sent for Marco and told him what I had learned. And we talked about the matter for a while, and decided that he should say something to the father and give him a little hope, but not so much that we couldn't withdraw, and find out from him the amount of the dowry. . . . Marco and Francesco [Tanagli] had a discussion about this yesterday (I haven't seen him since), and Marco should inform you about it one of these days, and you will then understand more clearly what should follow. May God help us to choose what will contribute to our tranquillity and to the consolation of us all. . . .

[September 13, 1465] . . . Marco came to me and said that he had met with Francesco Tanagli, who had spoken very coldly, so that I understand that he had changed his mind. They say that he wants to discuss the matter with his brother-in-law, Messer Antonio Ridolfi. . . . And he [Francesco] says that it would be a serious matter to send his daughter so far away [to Naples], and to a house that might be described as a hotel. And he spoke in such a way that it is clear that he has changed his mind. I believe that this is the result of the long delay in our replying to him, both yours and Marco's. Two weeks ago, he could have given him a little hope. Now this delay has angered him, and he has at hand some prospect that is more attractive. . . . I am very annoyed by this business; I can't recall when I have been so troubled. For I felt that this marriage would have satisfied our needs better than any other we could have found. . . .

[Filippo Strozzi eventually married Fiametta di Donato Adimari, in 1466.]

20. ILLEGITIMACY AND MARRIAGE, 1355*

Agnola, the illegitimate daughter of Piccio [Velluti's brother], was born in Trapani in Sicily, of the proprietress of a baker's shop, or rather a lasagna shop. While Piccio was

* Source: La cronica domestica di Messer Donato Velluti, ed. I. Del Badia and G. Volpi (Florence, 1914), pp. 147–50.

alive, he did not want to bring her here [to Florence], although my wife and I urged him to do so. After his death, Leonardo Ferrucci [Velluti's brother-in-law] went to Sicily and . . . found Agnola alive and her mother dead. He then asked me to bring her [to Florence]. But I had some doubt that she was really Piccio's child, seeing that he did not wish to bring her back, and also considering that in his will he left her 50 florins for her dowry, if she were truly his daughter. . . . But seeing that there was no other descendant in our immediate family except Fra Lottieri and myself and my son Lamberto, and my niece Tessa di Gherardo, and so that she would not fall upon evil ways, and for the love of God, I allowed her to come. She was then ten years old, and I welcomed her and I—and my family—treated her as though she were my own daughter. And truly she was the daughter of Piccio, considering her features and the fact that she resembled him in every way.

When she reached the age of matrimony, I desired to arrange a match for her, and she caused me a great deal of trouble. I was willing to spend up to 300 florins [for her dowry] but could not find anyone interested in her. Finally, after much time had passed, and with her situation not improving, she began to complain about me to relatives and others, saying that I didn't know how to get her out of the house [i.e., to marry her]. In the cloth factory which my son Lamberto was operating with Ciore Pitti, there was a factor named Piero Talenti, who was earning a [yearly] salary of 64 florins, and later he received 72 florins. And since I couldn't find any better prospect, I married her to him in May, 1355. . . .

Later there occurred the plague of 1363 . . . and first Piero's four children died, and then Piero himself, and I had to bury him. He left about 35 florins worth of house-

hold furnishings, and I had to provide mourning clothes
for Agnola, and I could not get back her dowry of 160
florins. . . . Since her husband's death, Agnola has lived
with me. I wanted to arrange another marriage for her, but
since she is both a widow and illegitimate, I have not been
able to find her a husband. So, to protect my honor and to
assist her in her need, Fra Lottieri arranged for her to become a tertiary in his order in December, 1366. . . .

II. Death

21. Deaths in the Sassetti Family, 1383*

I record that on July 31, 1383, there died the ill-famed
Letta, daughter of Federigo di Pierozzo Sassetti, in the
house of Giovanni di Noldo Porcellini, in Borgo Ogni Santi.
She was buried by the friars of the church of Ogni Santi at
the hour of vespers. May the devil take her soul, for she
has brought shame and dishonor to our family. May it please
God to pay whoever was blameworthy. And this is sufficient
to describe this evil memory, which has dishonored us all.
But man cannot change that which God, for our sins, has
willed. But we are contemplating a vendetta which will bring
some balm to our feelings.

I record that on August 1, 1383 it pleased God to call to
Himself Monna Filippa, the wife of Pollaio Sassetti. She
was buried in our tomb in S. Maria Novella under the vault

* Source: The diary of Paolo Sassetti; *ASF, Carte Strozziane*, series II,
vol. 4, fols. 67r–68v.

of the cloister, in the burial space belonging to Soldo di
Jacopo Sassetti and his family. She was put in that tomb
through the error of Fra Bernardo di Maso Manetti, a friar
of S. Maria Novella. He thought that he was honoring us,
but we were not pleased. . . . May our Lord God receive
her soul in peace, for she was a good woman and always
brought honor to our house.

I record that on Wednesday, August 26, 1383, it pleased
our Lord God to claim the blessed soul of our eldest brother
Bernardo. He was buried in S. Maria Novella in our marble
tomb. We gave him those honors which were permitted by
the Commune in time of plague. May God grant him a
blessed peace, amen.

On Saturday, the 23rd of the month, he named me his
procurator, with the same power which he had himself. He
also granted authority to Ser Michele di Ser Aldobrando to
make peace with Bindo di Giovanni Vecchietti. . . . Then
on Monday, the 25th, he made his will, drawn up by Ser
Michele. . . . In that testament, he recommended his soul
to the omnipotent God and the Virgin Mary, and his body
to the church of the Friar Preachers of S. Maria Novella.
He left . . . soldi to the walls of Florence and . . . soldi
to the building fund of S. Reparata. He left a sum of money,
between 75 and 100 lire, to be spent by me, Paolo, for the
love of God, as I see fit. And he did this in lieu of a vow
which he had made to go to [the basilica of] the Blessed
S. Antonio in Verona [an error: Padua], and he was not able
to go. To his wife Simone, he bequeathed her dowry . . .
and an additional 200 florins to his daughter Lena as a dowry
in the event that she marries. . . .

I record that on September 24, 1383, God called to Himself Rinaldo di Pollaio Sassetti. He died in the house of

Francesco di Giovanni di Giano, or rather of his sister, Monna Fiondina. At the hour of vespers, we buried him in our vault in the church of the friars of S. Maria Novella. . . . He did not make any testament, for ten years ago, he made one in favor of his sister, Monna Fiondina. And like the bad woman she is, she did not allow him to make another will, nor did she permit any of us to visit him. Without any reason or provocation, she has treated each one of us as though we were mortal enemies.

22. DEATHS IN THE PANZANO FAMILY, 1423–46*

I record the death of Antonio di Messer Luca da Panzano on September 12, 1423, at Pietrabuona, for he was vicar of Pescia. On September 15 we brought his body to Florence in a coffin, and that evening we buried him in our tomb in S. Croce. On September 17, we held a memorial service in our house in the Via dell'Anguillara; the clergy attended, and we displayed a flag with our coat of arms. And we provided his widow, Monna Martinella, daughter of Francesco di Mainardo de' Bardi, with twenty-six yards of black cloth and a leather cloak and five veils and two handkerchiefs. And we held a mass on the 18th. And we bought an arch decorated with our coat of arms and placed it over the grave. . . .

November 5, 1445. I record that my wife Lucrezia, from whom I have eleven children alive today, died this day, Friday evening, two and one-half hours after sunset. This

* Source: The diary of Luca di Matteo da Panzano; C. Carnesecchi, "Un fiorentino del secolo XV e le sue ricordanze domestiche," *Archivio storico italiano*, ser. 5, IV (1889), 156–59.

has caused me as much grief as though I were dying, for we have lived together for twenty years, one month, and eleven days. I pray to God most fervently that He pardon her. She died in labor; the child was apparently stillborn. But since the child was said to be breathing, it was baptized and named Giovanni. We buried it in the church of S. Simone.

We dressed my daughter Gostanza and Monna Caterina, the wife of Filippo di Ghezzi, with fourteen yards of cloth for a cloak, and a pair of veils and handkerchiefs. On Saturday morning at 11 o'clock, we held a vigil in our house with priests and friars. We buried her that day in S. Croce, in the vault of Messer Luca [Luca's grandfather] next to the fount of holy water. On the 8th, we had a mass said for her soul in S. Croce, with candles and as much pomp as possible. A large number of friends and relatives attended.

The loss of this woman was a grievous blow; she was mourned by the entire populace of Florence. She was a good woman, sweet-tempered and well-mannered, and was loved by everyone who knew her. I believe that her soul has gone to sit at the feet of God's servants. For she bore her final sufferings with patience and humility. She lay ill for two weeks after the child was born. May God with His great mercy make a place for her with angels.

On May 16, 1446, I, Luca da Panzano, ordered thirty masses of St. Gregory to be said, one each morning on consecutive days, for the salvation of my wife Lucrezia's soul. I commissioned my confessor, Fra Altaviano del Mangano, a friar of S. Croce in Florence [to say these masses]. Today I gave him two wax candles weighing a pound each to keep lighted during these masses. And for his services, I gave Fra Altaviano approximately one-half yard of Alexandria velvet.

23. A Pestilence Victim,
1374*

Now it occurs to us to recall Giovanni's third son, whose
name was Gualberto [Morelli]. He was born on . . . He
was of somewhat larger than average height for his age,
slender but not skinny, and possessing a good complexion.
He was a learned man who—I believe—studied law. According to my information, with his knowledge and his in-
herent virtue, he developed into a very worthy person. . . .
During the plague of 1374, the surviving members of Giovanni's family and the entire family of Paolo [Morelli]
fled to Bologna and lived together in one house, dividing
the expenses equally (to the great benefit of Giovanni's
family). But returning to what I was going to say, there
were some twenty of us, counting men, women, children,
nurses, and foreign servants. Gualberto was in charge of
providing the necessities and supervising expenditures, and
he was responsible for keeping records and maintaining an
account of the money which was given to him. He, a young
man of tender age, a stranger in a foreign land with little
background or experience in these matters, carefully administered to all of the needs of this group while he lived,
and kept accurate accounts of what he spent for everyone,
both great and small. . . .

Finally, realizing that he had been stricken by the plague
and aware that he was dying, he provided for the salvation
of his soul with the same care, requesting all of the Holy
Sacraments, and receiving them with the greatest devotion.
With good and holy Psalms, he devoutly recommended his
soul to God. Then, with good and gentle words, he begged

* Source: *La cronica di Giovanni Morelli*, pp. 242–43.

the pardon of all members of that household, recommending his soul to everyone, having no more regard for the great than for the small. Then, in the presence of the whole company, he accused himself . . . of having spent some 10 or 12 lire from the fund for his own affairs, and, as I said, denouncing himself in the presence of all, he returned the money to the cash box. Then he departed from this life, being in full possession of his faculties to the final moment. Together with the priest, he said the prayers with a loud voice so that everyone heard him. Then, sensing that he was at the point of death, he urged the priest to recite more rapidly. And by God's grace, having completed the prayers, he and the priest together spoke the last words, "Thanks be to God, amen." He closed his eyes and rendered his soul to God at that precise moment.

The obsequies were performed, and he was buried in the Franciscan church in Bologna, in a vault which was newly constructed on the right side, between the choir and the church wall. . . . I believe that there is a stone with our coat of arms, or rather, adjacent to the tomb in the wall nearby. Since he was honorably buried there, his brothers decided to leave his remains there, and not bring them home. . . .

24. THE DEATH OF A SON, 1459*

My dear son. On the 11th of last month, I received your letter of July 29, with the news that my dear son Matteo had become ill, and since you didn't tell me the nature of his malady, I became worried about him. I called Francesco

* Source: Alessandra Strozzi to Filippo Strozzi in Naples, September 6, 1459; *Lettere di una gentildonna fiorentina*, pp. 177–81.

and sent for Matteo di Girgio; and they both told me that he had a tertian fever. I gained some comfort from this, for if some other malady does not develop, one does not become mortally ill from a tertian fever. Then I heard from you that he was improving so that, while I was still concerned, my spirits did improve a little. I then learned that on the 23rd, it pleased Him who gave him to me to take him back. Being sound of mind, he willingly received all of the sacraments as a good and faithful Christian. I am deeply grieved to be deprived of my son; by his death, I have suffered a grievous blow, greater than the loss of filial love, and so have you, my two sons, reduced now to such a small number. . . .

Although I have suffered the greatest pain in my heart that I have ever experienced, I have received comfort from two things. First, he was with you; and I am certain that he was provided with doctors and medicine, and that everything possible was done for his health, and that nothing was spared. Yet, it was all to no avail; such was God's will. I have also been comforted by the knowledge that when he was dying, God granted him the opportunity to confess, to receive communion and extreme unction. He did this with devotion, so I understand; from these signs, we may hope that God has prepared a good place for him. I realize, too, that everyone has to make this journey; and they cannot foresee the circumstances [of their death], and they cannot be certain that they will die as did my beloved son Matteo (for whoever dies suddenly or is murdered . . . loses both body and soul). So I have been comforted, realizing that God could have done worse to me. And if by his grace and mercy, he conserves both of you, my sons, he will give me no more anguish.

. . . From your letter of the 26th, I know that you have been sorely tried in body and soul as have I, and as I shall continue to be until I receive word from you that you are taking care of yourself. . . . I know that you have had sleepless nights, and that you have suffered from this ordeal, so that you are now in a bad state. And I worry so much about this day and night that I cannot rest. . . . I beg you, for love of me, to calm yourself and guard your health, and don't concern yourself so much about the business. It might be a good idea to take a light purgative . . . and then to take some air, if it is at all possible. Do remember that your health is more important than your property. . . .

In burying my son with such ceremony, you have done honor to yourself and to him. Since no services are held here for those in your state [i.e., exiles], it was particularly important to give him a decent funeral there, and I am pleased that you have done so. I and my two daughters, who are disconsolate over the death of their brother, are dressed in mourning. . . .

III. Property and Inheritance

25. The Testament of Fetto Ubertini, 1348*

Be it manifest to all persons who hear or read this document that I, Fetto Ubertini, of the parish of S. Felice in Piazza of Florence, being of sound mind and body, hereby record my testament in my own hand in this document. This is my true and valid testament, and all others which I have made in the past I hereby declare to be null and void.

First, when it pleases my Lord Jesus Christ that I pass

* Source: *ASF, Conventi Soppressi,* 122 (S. Spirito), vol. 75, fols. 28r–30r.

from this life, I recommend my soul to Him and to His blessed mother St. Mary, and I order the burial of my body in the church of S. Spirito of the order of the Friars of St. Augustine, and [I desire to be interred] in the robes of that order.

Within six months from the date of my death, I order that 100 florins from my estate be given to my wife Pia, and to my son Fra Ubertino and to Fra Bartolino of Mugello, of the order of S. Spirito . . . and this money they shall distribute to God's poor and to have masses said, as it pleases them, for the benefit of my soul. I also order that every person, who can prove that he should have anything from me, be paid in full.

I bequeath to my wife Pia, daughter of Ubaldo Bertaldi, the sum of 125 florins in addition to her dowry, and also all of her clothing and accessories. And if she desires to remain a widow and live with our children, she may have an income sufficient to maintain herself and a servant in my house. . . . However, if she withdraws her dowry [from my estate], then I cancel the bequest of 125 florins, nor shall she receive living expenses for herself and a servant, but only if she leaves her dowry in my estate, and remains a widow, or becomes a tertiary.

To each of my daughters—Filippa, Antonia, Francesca, Andrea, and Tommasa—I bequeath the sum of 400 florins for their dowries if they intend to marry, or the sum of 225 florins if they become nuns. . . . I bequeath to my son Fra Ubertino of the Friars of S. Spirito of the order of St. Augustine the sum of 10 florins annually toward his living expenses. In the event that the order decides to send him to the university, then he shall have an additional 100 florins during four years, that is, 25 florins, annually, to buy those books which he needs. . . .

In the event that my daughter Agnola, wife of Lorenzo di Nutino, becomes a widow, I leave to her the property, with buildings, courtyard, arable land, and woodland in [the parish of] S. Maria a Soffiano, in a place called "A Lame," which I bought from Bartolo di Cino Benvenuti, and from which his widow Monna Grana receives the income during her lifetime, and after her death, this property reverts to me and my heirs. . . . And in the event that Agnola remarries with the consent of my sons, I leave to her, in addition to the above-mentioned property, the sum of 100 gold florins. . . .

So that the dowry which belongs to Lisabetta, wife of my son Maffeo, remains in my hands and may be used for my profit, I cede to Maffeo a farm . . . located in the Valdipesa . . . which he has been cultivating for several years without having clear title to the property. . . . And since I bore the expenses of his marriage with Lisabetta (which I estimate to have cost me 225 florins), I order that each of my sons who marry shall also receive . . . 225 florins from my estate. . . .

If my daughters become widows, and wish to return to my house, it is my will that they may do so, and they shall have that accommodation which is proper. They may remain there as long as they wish, either as widows or tertiaries, and if they do not recover their dowry, they shall receive from my estate the necessary means to sustain themselves as long as they live. . . .

After these bequests have been honored . . . I leave the remainder of my estate in equal parts to my sons Maffeo, Sassettino, Bartolomeo, Jacopo, Luca, Uberto, and Gregorio, and an equal share to legitimate sons whom I may have in the future. . . . As executors of my estate and guardians of my children under fourteen years of age, I designate my wife Pia, and my sons Maffeo, Luca, and Fra Ubertino. . . .

[This testament was witnessed by seven of Fetto's neighbors in his house, on June 18, 1348.]

26. THE TESTAMENT OF
MICHELE DI VANNI CASTELLANI,
C. 1370*

This is the record of what I have bequeathed to Vanni and Niccolò, my sons, because it is my desire that they do the same to Alberto and Giovanni and Matteo [his younger sons]. I gave to each son, Vanni and Niccolò, the sum of 2,000 florins, as it is recorded in the account book of my shop, in which these sums are credited to their accounts and debited to mine. And furthermore, when they took wives, I paid all of the costs of their wardrobes, their rooms, and the festivities. Moreover, if I die before I have given 2,000 florins to Alberto, Giovanni, and Matteo, I bequeath to each of them that sum from my estate. . . . Then, if God should grant them such life that they would marry, then let each receive the same expenses for their marriage as Vanni and Niccolò. . . . I further bequeath the sum of 1,000 florins to my daughter Antonia for the dowry, as I have already done for [her sisters] Caterina and Margherita. . . .

If I were to die at the time of this writing, God has shown me such grace and has made me guardian of so much of his substance that I leave my sons with great wealth. Therefore, it is my will that my heirs be required, in the event that any of my daughters be widowed, to establish them in my house, to allow them to live there as though it were their own, and to give them the wherewithal to live decently. And if it

* Source: *ASF, Conventi Soppressi*, 90 (S. Verdiana), vol. 132, no pagination.

should happen that any one of my daughters becomes a widow, and my sons do not treat them with the proper respect (in the judgement of Messer Lotto or Niccolò), then it is my will that my heirs pay her the sum of 50 florins annually during her lifetime. . . . And in the event that any one of my daughters is widowed and cannot recover her dowry, then my heirs are hereby ordered to provide her with another dowry of 1,000 florins, if she wishes to remarry. If, however, she recovers her dowry, then they are not required to give her anything, except as good brothers or good sisters might wish to do.

If God should call me to Himself, I also order my heirs to give each of my daughters a farm worth 500 florins, or a house of the same value. And furthermore I desire that the income from the farm or house go to them, with the stipulation that after their death, the property should revert to my male heirs. . . .

I also desire that my male heirs maintain in their house the children of Guido Federighi and of Gostanza, my sister, and to give them the wherewithal for their subsistence until they reach the age of fifteen. . . . If God should claim me within a year, I order my heirs to arrange for the marriage of my niece Andreuola, daughter of Guido, and to provide her with a dowry of 500 florins. If they grant her more, they will be contributing to her welfare, for she has no one else in the world—neither father nor relative—but ourselves.

Furthermore, it is my will that my sisters, Filippa and Cicilia, may return to live with my heirs if they have need, and they shall not be denied sustenance. I shall bequeath nothing else to them because I do not believe that they require anything. But my heirs shall give annually to Cicilia 50 bushels of grain and 200 pounds of pork and two cords of wood, without which she will not be able to live on the

income from her dowry. I also desire that she and the other
[Filippa] should perform deeds for my soul and pray to
God for me.

I see that Messer Lotto [Castellani] is a young knight and
is not as wealthy as his station requires. I therefore order
my sons and heirs to grant him 200 florins annually during
his lifetime if he wishes to accept it. However, I know that he
will not take this money except for the benefit of my sons,
and if he has need of it. Stefano [Castellani, brother of
Messer Lotto] is prospering and he does not need to spend
above his income, and therefore I shall not treat him in the
same manner as Messer Lotto. But when his daughter Ghita
reaches the age of matrimony, I order my heirs to give her
and her sister Catalana 200 florins each for their dowry. If
only one marries, then her dowry shall be 300 florins.

If, in the opinion of Messer Lotto and my sons and heirs,
Antonio di Lotto Castellani lives and works well, then he
shall be given the farm in Avignon . . . and also the houses
which I have bought from Pagolo di Ser Francesco. From
my estate I also bequeath him 150 florins to purchase household furnishings or for whatever purpose he desires. However, if Messer Lotto judges him unworthy of this benefit,
then my heirs are not bound to give him anything. I make
this bequest out of pity, because he has nothing of his own.
It is my will that the house of Stafole, in which is located the
hospital where Master Simone stays, shall be the haven of
Christ's poor. The income from the farm at Poggio a Men-
sola shall be used to sustain those who live there. I place
the burden for maintaining this house upon the consciences
and the souls of my heirs, and I charge them with keeping
it, as I have done, or better, in the service of God.

When our Lord Jesus Christ calls me to Himself, I pray
Him that out of His pity and mercy He pardon my sins and

receive me into His holy kingdom. I desire that my body be buried in the church of the Friars of St. Francis in Florence, if I die in the city or the *contado*. If I die elsewhere, then I wish to be buried in the Franciscan church of the locality. If there is none, then whoever arranges my burial can bury me wherever he wishes. Since I do not have a tomb in the Franciscan church, and since I wish my son to be buried with me, I order my heirs to build a chapel costing 1,000 florins in the church where I am buried, and there they should bury my body and that of my son Rinieri. This should be done with the counsel of my confessor, Fra Marco de' Ricci and of Fra Francesco of the Friars [of S. Croce in Florence].

If there be any person who petitions my heirs for repayment of my legitimate debts, he should be paid. I have not contracted any debts in this world save those which I have recorded in my own books, or in the yellow book which belonged to Vanni [his dead partner] in the shop. . . . And there it is written that I owe Giovanni di Ser Pierozzo 600 florins. . . .

I bequeath 100 florins to the bishop as compensation for money which I may have gained illegally, and this should be used in benefit of the souls of those from whom I received the money. But I do not believe that I obtained any [illicit income].

As my equal heirs, I name my sons Vanni, Niccolò, Alberto, Giovanni, and Matteo with the charges that I have recorded in this document or which I have yet to record. I pray God to grant them the grace to act for the benefit of my soul and theirs.

I bequeath 100 lire to the church of the order of St. Francis in Florence. To the Dominican, the Augustinian, and Carmelite Friars, I bequeath 25 lire each. To every [other] order of Friars of our city, I leave 10 lire; to every house

of monks or nuns, 5 lire; to every hospital in Florence, 2
lire, except that I wish to give 25 lire to S. Maria Nuova. I
bequeath 5 lire to each priest in the *pieve* [ecclesiastical dis-
trict] of Cascia, so that they may pray for my soul, as they
would pray for their friend. I bequeath 50 lire to Ser
Michele of Ruota, so that he will say a mass for my soul with
the priests of the *pieve*. I give 60 lire to Fra Federigo of
Bibbiena to spend on behalf of the convent of Vernia. I bequeath 25 florins to Master Battista of Poppi to refurbish the
chapel which I built.

27. THE TESTAMENT OF ANDREA DI FEO, STONEMASON, 1380*

Since death is an obligation that all men must pay, and no
one can avoid the peril of death, therefore the prudent and
discreet man, Andrea di Feo, stonemason, of the parish of
S. Piero Gattolino of Florence, being of sound mind, body,
and spirit, and wishing to make disposition of all his property and goods, has made this testament before witnesses.

First, he recommends his soul with devotion to Almighty
God and to the glorious Virgin Mary and to all the saints.
He desires that upon his death, his body is to be buried in
the convent of the Friars of S. Spirito, in whatever tomb is
selected by Master Martino [one of the friar witnesses].

Item, from his estate he orders payment made to all of his
creditors, whether the debt was recorded or not, and in particular the debts which are written in his green account
book. . . .

Item, for the love of God and the forgiveness of his sins,

* Source: *ASF, Conventi Soppressi,* 122 (S. Spirito), vol. 75, fols. 66v–71v.

he bequeaths a florin to each of the witnesses, for a total of 7 florins.

Item, so that God will show mercy to him and all of his departed relatives, he bequeaths to Master Martino of Signa the sum of 50 lire, to be given away by him (for the remission of his sins and those of the above-mentioned dead) to those poor religious or laymen or to those institutions of piety concerning which the testator has secretly informed Master Martino. If, however, Master Martino predeceases the testator, then he leaves 50 lire to Nofrio, Master of Holy Scripture, a friar of this order, to give to those poor religious or laymen whom he chooses. . . .

Item, he bequeaths 10 lire to Matteo di Ceci, of the parish of S. Maria de Casavecchia, for the love of God. Item, he bequeaths a piece of land in the *pieve* of Settimo to his relative, Lorenzo di Donato, of the parish of S. Piero Gattolino in Florence.

Item, in consideration of the fact that Cristofano di Piero, Andrea's partner in the stonemason's craft, treated him well and liberally and worked at his trade honestly with Andrea, he desires to reward Cristofano as follows. If Cristofano wishes, within five years of the testator's death, he may purchase the shop where they exercise their trade located on the Piazza de' Tornaquinci in the parish of S. Pancrazio. . . . The price is to be determined by the executors of his estate. . . .

Item, he leaves to his wife Simona, daughter of the deceased Domenico di Ciardo of Florence, her dowry of 220 florins. Item, he bequeaths the income from the house in which he lives to his daughter Simona, wife of Azino Chinucci, of the parish of S. Donato de Vecchietti of Florence, and to his daughter Magdalena, wife of Cenci di Francesco, of the parish of S. Felicita, in case they become widows and as long as they remain in that state. Moreover, he leaves to each of his daughters the sum of 10 lire.

For the remainder of his property to be divided in equal portions, he nominates as his heirs his legitimate sons who may be born posthumously to himself and his wife Simona, or any other legitimate wife.

Item, in the event that one or more legitimate daughters are born to him, he bequeaths to each the sum of 200 florins for a dowry, and until the date of marriage, they should be provided with food and clothing according to the possibilities of the estate. . . .

Item, to his wife Simona, as long as she remains a widow, he leaves the use and income of his house located in the parish of S. Piero Gattolino in Florence. Furthermore, in the event that no children survive him, he leaves to his wife Simona, while she remains a widow, 24 bushels of grain and 10 barrels of wine each year during her lifetime. . . . But in the event that she abandons the widowed state and marries again, then he leaves her only her dowry and her clothes and bedding. . . .

In the event that no legitimate sons are born to him, he bequeaths his entire estate to the Friars of the convent of S. Spirito. . . . These friars are required each Saturday of each week in perpetuity to select a priest of the order of Augustinian Hermits to celebrate a mass for the soul of Andrea and of his deceased kin in the church of S. Spirito, and this priest is required to say one mass each day of the week for the soul of the testator and his kin.

Item, the friars . . . must celebrate twice each month in perpetuity a solemn mass for the above-mentioned dead. And if in any month the friars do not celebrate the above-mentioned two masses, in the following month they shall celebrate three masses. . . . And if the masses are not celebrated during that subsequent month, then the testator stipulates that his estate shall pass to the hospital of S. Maria Nuova of Florence. The oaths of the masters of Holy Scripture in the convent will suffice to certify that these masses have been celebrated according to these instructions. If no masters are living in the convent, then the oaths of six of the oldest and most venerable friars will suffice as proof that these masses have been celebrated. . . .

28. Two Petitions for Legitimization, 1388–89*

On behalf of Andrea di Niccolò di Nino Rucellai of Florence, this petition is presented to you, lord priors. . . . He has an illegitimate son named Santi, aged nine years or thereabouts, born of his union with Sandra, daughter of Sandro of Florence. For some twenty years, she has lived with him in his house as his concubine, and since he has never had a wife, he loves her as though she were his legitimate spouse. And similarly, he loves his son Santi, and during his adolescence, he hopes to educate him in virtue and good customs as though he were legitimate. And since Andrea is now fifty years old or thereabouts and does not expect to have other children, and since he feels the greatest affection for Santi, he desires to do everything possible for him and to leave his property to him . . . and in every respect . . . to have him treated as his natural and legitimate son. Therefore, Andrea petitions your lordships . . . that he be allowed . . . to give his goods and his rights to Santi, either by means of a testament or by means of a gift or by any other method . . . and that in every respect . . . Santi is understood to be entitled to receive this property . . . as though

* Source: *ASF, Provvisioni*, 77, fols. 117r–117v; 78, fols. 259r–260r.

he were his legitimate and natural son. . . . If in the future a child should be born to Andrea and his legitimate wife, this provision is hereby nullified. . . .

On behalf of Niccolò di Sandro Bardi, this petition is presented to your lordships. . . . He has two sons named Carlo and Ugo, aged seven and eleven, who are illegitimate. He has great affection for his sons, particularly since he does not have any legitimate children, even though he has a wife. Niccolò desires to give property to Carlo and Ugo while he lives and to bequeath his estate to them in his testament, as though they were his legitimate and natural sons. In order to legitimize them, Niccolò thought of petitioning your lordships. . . . So he humbly requests that . . . notwithstanding the illegitimate condition of Carlo and Ugo, and despite the fact that they were born of a relationship both prohibited and condemned, Niccolò be permitted to give and bequeath to his sons . . . whatever property and rights he desires, while he lives and in his testament. . . . Furthermore [he requests] that Carlo and Ugo . . . henceforth be considered as legally entitled to receive this property and these rights, as though they were his legitimate sons. . . .

29. THE DIMINUTION OF AN ORPHAN'S ESTATE, 1397*

. . . [This is the petition of] Monna Caterina, daughter of Messer Giovanni Gherardini, widow of Bartolomeo di Ser Spinello of Castelfiorentino and mother of Giovanni. When Bartolomeo died, he left as his sole heir his son Giovanni, a little more than eighteen months old. Seeing her son wealthy and with large amounts of money owed to him, his

* Source: *ASF, Provvisioni*, 86, fols. 320r–321r.

mother Caterina decided to place her trust exclusively in the Commune, instead of relying upon herself and the boy's other guardians. She believed that the Commune would exercise great care and that her son's property would increase, as any sensible person would have a right to expect. So she petitioned the Commune to appoint the officials of the *Monte* [as administrators of her son's estate]. . . . However, instead of her son's property increasing, it declined by nearly one-fourth of its original value, and much of what was due him was never collected, since many of his debtors were foreigners who have either died or gone away. And whereas a minor under the Commune's tutelage should be treated leniently in the assessment of forced loans and in other levies, the contrary has occurred, and he has been so heavily burdened that he is on the verge of ruin. If something is not done to remedy this situation, the boy will live in poverty, which will be contrary to justice and would be a shameful thing for the Commune. Never has it happened that a minor under the Commune's tutelage was impoverished, while the Commune has gained a great deal of money from him.

Lord priors, I speak the truth when I say that the Commune has taken more than 36,000 florins from the boy's estate, and this you can verify at the office of the *Monte*. Moreover, the boy is currently so heavily assessed . . . that he cannot possibly pay his levy. Unable to find any remedy, Monna Caterina has been forced by necessity to appeal to you, lord priors, for justice, grace, and mercy. . . . The boy's property is fully described in the records of the officials responsible for administering the estates of minors, where you can learn the truth. [The petition, which was approved, requests that the Signoria examine the records of Giovanni's property and reduce his assessment accordingly.]

IV. Family Enmities

30. FATHER AND SON,
1380*

I record that on May 8, 1380, I, Simone di Rinieri de'
Peruzzi, made my will in Montepulciano, in the sacristy of
the Franciscan church . . . in the presence of seven solemn
and devout Franciscans. Having annulled all earlier testaments, I want this to be executed by my son Niccolò and my
other heirs, as I have today written with my own hand. And
I have so commanded him, and here I shall record its contents. I have left [this document] with Fra Simone of the
Franciscan Order of Montepulciano, in the custody of these
friars. And I composed this document on May 8, 1380 in
good conscience and with a calm and honest spirit, as a
father should act toward his children, for he should be a fair
judge and arbiter between them. If I were influenced by
rage or fury, I would have left my testament as it was, without adding the codicil, considering the numerous lies, tricks,
betrayals, and acts of disobedience of my son Benedetto
against me and my family up to the present time. These
have been recorded in part in my testament, and in part in
this secret book. In addition to my substance, which he has
spent and consumed, he has been the cause of much harm to
me [and] my family and relatives, as a result of his evil activities and disobedience. In addition to that, and without
any blame on our part, he has endangered our very lives.
Without my doing him any wrong, but rather rewarding him
for those things which he has done to the present time, I

* Source: The diary of Simone di Rinieri Peruzzi; *I libri di commercio
dei Peruzzi*, ed. A. Sapori (Milan, 1934), p. 522.

have decided to compose this document, notwithstanding any other testaments or other records which may be found in this book, written or declared by me to the present time. . . . I have done this . . . in good conscience and calm spirit, having justified myself to God, for the peace and tranquillity of my children, and to promote concord and justice among them. And through this document, I have benefitted my son Benedetto to a greater degree than my other son Niccolò, his brother. And this is the truth, and I swear it on my soul and my conscience.

Since I dictated the above-mentioned testament and the document which I shall record below, Benedetto has been exiled to Genoa. My relatives and I wished to abide by the terms of exile (which was to be for a year), as I have done, for I have always been obedient to my Commune. But he [Benedetto], inspired by a malignant spirit which has led him from bad to worse, disobeyed me, and, showing contempt for me and my family, rebelled against the Commune of our city. Therefore today, November 14, 1380, I have invalidated every document which I have made, as I declared above that I had written, and have destroyed them. And I desire that the terms of my [new] testament described below be executed, or any testament which I shall make in the future. And I curse my son Benedetto; may he be accursed to the extent of my power! . . . With lies, tricks, and betrayals, he has continually disobeyed and vituperated me, my Commune, and my family and relatives. As a result of his evil and iniquitous activities, we have suffered many dangers and we have lost honor, status, and security . . . May he be accursed by God, amen! And if he survives me, and I have not first chastised him as he deserves, may the just sentence of God punish him according to his deserts as a vile traitor.

31. SON AND FATHER,
1405*

I haven't written you in recent days because there was no need. I am writing this only to advise you of the wisdom and good judgment and the dishonorable conduct of our father Lanfredino.

Let me tell you that on the 4th day of this month, Basilio Baldini came to dine with Giacomo Pascilocha. And after they had dined, they sent for our father, and offered him some Malmsey wine and treated him with great respect. When they were well into their cups, Basilio told Lanfredino that it would give him great pleasure to arrange a peace agreement with Giacomo. He said that Giacomo had never meddled in our affairs, and that he had always been our friend and wished to remain so in the future. Lanfredino replied that he was willing, but that he didn't want this settlement to become public knowledge for ten days, because he knew that we would not be so eager to make peace, but he would arrange the matter himself. Giacomo then said that he would like to seal this agreement by drinking with me. Lanfredino replied that he should not be afraid, and then, in the presence of honorable witnesses, he promised that none of us would offend him. In summary, they drank together and made peace without the knowledge of wife or sons or relatives or friends.

Being unaware of this, I traveled to Ferrara and stayed there for three days on certain business of my brother-in-

* Source: Remigio Lanfredini in Venice to his brother Orsino in Florence; *BNF*, II, V, 7, fols. 137r–138r.

law. When I arrived home, I found our friend [Giacomo Pascilocha] in Piero's field. When he saw me, he dismounted from his horse and said: "I beg you to listen to a few words." I told him that I didn't want to hear him, and that if he accosted me, I would run him through [with a sword] from one side to the other. He replied that he couldn't force me to listen to him, but that if I struck him, even if it were not fatal, that I would destroy my family forever. And then he told me about the promise which Lanfredino had made to him. During this exchange, a certain Guglielmo del Barba happened to come along, and he told Giacomo that he was a beast, and that he should go about his affairs. So then we separated and I came home.

There I told Lanfredino: "You didn't know that I met Giacomo and he told me what you have said. By God's body, he wouldn't leave me before discussing this business with me, and he wanted to disgrace me before the whole world!" Lanfredino didn't reply to me but began to weep like the traitor he is. And then our mother said: "My son, suffer as much as you can, for God will so arrange matters that we will have a just vendetta." And we didn't discuss the issue further, but every time I spoke to Lanfredino, he began to cry like Cain, the traitor that he is. For I will never regard him as anything but a traitor and an evil man, and if I were to see him collapse at my feet, I wouldn't give him a penny!

After he had cried for a long time and had betrayed me twenty times, I asked him what these laments signified. And he said, "Remigio, you are my son and you should be content with my decisions; I did it for the best." And he wouldn't explain anything to me, but after moaning for a long time, he gave a reason to my mother, being too ashamed to tell me. "You see, Giovanna," he said, "I received an order from the Marquis [of Ferrara] to make peace with Giacomo Pascilocha. Explain this to Remigio, for I didn't want to tell him. He will believe the story from your lips." But Monna Giovanna replied, "Oh, Lanfredino, you are a traitor to your own kin! For you have disgraced your sons by making peace without informing them or me. Now you have taken away their property, their honor, and everything which they possess in the world."

Having learned everything about this business, I told Lanfredino what I thought and left him in a very bitter mood. I have come to Venice with a letter of recommendation and am trying to establish myself with some merchant. But I have only found one merchant who is going overseas, and he has offered me a salary of only 3 florins per month, and I wanted 4. So we did not come to any agreement. While I was staying at the inn, I met the chancellor of Messer Taddeo del Verne who wanted to hire someone, and I have agreed to serve as his accountant with a salary of 3½ ducats per month. . . .

I received a letter from Lanfredino, which I am enclosing with this letter. . . . When I left home, I told him never to call me his son, and I said that I would change my surname. In fact, I have been calling myself a Bellini from Florence, and my only goal now is to establish myself as a merchant to regain my reputation, and to demonstrate my desire to succeed and to restore past damages. . . . We can see that Lanfredino doesn't care a fig about us and gives no thought to either honor or shame. . . . By my faith, since he doesn't care about me, I care less about him. If I were to see him cut to pieces before my eyes, I would not raise myself from my seat. . . .

32. Disputes Among Heirs, 1385*

Dearest brother. I received your letter containing the information which you had received from other sources, saying in effect that my father, mother, and brother had died, and that I have become rich, etc. To which I can only reply that I have had such troubles, as you will see from my account, that I have been unable to write sooner.

It is true that after the death of my parents and my brother, the bishop initiated a process against Sandro's [Domenico's father's] estate, accusing him of usury. This has been a source of great embarrassment, and I am not yet absolved, nor will I be absolved without great loss. In addition to that, numerous creditors have appealed [to the court], some with documents and others with records, who demand the little that remains. Then there are others at the bishop's court who claim the usury which they had paid to Sandro in the past. So I have been very busy defending myself in these lawsuits, and you must excuse me for not writing earlier.

And while these troubles have been bad enough, those of my sister, concerning whom you have written me, are even greater. . . . A certain Monna Ghinga, the widow of Pocchegiate, together with her son, have used the excuse of their blood connections [with us] to persuade Druda [Domenico's sister] to believe that they would contract a marriage for her with the richest knight in Florence. Even though Sandro had left only 300 florins for her dowry and

* Source: Domenico di Sandro Lanfredini to Lanfredino di Orsino Lanfredini; *BNF*, II, V, 7, fols. 5r–5v.

no more, they would so arrange it that the entire inheritance would pass to her. Druda believed them and began to quarrel with me, so that, fearing something worse, I agreed to allow her to go with Ghinga and her son Nanni, thinking that she would return after a few days. But expecting to profit from this, they first looted the house and they have induced her to sue me in court right up to the present time. But I have the law on my side, and they haven't gained anything. Despite everything that she has done to me, I have been willing to forgive Druda and told her that if she returns home, I will endeavor to find her a husband who pleases her, and if the dowry of 300 florins which her father left does not suffice, then I would contribute 400 or 500 florins, if necessary, so long as she was properly established. But she would have none of it, but placed her faith in the words of those who have been flattering her. . . . Without my consent or even without asking me, they have married her to a certain Luca delle Calvane, who is a man of little worth, with five children from his first wife. . . . From this affair, I have had much grief, for I planned to arrange for her marriage with your advice during this coming Lent, as I have written. If I behaved badly during the illness of Sandro, my mother, and Lamberto, you can now understand if there is any truth in the story. . . . To whomever calls me a madman and a scoundrel, I reply that I am not afraid of shame. I also reply that I do not wish to make any excuses, except that I marvel at your willingness to put faith in letters written with malice and trickery by someone who not only has betrayed me, but who has sought to betray you.

That evil Nanni wrote you that I am rich. If this were true, I would be content. And since it would be to your benefit as well as mine, I believe that you would also be pleased. But you should know that Sandro's estate, counting my mother's dowry, is not worth 1,000 florins. Then subtract Druda's dowry, which I did not want to pay, but was forced to pay, since the sum of 300 florins was stipulated in the will. In addition, I have to pay more than 200 florins to the bishop and to those who are owed money for usury. . . . So consider how large is the balance which remains to me. . . .

33. A Broken Marriage, 1377*

To you, lord priors . . . of the city and Commune of Florence, with reverence and tears, this petition is presented by Monna Nicolosa, widow of Giovanni di Ventura, a mercer, of the parish of S. Reparata of Florence. It is true that Duccio di Agostino di Duccio de' Benegli of S. Martino la Palma took as his wife Monna Madelena, daughter of Giovanni [di Ventura]. And having taken her, Duccio beat her and maltreated her unmercifully, and wished to kill her without any cause. With the license of the priors then in office and with their messenger, Giovanni brought his daughter back to his house. It was then formally decreed by the priors and other good men that Duccio and Agostino had to give her a certain amount of food each year. Agostino had recently left S. Martino la Palma to stay in Florence, and last July, this hypocritical and perverse man and his son Duccio . . . conspired to kill Giovanni di Ventura, an artisan and a weak man, the father-in-law of Duccio, who only a short time ago was one of the priors, and has been an official [of his guild] on several occasions. Agostino ordered Duccio to assassinate Giovanni, and also told his son Felice to help him. . . .

* Source: I. Del Badia, ed., *Miscellanea fiorentina* (Florence, 1902), I, 11.

Moreover, Agostino loaned his horse, saddled and ready, to Duccio at his house in Florence, on which Duccio fled to Pisa immediately after the homicide, to the house of his relatives there. Desiring to put into execution this evil plan, Duccio with his companions . . . assaulted Giovanni di Ventura on a plot of land in the parish of S. Maria de Falgano di Valdisieve. . . . They struck and wounded Giovanni with knives, as a result of which he fell to the earth dead. And if it had not been for the outcry which arose, they would have gone to the farmhouse to burn it down and kill Giovanni's wife and children. . . .

Agostino and Duccio all belong to a powerful clan, the house of Benegli in S. Martino la Palma, and they are among the wealthiest and most powerful members of that family, of those who live in the *contado*. And there are more than sixty men with arms, rich and powerful, and they continue to threaten to kill Giovanni's sons. Moreover, Duccio and Agostino have forbidden anyone to cultivate the farm which belonged to Giovanni, so that the land lies idle, and they [the members of Giovanni's family] have nothing for their sustenance. So, having killed the father, [and] retained the dowry of the daughter, they now wish to starve the family, and they will continue to persecute them into the next world. . . .

34. The Murder of a Brother, 1393*

. . . We condemn . . . Tommaso di Messer Guccio di Dino Gucci of the parish of S. Lucia Ogni Santi. . . . While

* Sources: *ASF, Atti del Esecutore degli Ordinamenti di Giustizia,* 1170, fols. 55r–58v; R. Piattoli, "L'origine dei fondaci datiniani di Pisa e Genova," *Archivio storico pratese,* VII (1927), 180.

Tommaso was in prison . . . and realizing that he had
been offended and injured many times by his brothers,
Giorgio and Salvano . . . he saw no other way to leave
prison except by the death of one or both of them. . . . He
decided to arrange for the death . . . of Giorgio who was
the primary cause of his misfortunes. . . . Six months ago,
a certain Englishman named Richard was captured and detained in prison . . . and Tommaso had several conversations with him and established a friendly relationship
with him. When Richard was about to leave prison, Tommaso told him of his plan and asked him to arrange with
one of his friends or associates to kill his brother Giorgio,
and he promised to pay him 100 florins if the assassination
was successful. Then Richard promised to do what Tommaso
asked, and the two men were in agreement. But after Richard
was released from prison, he left Florence and did not keep
his promise to Tommaso.

Realizing that he had been deceived by Richard, Tommaso
persisted with his evil and iniquitous plan . . . and became
friends with a certain Jacopo di Bartolomeo, of the parish of
S. Ambrogio, called "El Maxina". Tommaso knew that Jacopo had a nephew, Nanni di Simone . . . who was capable
of doing what Tommaso desired, and he suggested to Jacopo
that he ask his nephew to serve him. . . . In September
1392, Nanni went to Tommaso and told him that he would
do everything that Tommaso requested. Knowing that a
certain stone-cutter from Fiesole called "El Straza" was a
criminal type and an enemy of his brother, Tommaso said
to Nanni: "I have need of your services for a project which
is very important to me, and if you help me, you will find
that I will be your good friend and will serve you so that
you will be content and you will never lack for anything."
Then Nanni told Tommaso: "I am ready to do everything

that you command." Tommaso said, "Nanni, I want you to find a stone-cutter of Fiesole named "El Straza" who used to work at S. Reparata and then had to leave the territory for certain reasons. Now I hear that he is in Bologna and I want you to find him. On your return, you should contact my servant, Martelaccio. . . ."

Nanni then went to Bologna but he could not find "El Straza" and so he returned to Florence and told Martelaccio . . . who went to the prison to inform Tommaso. . . . Then Tommaso said, "Martelaccio, I have need of your services at this time. I am determined to kill my brother Giorgio who has kept me in prison, and has treated me as badly as possible. I have tried to arrange for his assassination, but I have not been successful. Now I appeal to you to go to Nanni and work with him to accomplish this. . . ." Martelaccio replied, "Tommaso, in this affair or anything else, I am willing to do what you want, insofar as I am able." Then he went to Nanni and told him everything that Tommaso had said. . . . So while Giorgio was in the palace of the Signoria . . . and remained there until one hour after sunset, they went to a location . . . in the parish of S. Trinita in a district called Parione, by the route which Giorgio customarily followed when he returned from the palace to his home. . . . When Giorgio approached the spot where Nanni and Martelaccio were hidden, Nanni attacked him with a knife . . . and wounded him in the chest . . . and Giorgio fell to the ground and died. . . . [Tommaso confessed to his role in the crime; he was sentenced to death and the confiscation of his property. The two assassins escaped and were condemned to death *in absentia*.]

[Domenico di Cambio in Florence to Francesco Datini in Prato.] Yesterday after dinner Tommaso di Messer Guccio

[Gucci] was taken to his execution; never has there been such a crowd as witnessed this execution. His escort was not able to pass through [the piazza of] S. Croce, on account of the throng, so they went along the Via Ghibellina, and Tommaso was taken from them and he fled into S. Croce. If it had not been for Filippo di Ugucciozzo, who recaptured him, he would have escaped. Then the Signoria sent their officials there and brought him back to the palace of the Signoria, whereupon the crowd assembled in the piazza [della Signoria]. Then the captain of the *popolo* appeared with his armed retinue and ordered the crowd to disperse. . . . Seeing that the people had left, the Signoria placed Tommaso in the hands of the executor and he was executed. . . . As Tommaso was being returned to the palace, a crowd of some 200 boys armed with stones surrounded the house of Messer Guccio and broke open a door and tried to set fire to the house. They shouted: "We want to kill the wife of Messer Guccio [Tommaso's mother], who is guilty of Tommaso's death." If the Signoria had not sent four troops of police, they would have burned down the house.

Later, when Tommaso's body was taken to the church, those who were carrying it wanted to throw it into Messer Guccio's house, and they would have done this if the podestà with his entourage had not been there. The podestà commanded them to carry the body to the church and then ordered the friars to bury the corpse immediately. . . . When you read this letter, I ask that you destroy it, in honor of Messer Guccio's family, which did not deserve the death of one of their brothers.

PART THREE

COLLECTIVITIES

While the family was the primary unit of social organization
in Florence, every citizen belonged to other corporate bodies
which claimed his allegiance. He was a member of Florence's
Christian community, and he had a more specific attachment
to the parish church or the monastery of his neighborhood.
Ordering and regulating his secular activities were his guild
and the Commune. Guild affiliation was a prerequisite to
membership in the political community, and to the right to
hold communal office. A relic from a past age of factional
strife was the Parte Guelfa, a political organization which
had been very powerful in the early fourteenth century, but
which had lost much of its influence and vitality by 1400.
Periodically, the Parte sought to establish and enforce standards of loyalty to Guelfism, and to extirpate the political
heresy of Ghibellinism. These organizations were "establishment" societies to which the solid and respected citizens
of Florence belonged. Outside this structure were other
groups, with varying degrees of cohesion and permanence.
We know little about them since their members were re-
cruited from the ranks of the poor and the illiterate. Repre-
sentative of this type of collectivity was the community of
heretics known as the Fraticelli (Part Eight, nos. 123-125).
But there were other clandestine groups which flourished
in the subterranean levels of Florentine society and which
have left few traces in the sources: workers' societies, youth

gangs, organizations of the beggars and vagabonds, sorcerers' cults.

On certain festive occasions, and particularly on the feast day of Florence's patron saint, John the Baptist, the corporate communities which made up the social order joined together in a demonstration of fraternity and solidarity (no. 35). In times of crisis, however, this façade of harmony broke down, as competing groups fought each other in the city's streets and squares (no. 36). The ultimate victor in this power struggle was the Commune, which claimed to speak for the whole community even though it was itself controlled by a small minority. The Commune adjudicated disputes between the feuding corporate groups; it suppressed those which threatened (or appeared to threaten) its hegemony (no. 39). The demands made upon its members (nos. 37-38) were not unlike those imposed by the modern state.

I. Corporations and Community

35. AN OCCASION OF SOLIDARITY*

When springtime comes and the whole world rejoices, every Florentine begins to think about organizing a magnificent celebration on the feast day of St. John the Baptist [June 24]. . . . For two months in advance, everyone is planning marriage feasts or other celebrations in honor of the day. There are preparations for the horse races, the costumes of the retinues, the flags and the trumpets; there are the pennants and the wax candles and other things which

* Source: Gregorio Dati, *Istoria di Firenze dall'anno MCCCLXXX all'anno MCCCCV* (Florence, 1735), pp. 84-89.

the subject territories offer to the Commune. Messengers are sent to obtain provisions for the banquets, and horses come from everywhere to run in the races. The whole city is engaged in preparing for the feast, and the spirits of the young people and the women [are animated] by these preparations. . . . Everyone is filled with gaiety; there are dances and concerts and songfests and tournaments and other joyous activities. Up to the eve of the holiday, no one thinks about anything else.

Early on the morning of the day before the holiday, each guild has a display outside of its shops of its fine wares, its ornaments and jewels. There are cloths of gold and silk sufficient to adorn ten kingdoms. . . . Then at the third hour, there is a solemn procession of clerics, priests, monks, and friars, and there are so many [religious] orders, and so many relics of saints, that the procession seems endless. [It is a manifestation] of great devotion, on account of the marvelous richness of the adornments . . . and clothing of gold and silk with embroidered figures. There are many confraternities of men who assemble at the place where their meetings are held, dressed as angels, and with musical instruments of every kind and marvelous singing. They stage the most beautiful representations of the saints, and of those relics in whose honor they perform. They leave from S. Maria del Fiore [the cathedral] and march through the city and then return.

Then, after midday, when the heat has abated before sunset, all of the citizens assemble under [the banner of] their district, of which there are sixteen. Each goes in the procession in turn, the first, then the second, and so on with one district following the other, and in each group the citizens march two by two, with the oldest and most distinguished at the head, and proceeding down to the young men in rich garments. They march to the church of St. John [the Baptistery] to offer, one by one, a wax candle weighing one pound. . . . The walls along the streets through which they pass are all decorated, and there are . . . benches on which are seated young ladies and girls dressed in silk and adorned with jewels, pearls, and precious stones. This procession continues until sunset, and after each citizen has made his offering, he returns home with his wife to prepare for the next morning.

Whoever goes to the Piazza della Signoria on the morning of St. John's Day witnesses a magnificent, marvelous, and triumphant sight, which the mind can scarcely grasp. Around the great piazza are a hundred towers which appear to be made of gold. Some were brought on carts and others by porters. . . . [These towers] are made of wood, paper, and wax [and decorated] with gold, colored paints, and with figures. . . . Next to the rostrum of the palace [of the Signoria] are standards . . . which belong to the most important towns which are subject to the Commune: Pisa, Arezzo, Pistoia, Volterra, Cortona, Lucignano. . . .

First to present their offering, in the morning, are the captains of the Parte Guelfa, together with all of the knights, lords, ambassadors, and foreign knights. They are accompanied by a large number of the most honorable citizens, and before them, riding on a charger covered with a cloth . . . is one of their pages carrying a banner with the insignia of the Parte Guelfa. Then there follow the abovementioned standards, each one carried by men on horseback . . . and they all go to make their offerings at the Baptistery. And these standards are given as tribute by the districts which have been acquired by the Commune of Florence. . . . The wax candles, which have the appearance of golden towers, are the tribute of the regions which in most ancient times were subject to the Florentines. In order of dignity, they are brought, one by one, to be offered to St. John, and on the following day, they are hung inside the church and there they remain for the entire year until the next feast day. . . . Then come . . . an infinite number of large wax candles, some weighing 100 pounds and others 50, some more and some less . . . carried by the residents of the villages [in the *contado*] which offer them. . . .

Then the lord priors and their colleges come to make their offerings, accompanied by their rectors, that is, the podestà, the captain [of the *popolo*], and the executor. . . . And after the lord [priors] come those who are participating in the horse race, and they are followed by the Flemings and the residents of Brabant who are weavers of woolen cloth in Florence. Then there are offerings by twelve prisoners who, as an act of mercy, have been released from prison . . . in honor of St. John, and these are poor people. . . . After all of these offerings have been made, men and women return home to dine. . . . [There follows a description of the horse race which takes place in the afternoon.]

36. A COMMUNITY IN DISORDER*

On Monday night, January 13 [1382], Messer Giorgio Scali, with armed men from the two new guilds [of artisans which had been created in 1378] . . . and with their Ghibelline followers went to the palace of the captain [of the *popolo*], all together about four hundred men. From his custody, they took Scatizza, a cloth shearer, who on the following morning was to be executed by the captain. . . .

* Source: *BNF, Fondo Panciatichiano*, 158, fols. 140r–141r.

He had confessed that he was planning to kill all the Guelfs and deliver the city to Messer Bernabò Visconti, lord of Milan. The next morning, the captain went to the palace of the Signoria and, narrating to the priors what had happened the night before, he resigned his office. . . . This greatly displeased the priors, their colleges, and the good citizens, and there was much talk throughout the city. . . . On Thursday morning, January 16, 1382, the captain received authority to punish whoever erred, and his office was returned to him. . . . After dinner, the captain had Giorgio Scali captured, and there was a lot of talk among the Ghibellines. . . . The militia captains armed their companies for the security of the city, and so that no disorders would break out. . . .

On Friday morning, January 17, Messer Giorgio Scali was executed for treason on the wall of the captain's courtyard. He confessed that he was going to surrender the city to Messer Bernabò Visconti of Milan, and that on the 21st, he was going to ravage the city and rob and kill all of the Guelfs. . . . On Saturday, the 18th, the cry went up: "Long live the Parte Guelfa," but no banners were displayed. And the Guelfs, all armed with swords in hand, ran through the city streets. . . . The city was peaceful and that night the Guelfs fortified themselves.

. . . On Monday morning, the 20th, Messer Donato di Ricco and Feo, the armorer, were executed on the wall of the courtyard, and immediately a disturbance broke out and [the people] shouted, "Long live the Parte Guelfa and death to the Ghibellines!" And they ran through the city streets with three flags of the Parte Guelfa. . . . The city was in arms and all of the Guelfs were in the piazza. . . . At vespers, the standard of the Parte Guelfa was given to Giovanni Cambi, and with that [banner] displayed, the entire populace marched in procession—the worthy citizens, the soldiers, the people—in an atmosphere of joy and celebration. . . . That night the city was peaceful. On Tuesday morning, the 21st, members of the guild of cloth manufacturers armed themselves, and together with the prominent citizens, they assembled in the Mercato Nuovo, and they demanded that the two new guilds be disbanded, and this was done. The houses where they met were ransacked, with all of their furnishings, arms, and papers. . . .

Then on Wednesday morning, the 22nd, the fourteen lower guilds [of artisans and shopkeepers] assembled and marched to the Piazza della Signoria. [The priors] marveled at this and asked them what they wanted. They replied that they had heard that the magnates desired to ransack the city, and they said this to disguise the fact that they wished to restore the two disbanded guilds, for they feared that they too would be barred from office. The members of the cloth manufacturers' guild armed themselves and marched to the piazza where they attacked the butchers. There was a great struggle, in which two died and several were wounded. The flags [of the Commune] and of the Parte Guelfa were brought out of the palace [of the Signoria] and carried several times around the piazza, and as a result, the people became calm. And all of the flags of the guilds were collected and brought into the palace of the Signoria.

On Thursday, the 23rd, the Signoria issued a decree that every citizen should stand with his arms and on the alert, for they feared that the fourteen lower guilds would attempt to restore the two disbanded guilds. And the seven greater guilds assembled, together with the rich and prominent citizens, in the Mercato Nuovo with a large force. . . . On Friday, the 24th, the shops, factories, and moneychangers' tables were all open and trouble erupted, whereupon the seven greater guilds assembled with the rich and worthy citizens in the Mercato Nuovo. . . . On Saturday evening, the 25th, the Guelfs marched through the city with torches and lanterns, but no one did or said anything against them. . . . And many pacts were concluded among the Guelfs, who agreed to stay united in peace and amity to maintain their status.

II. The Commune

37. CIVIC SPIRIT*

[July 4, 1388] Matteo di Scelto Tinghi said that he is prepared to suffer death for liberty, and to give 500 florins [to the Commune] now, and later another 500, and then, at intervals, all that he possesses.

[May 22, 1413] Piero di Messer Luigi Guicciardini said that although he has nearly been ruined by taxes levied in the past, nevertheless he is prepared to offer the remainder of his possessions, and his body and soul, and others should be urged to do likewise, so that we can live in freedom.

[May 24, 1413] Messer Rinaldo Gianfigliazzi said that our homeland (*patria*) is more precious than our children, and everything should be done for its wellbeing, so that we will bequeath to our posterity that which we received from our ancestors.

[December 6, 1413] Berardo di Buonaccorso Berardi said that he fears that as a result of our maladministration, either

* Source: *ASF, Consulte e Pratiche*, 26, fol. 224r; 42, fols. 14v, 17v, 94v.

divine anger or fortuitous circumstances will bring about our ruin, considering our actions which provoke God's wrath, and comparing the works of our ancestors with ours at the present time. For in the past, many sought to gain political power and office for glory and fame; today no one seeks it except for private advantage and profit. . . . It is to be feared that if it is not checked, civic dissension will lead to our ruin. Everyone says that evil will befall us, but no one offers a remedy. . . . Our only hope for safety lies in concord; dissent must be suppressed, and the Signoria should delegate some citizens to achieve this. . . .

38. A PATRIOTIC APPEAL, 1401*

. . . You say that you do not intend . . . to return to Florence . . . because of the excessive tax burdens which have been imposed on you by the Commune, and because in your opinion, these will not be reduced. It is true that the Commune has been in disorder, but it is my feeling that at the present time order has been restored, and every day measures are taken to reduce expenditures and increase revenues. . . . Our city needs the equalization of the tax burden, so that everyone pays his proper share. I think that, with God's grace, my colleagues . . . will do everything to achieve this, and I believe that they will succeed. . . . And considering that everyone is obligated to his country, and should never abandon it, particularly in time of adversity, I tell you that I am one of those who advises you not to forsake yours. If you do, you will be censured by God and by the world, because you do not have any valid reason.

* Source: Domenico Giugni in Florence to Francesco Datini in Bologna; *Archivio di Stato, Prato, Archivio Datini,* 719, no pagination.

Those who levy taxes say that they wished to treat you
equitably, and I believe that they did so, and until you
have evidence to the contrary, you should not complain.

39. THE DISSOLUTION OF THE CONFRATERNITIES, 1419*

. . . The lord priors . . . desire to eliminate the cause
and occasion of scandals and to remove all suspicion from
the minds of the authorities so that everyone can live peace-
ably. They have learned that as a result of the meeting of
certain confraternities, the spirits of the citizenry have been
perturbed, divisions have arisen, and many other incon-
veniences have occurred. Desiring to provide the proper
remedy, they . . . have decreed . . . that every confraternity, whether penitential or dedicated to singing lauds
. . . which is accustomed to assemble in the ecclesiastical
foundations of the city of Florence . . . is henceforth to be
dissolved and banned, and its meetings categorically prohibited. Whoever has . . . the custody of any of the books
or documents containing the names of the confraternity's
members, or their constitutions, observances, and regulations
must bring them to the chancellor of the Commune of
Florence during the month of October. . . .

Item, the lord priors . . . are authorized, between now
and the end of November, to dispose of all property, both
real and personal, belonging to these confraternities . . .
for the benefit of the souls, and for the remissions of sins, of
those who had given that property to those confraternities. . . .

Item, all of the furnishings in the buildings of these con-

* Source: *ASF, Provvisioni*, 109, fols. 160v–161v.

fraternities are to be totally destroyed . . . and the places of assembly . . . are to be used for other purposes or for habitation, or they are to be closed . . . so that no congregation or meeting can be held in them. . . .

Item, none of the confraternities may assemble or congregate in any other location, whether ecclesiastical or secular, within or outside the city of Florence. . . .

Item, no person, lay or clerical, of whatever dignity, status, quality, or eminence may allow any company to assemble in his house. . . .

Item, no confraternity may be newly created or established in the city of Florence or within a three-mile radius. . . . This provision does not apply . . . to any confraternity which is newly established with the license and consent of the lord priors. . . . [Within each] confraternity which is accepted, confirmed, and approved by the above-mentioned license . . . the members thereof . . . are prohibited from . . . interfering by word or deed in matters pertaining to the Commune of Florence, to the Merchants' Court, to any guild . . . in the city of Florence, or to the administration of any of them. . . .

III. *The Parte Guelfa*

40. A GUELF ASSOCIATION,
c. 1350*

In the name of God and of the Virgin Mary. May it be manifest to whoever shall see or read this document that

* Source: C. Guasti, ed., *Le Carte Strozziane del R. Archivio di Stato di Firenze* (Florence, 1884–91), I, 98–100.

. . . all of us in the past have been united—as relatives, neighbors, and friends—by one spirit, and [that we are] faithful and devoted [members] of the Holy Church, supporters of the *popolo* and the Commune and the liberty of Florence and of the Parte Guelfa. We therefore . . . promise and swear to help each other, and to provide as much support as is necessary, as do those who are united by ties of blood. In order to preserve fully this agreement among ourselves, we have drawn up this document, signed at the end by each of us, in which there is contained, chapter by chapter, our intentions and desires, to wit:

First, we agree and desire that there shall be compiled an assessment of _____ gold florins, so that every expense which might occur can be paid from this money. . . .

Item, we shall choose or elect three arbiters, whose responsibility it is to recognize and settle everything which might arise among us. . . .

Item, none of the signatories shall engage in any dispute or quarrel, without the consent of the abovementioned arbiters. If anyone violates this provision, the arbiters may correct and punish him, as they wish.

Item, if any one of us is offended or outraged by any person, each and every one is obligated to help, defend and avenge him, with his life and property, and to respond to that quarrel as though it were to his own person. No one is allowed to make any agreement or peace settlement without the decision of the abovementioned arbiters.

Item, if any of the signatories commits an offense, outrage, or villainy against any person, as a consequence of which he must carry arms, then everyone must carry them, and each one accompany and assist the other, as true brothers and blood relations. . . .

Item, if any one of us has a lawsuit in the palace [of the

Signoria] with an influential person, or is involved in a serious case, then each one is obliged to accompany him and to render aid and counsel, like true brothers and blood relatives, at the request of those who are involved in these suits.

Item, if any one or more of us is fined for any cause which resulted from an act committed in support of, or on behalf of, any one of us, or all of the signatories, and if that was done by command or decision of the arbiters, in that event the fine should be paid for all of the signatories, in accordance with their assessment. . . .

And we are in agreement, and we desire, promise, and swear on the Holy Gospels to observe and maintain the abovementioned things, and never to violate them, but henceforth to be loyal and faithful the one to the other, in quarrels and in peace, in which concord may God favor and maintain us through his mercy.

41. GUELFS AND GHIBELLINES, 1347*

The lord priors have heard and comprehended the expositions and supplications made to them . . . by zealous Guelfs who are loyal to the Holy Roman Church, to the effect that the Guelfs of the city, *contado*, and district of Florence . . . have always striven for the glory and honor of Mother Church and they intend to continue to do so with all of their power. [They assert that] there are some who are not only rebels of Mother Church, but also of the *popolo* and Commune of Florence, who have insinuated themselves into the administration and government of the city of Florence and

* Source: *Delizie degli eruditi toscani*, ed. Ildefonso di San Luigi (Florence, 1770–89), XIII, 314.

with iniquitous and deceitful words and operations, endeavor
to separate devoted and faithful children from their vener-
ated mother. . . . So the abovementioned lord priors desire
to have the Holy Roman Church as the mother of her Guelf
children, and to prevent those seeking to sow discord from
achieving their goals and from interfering in the administration of the Florentine republic, which is to be ruled and gov-
erned by true Guelfs. . . . In honor, praise, and reverence
of the omnipotent God and the glorious Virgin, and in
exaltation and augmentation of Mother Church and the
magnificent Parte Guelfa . . . they provide, ordain, and
decree the following:

First, no Ghibelline who has been condemned and out-
lawed for rebellion since November 1, 1300 . . . or who
has rebelled (or will rebel in future) . . . against the *popolo*
and Commune of Florence . . . or his son or descendant
. . . in the male line . . . may hold any office of the *popolo*
and Commune of Florence or any office in the Parte Guelfa
or . . . in any guild. . . .

If any doubt should arise concerning any person or persons who are drawn for, or elected to any of the above-mentioned offices, that he might be or is said to be one of those
prohibited, then there should be held . . . a deliberation
of the lord priors . . . [with their colleges] . . . whether
or not that person should be removed from office. And if it
is decided by a majority of them by secret vote . . . then
he is to be removed from that office. . . .

Anyone may accuse [or] denounce [a person] and notify
[the authorities] about the abovementioned cases . . . and
the podestà, captain, and executor . . . must take cognizance of this and proceed by means of an inquisition, and
punish and condemn [the guilty]. . . . And for proof, the
testimony of six reputable witnesses suffices. . . .

42. THE DECLINE OF THE PARTE GUELFA, 1413*

In November of that year, the captains of the Parte Guelfa took counsel with a large number of Guelfs who had been assembled and also with the two regular councils. . . . With their colleges and with ninety-six Guelf co-adjutors they assumed the authority for reforming offices of the Parte with a new scrutiny, after burning and annulling all of the previous scrutinies. They were motivated to do this, because the Parte had lost much of its accustomed honor and reputation. So low indeed had it fallen that the captains had difficulty in recruiting citizens to accompany them on their processions to make the customary offerings. This resulted from the disdain felt by good and true Guelfs at seeing many Ghibellines and parvenus of low condition occupying the offices of the Parte Guelfa.

[November 16, 1413] Piero Baroncelli said that nothing is more desirable than to live in peace, to value and to conserve the status [of everyone], and to unite the citizenry. The captains [of the Parte Guelfa] say that they desire to achieve this, and that they seek to reform the Parte because it is not in a good condition. Everyone should rejoice, and if toward this end they hold a new scrutiny [for offices], that is proper. . . . But it is displeasing to hear that . . . the scrutinies should be burned, and it is even worse to hear that all scrutinies of the Commune should be burned. Everyone must deplore this. All of the troubles which have occurred in the city since 1378 had their origin in this

* Sources: *Two Memoirs of Renaissance Florence,* ed. Brucker, pp. 98–99; *ASF, Consulte e Pratiche,* 42, fol. 88r.

[tampering with elections], and it has almost brought the city to destruction. On no account should it be done. Let the Signoria agree with the captains [of the Parte Guelfa] and others to have a new scrutiny . . . but no burnings. The palace [of the Parte Guelfa] is on a par with this palace [of the Signoria] in the government of the city. . . .

Rinaldo di Filippo Rondinelli said that as a result of our actions, God must regard us with loathing. We take no account of our condition, nor of the imminent dangers which threaten us. Daily we seek changes. . . . There are errors in the scrutinies of the Parte, but this results from unwise nominations. The present [reform] is not useful; rather, the Parte should be strengthened. . . . The captains should proceed with holding a new scrutiny, but nothing should be burned . . . and the Signoria should so instruct the captains. . . .

Messer Lorenzo Ridolfi said that everyone ought to honor and exalt the Parte. He who is not willing to do so is not a citizen but a rebel. . . .

Messer Rinaldo Gianfigliazzi said that as a result of the Parte's poor condition, the captains are not obeyed by the citizens when they call them to assembly, or when they ask for oblations. Since the society does not function properly, many refuse to go. . . . He and his three sons are in the bags [i.e., they were nominated for Parte office], and he has seen three or four men chosen as captains whose relatives, being Ghibellines, could not bear arms in the *contado* . . . which is a scandal to the Parte Guelfa. . . .

IV. The Guilds

43. THE CORPORATION OF WINE MERCHANTS*

[Chapter 18] It is also decreed and ordained that the consuls [of the guild] are required, by their oath, to force all of the winesellers . . . who sell at retail in the city and *contado* of Florence to swear allegiance to this guild and for this guild. And for this purpose they must make a monthly search through the city and the suburbs of Florence, and if they find anyone who is not matriculated in the guild, they must require him to swear allegiance. . . . And whoever, as has been said, is engaged in this trade, even though he is not . . . matriculated in the guild . . . is considered to be a member of the guild. . . . And each newly matriculated wineseller . . . must pay . . . 5 lire to the guild treasurer . . . as his matriculation fee. . . . If, however, he is a father or son of a guild member, then he is not required to pay anything. . . .

[Chapter 20] The consuls, treasurer, and notary of the guild are required to assemble together wherever they wish . . . to render justice to whoever demands it of the men of this guild, against any and all those . . . who sell wine at retail . . . in the city, *contado*, and district of Florence. . . . [They must] hear, take cognizance of, make decisions, and act on everything which pertains to their office, and accept every appeal which is brought before them by whosoever has any claim upon any member of the guild. . . . They

---

* Source: *Statuti delle arti dei fornai e dei vinattieri di Firenze* a cura di Francesca Morandini [*Fonti sulle corporazioni medioevali*, V], (Florence, 1956), pp. 82–87, 89–90, 103. Printed by permission of Casa Editrice Leo S. Olschki.

must record [these acts] in their protocols and render justice
with good faith and without fraud on one day of each week.
. . . . With respect to these disputes, the consuls are required
to proceed in the following manner. If any dispute or quarrel
is brought against any member of the guild . . . and it involves a sum of 3 Florentine lire di piccolo or less, this dispute is to be decided summarily by the consuls, after the
parties have sworn an oath, in favor of whoever appears to
be more honest and of better reputation. . . . If the dispute
involves 60 soldi or more, the consuls, after receiving the
complaint, are required to demand that . . . the defendant
appear to reply to the complaint. . . . [Witnesses are to be
called and interrogated in such major disputes, and the consuls must announce their judgment within one month.]

[Chapter 21] It is decreed and ordained that each wineseller shall come to the assembly of the guild as often as he
is summoned by the consuls. . . . The consuls are required
to levy a fine of 10 soldi . . . against whoever violates this
[rule], and the same penalty is to be incurred by anyone who
fails to respond to the consuls' order to come to the guild's
offering in a church. . . . And if necessity requires that
. . . the members of the guild assemble under their banner
to stand guard, or to go on a march, by day or night, in the
city and *contado* of Florence or elsewhere, every member of
the guild is required to appear in person, with or without
arms as ordered, with their standard-bearer and under their
banner, or pay a fine of 10 lire. . . .

[Chapter 35] For the honor of the guild and of the members of the guild, it is decreed and ordained that whenever
any member of the guild dies, all guild members in the city
and suburbs who are summoned by the messenger of the
guild . . . are required to go to the service for the dead
man, and to stay there until he is buried. . . . And the

consuls are required to send the guild messenger, requesting
and inviting the members of the guild to participate in the
obsequies for the dead. . . .

44. A Charitable Enterprise,
1421*

[October 20, 1421] . . . This petition is presented with
all due reverence to you, lord priors, on behalf of your devoted sons of the guild of Por Santa Maria [the silk guild]
and the merchants and guildsmen of that association. It is
well known to all of the people of Florence that this guild
has sought, through pious acts, to conserve . . . and also to
promote your republic and this guild. It has begun to construct a most beautiful edifice in the city of Florence and in
the parish of S. Michele Visdomini, next to the piazza called
the "Frati de' Servi." [This building is] a hospital called
S. Maria degli Innocenti, in which shall be received those
who, against natural law, have been deserted by their fathers
or their mothers, that is, infants, who in the vernacular are
called *gittatelli* [literally, castaways; foundlings]. Without
the help and favor of your benign lordships, it will not be
possible to transform this laudable objective into reality . . .
nor after it has been achieved, to preserve and conserve it.

And since [we] realized that your lordships and all of the
people are, in the highest degree, committed to works of
charity, [we have] decided to have recourse to your clem-
ency, and to request, most devotedly, all of the things which
are described below. So on behalf of the above-mentioned
guild, you are humbly petitioned . . . to enact a law . . .

* Source: L. Passerini, *Storia degli stabilmenti di beneficenza e d'istruzione
gratuita della città di Firenze* (Florence, 1853), pp. 942–45.

that this guild of Por Santa Maria and its members and guildsmen—as founders, originators, and principals of this hospital—are understood in perpetuity to be . . . the sole patrons, defenders, protectors, and supporters of this hospital as representatives of, and in the name of, the *popolo* and Commune of Florence. . . .

Item, the consuls of the guild . . . have authority . . . to choose supervisors and governors of the hospital and of the children and servants. . . .

45. GUILD RIVALRY, 1425*

The above-mentioned consuls, assembled together in the palace of the [Lana] guild in sufficient numbers and in the accustomed manner for the exercise of their office . . . have diligently considered the law approved by the captains of the society of the blessed Virgin Mary of Orsanmichele. This law decreed, in effect, that for the ornamentation of that oratory, each of the twenty-one guilds of the city of Florence . . . in a place assigned to each of them by the captains of the society, should construct . . . a tabernacle, properly and carefully decorated, for the honor of the city and the beautification of the oratory. The consuls have considered that all of the guilds have finished their tabernacles, and that those constructed by the Calimala and Cambio guilds, and by other guilds, surpass in beauty and ornamentation that of the Lana guild. So it may truly be said that this does not redound to the honor of the Lana guild, particularly when one considers the magnificence of that guild which has

* Source: Deliberations of the consuls of the Lana guild; *ASF, Arte della Lana*, 49, fol. 109v.

always sought to be the master and the superior of the other guilds.

For the splendor and honor of the guild, the lord consuls desire to provide a remedy for this. . . . They decree . . . that through the month of August, the existing lord consuls and their successors in office, by authority of the present provision, are to construct, fabricate, and remake a tabernacle and a statue of the blessed Stephen, protomartyr, protector and defender of the renowned Lana guild, in his honor and in reverence to God. They are to do this by whatever ways and means they choose, which will most honorably contribute to the splendor of the guild, so that this tabernacle will exceed, or at least equal, in beauty and decoration the more beautiful ones. In the construction of this tabernacle and statue, the lord consuls . . . may spend . . . up to 1,000 florins. And during this time, the lord consuls may commission that statue and tabernacle to the person or persons, and for that price or prices, and with whatever agreement and time or times which seem to them to be most useful for the guild. . . .

PART FOUR

VIOLENCE AND ITS CONTROL

Renaissance Florence was a disorderly community, prone to violence both individual and collective. The most cursory perusal of the criminal court records reveals that violence was endemic, and that Florentines of all social ranks and conditions acted out their angry impulses in ways that may have been psychically healthy, but which continually threatened the public order. It is not difficult to discern some basic causes for the violent tenor of life (to borrow Huizinga's phrase) in Florence, or indeed in any European city of that time. Even after the fourteenth century plagues had decimated the urban population, people lived together in very close quarters, struggling for survival in an atmosphere that was rarely tranquil. Many violent acts, so the records show, were committed by poor workers and vagabonds, driven to crime by hunger or by the frustrations and anxieties of an existence which was so precariously marginal. From the peasant communities outside Florence came a stream of rural émigrés, who swelled the ranks of the urban poor and added yet another unstable element to the city's population. In times of famine, plague, or political unrest, the underprivileged could coalesce into a dangerous mob whose capacity for destruction was unlimited. In the higher levels of Florentine society, men indulged in violent behavior for reasons other than hunger or economic exploitation. The honor of an individual and his family was a serious concern, and in

defense of that precious commodity, Florentines resorted to
arms and pursued vendettas for generations (no. 51). In
members of old and prominent families, particularly those
with feudal backgrounds and traditions, a sense of pride and
self-esteem frequently manifested itself in a style of behavior
which was arrogant and domineering (nos. 55, 58).

To restrain disorder, to apprehend and punish malefac-
tors, the Commune elected three foreign magistrates—the
podestà, the captain of the *popolo*, and the executor—who
functioned both as judges and policemen. Each of these officials, normally appointed for a six-month term of office,
commanded a retinue of armed men who maintained order
and executed the decisions of the courts. In times of crisis,
these forces of public security might be augmented by the
civic militia (the sixteen military companies) or by foreign
troops hired by the Commune. In the towns and rural areas
of the Florentine dominion, the responsibility for maintaining peace and order was borne by those magistrates, Florentine citizens, who occupied the offices of vicar, podestà, and
captain in those administrative zones into which Florence's
subject territory was divided (nos. 61–63).

The limited effectiveness of the Commune's measures to
maintain order and restrain violence is clearly suggested by
these documents. Only a minority of those convicted of
crimes of violence ever paid the penalty for their deeds; the
others fled the city and the jurisdiction of the courts. Those
criminals who possessed wealth, status, and influence were
naturally in the best position to escape punishment. To force
such men to submit to authority and to restrain their pen-
chant for disorder, the Commune established legal mecha-
nisms which offend our contemporary sense of justice, but
which most Florentines considered necessary. Between 1293
and 1295, the Commune enacted the Ordinances of Justice,

designed to curb the lawless and arrogant behavior of those families, identified by name, with a reputation for violence and the maltreatment of impotent *popolani*. Members of these magnate families were excluded from major communal offices. They were also required to post bond for good behavior, and they could be punished for the misdeeds of their relatives. The executor of the Ordinances of Justice was responsible for enforcing this legislation. In addition to his normal duties as judge and police official, he was required to investigate all anonymous denunciations of magnates (nos. 56, 57), to determine whether the Ordinances had been violated.

I. Patterns of Violence

46. A SOLDIER'S CRIMES, 1379*

. . . We condemn . . . Domenico Pellegrini of Bologna, a cavalryman of the Commune of Florence. . . . Inspired by a diabolical spirit, Domenico went to the house of Giovanni di Noldo Porcellini, of the parish of S. Lucia Ogni Santi . . . and entered that house. Once inside the house, Domenico went into a room where he met Monna Anastasia, the wife of Giovanni di Noldo, an honest woman of good condition. He seized Monna Anastasia and threw her upon a bed and raped her. . . . Then he saw a chest belonging to Monna Anastasia in which she kept her jewels, and from this chest he stole a gold ring and an emerald ring of gold. . . .

* Source: *ASF, Atti del Capitano del Popolo,* 1197 bis, fols. 132v–133v.

Item, Domenico again planned to commit adultery with
Monna Anastasia and so he again visited the house of Giovanni. . . . While he was in the house, Giovanni di Noldo
discovered him there, and with a sword which he had in his
hand, Domenico struck Giovanni on the head and wounded
him with a great effusion of blood, to the grave detriment
of Giovanni, a worthy merchant and guildsman of the city
of Florence. . . .

[Domenico confessed to these crimes.] In order that Domenico should not exult over these crimes, and so that the
punishment will serve as an example to others, and considering that Domenico is a foreigner and a man of base condition . . . and Monna Anastasia is an honest woman of good
condition, and considering too the character and the number
of the crimes, we order . . . that Domenico be taken to the
customary place of justice and that there he is to be beheaded. [Sentence executed.]

47. A PRIVATE QUARREL, 1396*

. . . We condemn . . . Serpe di Cione of the parish of
S. Lucia de' Magnoli of Florence. . . . During a quarrel
which broke out between Serpe and Bonaiuto Lorini, a shirt-
maker of the parish of S. Niccolò, Serpe, being armed, assaulted Bonaiuto with the intention of killing him. . . .
To facilitate his nefarious enterprise and also to aid in his
escape from the Communal authorities, Serpe had a horse
with him, and seeing that Bonaiuto was running away, he
cried: "Traitor, you will not escape for I will kill you!" The
fleeing Bonaiuto entered the house of Tommaso di Giunta,

* Source: *ASF, Atti del Capitano*, 2044, fols. 51r–52r.

of the parish of S. Niccolò . . . and Serpe descended from
his horse and entered the house and with an unsheathed sword
in hand, he stood over the prostrate Bonaiuto . . . who
cried: "Mercy! For God's sake, don't kill me!" . . . And
with his left hand upon Bonaiuto's throat and his right hand
brandishing the sword, Serpe said to Bonaiuto: "Traitor, now
the time has arrived when we shall see if you are a man like
my father!" And Bonaiuto replied: "Your father is a better
man than I. For the love of God, I beg you not to kill me."
Then Serpe struck Bonaiuto several times with the sword and
also with his hand and said: "I want you to say three times
that you are a traitor and that you owe your life to me."
Then the terrified Bonaiuto, seeing himself on the verge of
death, repeated this phrase three times: "I am a traitor and
I acknowledge that I owe my life to you." And if, on account
of this turmoil, several men had not arrived to prevent it,
Serpe would undoubtedly have killed Bonaiuto. . . . By
means of force, terror, and illicit threats, Serpe had extorted
an obligation of personal servitude and subjection from
Bonaiuto . . . and against his will held him prisoner in a
private place . . . in violation of the good customs of the
citizens of this city. [Serpe escaped the authorities; he was
fined 600 lire *in absentia.*]

48. THE EXPLOITS OF A HIGHWAYMAN, 1391*

. . . We condemn . . . Paoletto di Jacopo Nuti, of the
parish of S. Maria Maggiore of Florence, . . . a notorious
robber, murderer, and a traitor of his native city of Florence. . . . With an associate, he assaulted a certain Leone

* Source: *ASF, Atti del Esecutore,* 1141, fols. 7r–8r.

of Florence in a public street called the Via de' Servi in the vicinity of a cloth-stretching shed which stands in that street. . . . With a steel knife which he held in his hand, he struck and inflicted several wounds upon Leone, from which he died. . . .

Item, this Paoletto with certain other associates . . . went to a village near the castle of Radda in the Florentine *contado,* and called a certain Bartolo of this village, saying that he and his comrades were servants of the Baroncelli [family] of Florence. Paoletto and his associates then used force to rob Bartolo of 37 lire. . . .

Item, this Paoletto with two of his comrades seized a certain native of Catingnano of the Florentine *contado* . . . near the castle of Montopoli, at a place called the Castello del Boscho, and they robbed this man of 16 lire. . . .

Item, this Paoletto with three associates assaulted and wounded a Lombard . . . in the city of Florence in the district called "the well of the Toscanelli" from which wounds he died. . . .

Item, Paoletto and two of his associates . . . were at a place called Pontasieve in the Florentine *contado* and hid themselves at a spot two miles from the bridge. They seized a man from Porciano in the Casentino who was traveling along the public road and by force and violence robbed him of 50 florins. . . .

Item, this Paoletto and two associates came to a place called Scupitino and there they seized a pair of oxen valued at 40 florins. They took the oxen into Bolognese territory and sold them for 27 florins. . . .

Item, Paoletto with certain associates came to the Porta Croce in the night and broke into the house of a baker located outside the gate, and with force and violence robbed the baker of 100 lire. . . .

Item, with the intention of assassinating a certain Antonio

di Vischio of the Florentine *contado*, Paoletto went with his associates to a village in the Pistoiese *contado* called the Ponte Agliani. . . . With their arms they attacked and wounded a certain Paolo, an inhabitant of that village, believing that he was the Antonio whom they wished to kill. And as a result of these blows, Paolo died. . . .

Item, while this Paoletto and certain other associates were in the army of Messer Bernardo de Sala, Gherardo de Alderiis, and other captains of that band in Sienese territory, they learned that Messer Bernardo and the other captains had given safe-conduct to a certain German merchant and two of his companions who wished to travel to Rome. Paoletto and his associates followed and seized these travelers and took them and their horses by force to the castle of Montecerchi which belongs to Bartolomeo of Petramala. And in this castle they stole 1,800 ducats and the horses from this German and his companions, all of which they kept, except for 800 ducats and the horses which Bartolomeo of Petramala received. . . .

Item, this Paoletto went to a certain villa near Bagno a Ripoli in the Florentine *contado*, and there kidnapped a certain person from that villa and took him to Montescalari in the Florentine *contado* and there ransomed him for 600 florins. [Paoletto was also convicted of conspiracy and rebellion; he was hanged.]

49. THE DEPREDATIONS OF A MAGNATE, 1404*

. . . We condemn . . . Carlo di Luigi di Messer Roberto Adimari, of the parish of S. Michele of Florence, a magnate, an outlaw, and condemned in both person and

* Source: *ASF, Atti del Podestà*, 4003, fols. 54r–55r.

property by the city of Florence, a murderer, kidnapper, and violator of virgins, [a man of] the most evil way of life, status, and reputation. . . . With certain of his companions . . . on Sunday, October 17, [1403], he came at night to a village called Villa Magna and approached the home of Monna Lucia Ducci of that village. With a loud voice he began to call: "Open up! Open up! Open this door for we want to take those outlaws who are inside!" They continued to knock upon the door and broke it open with force and violence and then entered the house. Carlo seized Monna Lucia, who had risen from her bed when she heard the clamoring and the knocking. Then, leading her outside the house to a small loggia by the door, he attacked her with a sword which he carried and cut off her head and threw her body—and also her head—into a stable where the animals lay.

He then entered the house and, with his companions, seized Angela di Matteo de Villa, called Missiano, a girl of fifteen or sixteen years of age, whom Monna Lucia had raised for several years and was planning to marry and provide her with a dowry for the love of God. He held Angela in this house against her will and, despite her resistance, he had carnal relations with her. Then Carlo and his companions ate and drank at their pleasure in that house, and desiring to abandon it, they stole some cloth of linen and of wool . . . and one gold florin and some poultry which belonged to Monna Lucia. . . . The total was valued at 13 florins. Then Carlo took Angela by force to his palace located in the village of S. Andrea a Candecchio in the Florentine *contado*, and there on several occasions he had relations with her and held her there by force until the time when he, with Angela, was captured by an official of the podestà . . . on October 29. When he was seized, he was planning to go to the city of Lucca and to take Angela with him against her will. With Carlo's knowledge and consent, his companions took the cloth and other stolen items to Florence on the day following the robbery, and sold them to certain linen merchants. . . .

Item, Carlo had a conversation . . . with two brothers, Balestraccio and Moncioni, the sons of Niccolò Vogli of Ulmeto in the Florentine *contado,* and with the brothers Francino and Andrea, sons of Duca, of the parish of S. Cristoforo in Perticaria, for the purpose of planning and committing a homicide. Knowing that Bartolomeo di Monte di Messer Cipriano was staying in the house of Paolo di Pagnono de Furiandolis, these men armed with weapons . . . seized one of Paolo's neighbors and persuaded him to knock on Paolo's door so that they might enter the house where Bartolomeo was staying. Impelled by fear, this neighbor knocked on Paolo's door, saying: "Open up; this is so-and-so," whereupon those inside recognizing his voice, they opened the door. Paolo and the others were stationed outside the door and with a great rush they stormed into the house and found Bartolomeo standing next to the fire. They attacked and assaulted him and inflicted several wounds upon him, and he died even before they had left the house.

. . . Carlo and his companions . . . burnt down . . . two houses belonging to Guglielmo Altoviti of Florence, one of which was located in a place called Palazzuolo in the Florentine *contado,* and the other a short distance away in a place called "Le Lami." . . .

Item, Carlo and his companions burned down the house of Antonio Rondelli. [Carlo confessed to these crimes and was executed. He and his associates were also found guilty of murdering the abbot of the monastery of Candecchio.]

50. AN ESCAPADE IN THE APENNINES, 1400*

[This criminal process was instituted against twelve residents of a mountainous Apennine district, in the court of Pere Baldovinetti, "vicar of the province of Florence in the region of Romagna."] On July 19, the accused banded together . . . with the intention of murdering Messer Jacopo di Conte of Portica, rector of the church of S. Marina in the province of Florence. They had surrounded the church, awaiting the exit of Messer Jacopo from his accustomed habitation. And after waiting in vain until after midnight, the accused gathered in the square in front of the church. Then Bartolo de Cornialeto and Belloso de Presco said to their comrades: "Since we can't have the priest, let us seize Monna Rigarda, his mother, and Bartola, his sister, and take them with us." To these words Cerusio replied: "It seems to me that before we kidnap these women, we should discuss this affair with two of our friends (whose names will not be revealed at the present time) and tell them of our plan. If they advise us to proceed with our plan, then let us pursue it vigorously, and they will help and defend us, as they have done with respect to our other affairs in the past." Hearing these words, the other members of the groups said: "This is a good idea, since those friends are very influential in this region and they can help us and we need not have any fear." They agreed among themselves that Cerusio Garzetti would go . . . to these friends and inform them of their plan, and that on the following Tuesday, they would all meet at the home of Bartolo de Cornialeto to carry out the advice of the two friends. . . .

* Source: *ASF, Giudice degli Appelli*, 97, fols. 129r–130v.

At dusk on the following Tuesday, everyone assembled at the home of Bartolo de Cornialeto . . . and Cerusio said: "Today I was with my friend and told him that we had decided to seize the mother and the sister of the priest of S. Marina and to shame them and thus to disgrace the priest. And my friend replied: "Go ahead and do it and don't have any fear if you do it. This will be a beautiful vendetta and you will disgrace his family. I will give you whatever help I can, but the dogs are so well chained that there is no need for concern." Likewise, Giovanni de Valle Morotta said that he visited another friend and informed him of the plan, and the friend responded: "Go and commit every disgrace and evil against the mother and sister of the priest that you can, and at least kidnap the sister, for you could not do a more shameful thing to him. I will support and defend you to the best of my ability."

With the counsel and persuasion of these friends, the accused broke down the door of this house, then entered with force and violence, and went to the bed where the two women lay. They seized Bartola, who began to shout: "Help! Help! What have I done that you want me? For the love of God, I beg you to leave me alone. Do not shame me nor take away my virginity!" But the accused did not release Bartola but took her with them to the house of Bartolo [de Cornialeto] with the intention of deflowering her, a virgin and a respectable maiden. At dawn on the following day, they took this Bartola, like a lamb among a pack of wolves, into a forest called Mirabello . . . and there they held her for an entire day and raped her. . . . The next evening, they took her out of the forest to the home of Bartolo, where they dined. Afterwards, they led her to the home of Cerusio Garzetti . . . and then took her to the church of Mandriola, where lived Fra Raimondo, the rector of this church. They held her there for the entire day, and violated

her body against her will, her virginity and her good reputation. [Four members of the band were sentenced to death
in absentia. The others were fined.]

II. *The Vendetta*

51. THE MEDIEVAL INHERITANCE*

According to the records which I have discovered, Gino
di Donato [Velluti] was killed by Mannello, called Mannel-
lino, de' Mannelli, in September or October, 1267 [because
he had procured the cancellation of a judicial ban against
an enemy of the Mannelli]. . . . For our part, we did not
wage a vendetta until June 24, 1295, the feast day of St.
John the Baptist. On that day (according to information I
found written on certain sheets of paper belonging to Velluto [Velluti], who was involved in the vendetta), Velluto
saw that Lippo di Simone de' Mannelli was riding to participate in the race held on that holiday. He was just leaving
the arched street, some forty yards from the Ponte Vecchio,
on the north side of the river, in the parish of S. Stefano,
when he was attacked by our neighbor, Cino Dietsalvi . . .
and by Lapo, Gherardino di Donato, and my father Berto
[Velluti]. Lapo and Berto pressed close to him and
wounded him mortally, with more than twenty blows. Then
they fled to the Borgo S. Apostolo, to the houses of the
Buondelmonti. Even though there was a great uproar, they
made their escape without incident, thanks be to God.

For that vendetta and killing, Chele di Cecco Mannelli,

* Source: *La cronica domestica di Messer Donato Velluti*, pp. 10–12, 14–15,
18–21, 62–70.

being Lippo's closest relative, accused my uncle Filippo,
called Lippo, of being the man responsible for this homicide.
He also accused Lapo, Gherardino, and Berto [Velluti],
Cino Dietsalvi, and Lapo Filigherini, our intimate friend
and neighbor, of participating in the murder, and our relative and friend, Fenci di Gherardo Malefici, of providing
aid and comfort [to the assassins] by preventing their cap-
ture. In response to this accusation, my uncle Filippo and
Lapo Filigherini appeared [before the court] to excuse themselves. And even though twenty-four witnesses, both male
and female, testified against them, nothing was proved
against them and they were absolved, may God be
praised. . . . However, Lapo, Gherardino, Berto, and Cino
did not appear; Lapo and Berto were fined 5,000 lire each,
and Gherardino and Cino, 1,000 lire each. . . .

Afterwards, when the Mannelli had made a peace agreement with our ancestors through a procurator . . . according to the form of the statutes of the Florentine Commune,
they still regarded our relatives with rancor and hostility. So
the Commune forced them to make another peace agreement, this time in person, and also to guarantee that the
peace would be kept. This ceremony was held in [the church
of] S. Piero Scheraggio, in the presence of the priors and of
the captain of the *popolo*. This they did with great reluc-
tance and because they were forced to do so. For at that time
they were so strong and powerful in numbers and possessions
that they considered themselves outraged because our family
had committed a vendetta against them. . . .

After that peace agreement was concluded, the Mannelli
continued to lord it over us. On account of their exalted
position, they regarded us with loathing, since they had been
forced by the Commune to sign the accord with us. . . .
And they continued to behave in this barbarous manner, so

that my father Berto was in danger from them, as I learned
from his papers, and in particular, from one letter sent to
him in Avignon by Piero and Matteo Velluti. He was planning to return from England by way of Genoa, and they
warned him that some of them [the Mannelli] had learned
of his trip, and if they had known his route, they would have
killed him. They reported that they had heard this from
someone who could be trusted. . . .

I myself had further proof [of their hostility], for once
upon my return from Bologna, I greeted Zanobi and Coppo,
the sons of Messer Lapo Mannelli, and another member of
their family named Gamaretto, and none of them returned
my greeting. And I learned from Jacopo di Guiduccio Mannelli (who had married Pasqua, the daughter of Tuccio Ferrucci, my wife's uncle) that they were hostile toward our
family. . . . [In 1349, Velluti was a member of one of the
colleges; he was asked by a friend, Filippozzo Soldani, to
procure the cancellation of the magnate status of Bertone
Mannelli.] And he begged me to do this, and when I did
not give him a straight answer, he sent Bertone and others
[of the Mannelli] to me to beg my pardon, and to say that
they wished to be like brothers to me. I accepted the apology,
and worked on his [Bertone's] behalf as though he were my
brother, and he was made a *popolano*. . . . Since then, we
have been as close as brothers without quarrels, and I have
served them, and particularly Zanobi and his family. . . .

Velluto [Velluti, first cousin of Donato's grandfather]
was killed by the Berignalli family in 1310, when he was
about thirty years old. The cause of his death was as follows.
Dino del Mangano, friend of the [Velluti] family, was involved in a quarrel with Giovanni Berignalli, a cloth manufacturer and merchant, and three or four of his sons, his
brothers, and relatives. With the aid of Lorenzo di Dietaiuto
Velluti, Dino had won this dispute with Giovanni. Giovanni

wanted to gain revenge on Lorenzo, and near [the church of] S. Spirito, he encountered him with Velluto [Velluti]. Giovanni attacked Lorenzo with a knife but he ran away, and when Lorenzo wanted to pursue him, Velluti held him. Then Giovanni shouted, "Let me free," and when Velluto would not release him, he gave him two blows in his flank.

Velluto was carried to his house, and our relatives—Lapo, Lorenzo, and the others—persuaded him to make his will. Our branch of the family was as closely related to him as theirs, and we had as much claim to be his heirs as they, but he made them his heirs and treated us as though we were bastards. . . . My uncle Gherardo . . . went to Velluto, who was still alive, and complained about this, but he refused to change the will. Whereupon, in the presence of that company, he said: "As you have treated us while alive, so shall we treat your memory after your death." That night he died, and neither Gherardo nor our women attended his funeral. Instead, a few days later he had conversations with several of the Berignalli, and never did anything to harm them. Fruosino [Velluti, Velluto's son] accused four of the Berignalli, but only Giovanni was condemned. When my father Lamberto heard all this, he warmly commended Gherardo for what he had done, saying that he had never done anything more praiseworthy. He complained bitterly of the actions of his relatives, and how they had repaid him for having involved himself in the vendetta against the Mannelli. For he had not been the principal offended [in the murder of Gino Velluti]; yet he had been the leader in the vendetta, and paid the fine. . . . And he never involved himself in Velluto's vendetta, but rather continued to speak to the Berignalli after he had returned to Italy. He also commanded us, his sons, not to involve ourselves in this affair, and placed his curse upon whoever did the contrary. But my brother Piccio disobeyed him, and engaged his own honor as if it [the assassination] had happened to him. Would to God that it was only his [honor] that was involved, but it all ended badly, as happens to those who disobey their fathers.

Velluto left 500 florins to whoever would avenge him. . . . But our side of the family did not wage the vendetta, although they expected us to act as we had done toward the Mannelli. But our father and his sons (with the exception of Piccio) refused to have any part of it. When my father was in Tunis, Filippo in Pisa, and I in Bologna, Piccio was persuaded by his relatives to commit this vendetta. . . . Piccio requested the assistance of one of our intimate friends, the baker Giunta di Mazzone . . . who, believing that he was helping us, promptly agreed. . . . So one day, this Giunta went with Piccio and Cino di Lapo Velluti to Ciardo's tavern for this business, and after spending some time there, they walked toward the monastery of S. Orsola. There was Niccolò Berignalli, and Giunta gave him a blow in the throat, from which he died instantly. Cino and Piccio were not armed with knives, so they fled. . . . The year was 1333 or 1334.

Then came the lordship of the Duke of Athens [1342–1343], and he cancelled the bans on outlaws and required everyone to make peace. Therefore, we and our relatives were forced to make peace. . . . If for no other reason than my father's command and his curse, no one of their descendants shall be molested. . . . And like my father before me, I thereby repeat this command and leave my curse, although I don't believe that any of that family survives. The vengeance of God has been sufficient for us. We are an honorable and wealthy family, while they have nothing, neither men nor possessions. And this is enough about Velluto; for our honor and welfare, it should have pleased God that he had not been born.

52. THE STROZZI AND THE LENZI,
1387–92*

In that year [1387] in the month of October, a cloth
dealer named Piero di Lenzo, who was one of the standard-
bearers of the companies, was gambling at cards with Michelozzo dell' Ambo outside the Porta a Faenza in a place called
"alle Panche." He was losing and he complained that he
always lost and would never play with Michelozzo again.
Then Pagnozzino degli Strozzi, who was a violent and arrogant man, said to him: "You ought to complain about
Michelozzo's gambling, for he is the most audacious and
successful gambler [in Florence]." Piero di Lenzo replied,
"I will complain about my losses, and you complain about
yours, if you have anything to complain about." Pagnozzino
thought that Piero was criticizing him, for a short time before, he had been wounded in the hand by one of [Piero's]
relatives. So he put his hand on his sword . . . and gave
Piero such a blow that he cut off his hand, and he struck his
head with such force that pieces of bone were scattered about
. . . and after ten days, Piero died. Pagnozzino did not
realize that he was a standard-bearer or he might have acted
less violently. This affair displeased all of the good citizens
because Piero, being a standard-bearer, had not been treated
with respect by that evil man.

[October 8, 1387] We, the lord priors . . . have considered the enormous crime and the atrocious offenses per-

---

* Sources: *Rerum Italicarum Scriptores,* ed. Muratori, XXVII (Florence,
1770), cols. 137–38; *ASF, Provvisioni,* 76, fols. 121r–125r; *ASF, Carte
Strozziane,* series III, vol. 132, fol. 1r; *ASF, Signori e Collegi, Missive,* 23,
fols. 45v–46r.

petrated during the present month of October against the person of Piero Lenzi, cloth manufacturer and Florentine citizen . . . by that son of iniquity, Pagnozzo di Pagnozzo Strozzi. [We have further considered] the grievous wounds inflicted by Pagnozzo, armed with weapons, the effusion of blood from the head and the left arm of Piero Lenzi, and the amputation of his left hand. With particular respect to the office which Piero held and holds, such offenses require more serious penalties than those regularly assessed for these crimes. Therefore, we desire to provide for the good and peaceful state of the city of Florence, and to promote the honor of this Commune, by providing graver penalties for these crimes than those stipulated in the statutes, to serve as an example to others so that they will abstain from any similar activity. . . .

It is first decreed that Pagnozzino (or Pagnozzo) and Nofri, the sons of Pagnozzo Strozzi, are henceforth in perpetuity to be considered magnates . . . and are subject to all of the penalties and limitations . . . which are currently in force against magnates, of whatever kind.

Item, Pagnozzino and Nofri are henceforth declared to be, in perpetuity, rebels of the *popolo* and Commune of Florence . . . and they may be condemned to death for rebellion by the podestà or by any of the other magistrates. . . . However, this condemnation of rebellion . . . does not apply to the sons or male descendants of Pagnozzino and Nofri . . .

Item, all of the property both real and personal of Pagnozzino and Nofri is declared to be confiscated by the Commune of Florence. . . . And the houses inhabited by Pagnozzino and Nofri, whether in the city or the *contado*, are to be completely destroyed. . . . And in future, no one shall dare to build anything on their locations. . . .

Item, every member of the Strozzi family and every masculine descendant now alive or born in future is declared to be a magnate in perpetuity. . . . But whenever any member of the Strozzi family shall kill, or shall bring alive to the podestà in the city of Florence . . . the abovementioned Pagnozzo and Nofri, or either one of them, then in that event, the members of the Strozzi clan, having been declared magnates, shall regain their *popolano* status. . . .

Item, Giovanni and Piero Lenzi . . . and their children and descendants are hereby authorized with impunity to pursue a vendetta . . . and to offend by any means and to any degree Nofri and Pagnozzino and their sons and male descendants, and also any other member of the Strozzi clan . . . no matter how remote the relationship. . . . The offenses committed by Giovanni and Piero Lenzi and their relatives and descendants shall be considered as having been committed for this vendetta. . . . And for any offenses committed by Giovanni and Piero Lenzi and their relatives and descendants . . . against Nofri and Pagnozzo, their sons and male descendants . . . or against any member of the Strozzi family, no vendetta may be waged in revenge . . . [by the Strozzi]. . . . Within fifteen days of the commission of such offense, each member of the Strozzi family shall be required (under penalty of 2,000 florins) to make peace with Piero and Giovanni Lenzi and their sons and male descendants. . . .

[Currado degli Strozzi in Florence to Messer Lionardo degli Strozzi in Carmignano, May 1, 1388.]

Last night as our band returned from Pistoia and reached the Rifredi bridge, the servant of Nofri [Strozzi] remained behind to give his horse a drink. Then as he was traveling to catch up with the band, two men with lances came out of

Masicciuolo's tavern, which is above [the house] of Monna Belloza. They thought that he was one of us [i.e., a Strozzi], and they attacked him with lances, so that he fell from his horse into a ditch filled with water to the height of his waist. They gave him several blows with sickles and with lances, but he was protected by his breastplate and his helmet, and being a valiant lad, he defended himself. Another member of Nofri's household, Meo, came upon the scene and said [to the assailants]: "You have killed Nofri's servant," whereupon a great outcry arose. Meo remounted and rode after the band, which then returned to rescue him. And in that house were several relatives of G[iovanni] di Lenzo, who fled. When our group arrived here in Florence, Master Lodovico [a physician] found a great wound in his throat and judged it to be mortal, since it appeared to him that a vein had been cut. There were other wounds in the arm and leg, but these are not serious. One can see the marks of many blows on the helmet and on the hood.

The judge has accepted the jurisdiction over this crime and will institute a process. G[iovanni di Lenzo] will defend himself by saying that he was authorized [to commit the assault]. But this is a lie, because he was in the service of Nofri who was excused [from the judicial vendetta against the Strozzi]. Furthermore, he was assaulted when he was not in our company. The fine will be heavy; I don't know how G[iovanni] will pay for them [the assailants]. . . . We are seeking for ways and means to satisfy our honor. We will see how the affair develops, and according to what occurs, we will proceed prudently to protect ourselves. We have everything in order. . . .

Giovanni di Lenzo has gone to the Signoria to complain that Nofri told his retainers: "Kill any member of G[iovanni's] household whom you meet." Then we went to the

Signoria and told the truth, which is believed by everyone who hates him. He is ready to commit suicide, for he has seen how the case goes, and he sees himself denounced by everyone. The process was initiated immediately by the podestà. I am very hopeful, and once the process moves to the trial stage, it will be bread in the oven. According to the legal advice which we have, if they attempt to defend themselves by the law [against the Strozzi], we will argue that it is not valid, so that the court will pronounce against their objection on the ground that the law is invalid. And by this means, we will free ourselves from them. It is necessary to keep this secret, and only three of us are cognizant of it. Several citizens have warned us to be on our guard, because one side or the other could have the favor of the Signoria. So there are twenty of us and eight servants, and we have sent all of the children away. . . .

Everyone has rallied round to help, and Messer P[azzino degli Strozzi] and N[ofri Strozzi] act as though one of their own sons was wounded. They denounce G[iovanni di Lenzo] in the strongest terms. We will not suffer this indignity. Our lawyers are prepared and there is plenty of money. But their lawyers will attempt to enforce the law against us. I deplore this incident for its effect on the family, but it has been like a tonic for us. I see those who were asleep now aroused, as a result of this incident. I see everyone [of the Strozzi] united and generous with money.

[The Florentine Signoria to Messer Piero Gambacorti, lord of Pisa, September 18, 1392.] Dearest friend and illustrious knight, a very grave matter has been brought to our attention, concerning which our ambassadors have informed us, namely, that you are displeased by Florentine citizens who engage in quarrels and disturb the tranquility of your city. It is our belief that these disturbances have not been caused by our merchants but rather by our exiles and other men of base condition. This displeases us . . . and we are prepared to do anything you suggest to remedy this situation.

We have also learned, dearest friend, that you have seized a certain Paolo di Francesco, for the murder of the son of Pagnozzino [Strozzi]. . . . You must be aware that this act was committed as a result of a vendetta . . . arising from a public offense committed against our Commune. . . . Through our ambassadors who have just returned, and through Vieri Adimari and Giorgio di Messer Guccio [Gucci], we have appealed to you to do justice with mercy in this case. . . . For this offense was a public rather than a private act, since Pagnozzino killed one of our standard-bearers. As a result, a vendetta was authorized. Therefore, dearest friend, we appeal to you as fervently and cordially as we can, on the grounds of our honor, of justice, and of the desires of our *popolo*, that you spare Piero's life, for his death would be an offense against our *popolo*. . . .

53. The Revenge of Luca da Panzano, 1420*

I record that, out of devotion and reverence for the Almighty God, I fasted on the day of the Annunciation, March 25, 1420, and for the remission of my sins and those of our ancestors, [I have vowed] to fast for seven years [on the day of the Annunciation] in honor of the Virgin.

I record that, on May 5, 1420, being podestà of Tizana, I

* Source: The diary of Luca da Panzano; *Archivio storico italiano*, ser. 5, IV (1889), 149–53.

received permission from the Signoria . . . to be absent from the Florentine *contado* for one month, to go to the baths at S. Filippo. As an excuse, I said that I was ailing.

During the night of May 10, I left Tizana and went toward Florence, on the way to Naples, for I had heard that our enemy was there. On May 15, Panicho and I left Florence on foot to go to Naples by the Casentino route. On the 19th, we were at Castiglione Aretino and there we awaited Maso and Guglielmo of S. Godenzo, who were to come there. They met us there on the 21st. We then traveled toward Naples, by way of Perugia, Norcia, and the Abruzzi. On the first day of June, we four entered Naples and settled ourselves and our arms in the Via Francesca, at Ruggiello's inn.

On the 2nd, I entered into conversation with the innkeeper concerning our merchants and fellow countrymen. And I learned from him that the traitor, Nanni di Ciecie, was living in Naples. On the 3rd, we learned from another person that Nanni had returned to Paghone's Inn in the company of Palla di Messer Palla Strozzi, who was the ambassador of the Commune [of Florence]. . . . And I received more assurance from the innkeeper's son. For when Nanni was passing our hotel, the boy said: "Be careful that you don't gamble with that man from the Del Nero family, who is called Nanni di Ciecie, for he plays with crooked dice." And that same day, we went to meet our ambassadors, to see if Nanni di Ciecie was with them, and he was there. . . . We therefore decided to assassinate him if he ventured outside the gate of the Carmine of Naples, but he did not go. . . .

On the 15th, we were joined by my brother Matteo and Niccolò di Biagio da Panzano. We met them and told them to inform the Court [of Queen Joanna] of their presence in Naples. I then asked them the reason for their coming.

They said that they had obtained some poison [for their arms] because they had wounded Antonio del Gatto Capucci in the territory of the Count of Moncione, and they believed that he would be cured. And in order that this would not happen again, they had procured this poison. Joining them when they wounded Capucci was Bettino di Lanfranco da Panzano. And they engaged in this vendetta on behalf of Lanfranco di Totto da Panzano, who was wounded by the Capucci in the Borgo del Panzano. He received many wounds and was left for dead. . . .

On that day, the army of Attendolo Sforza arrived to give battle at the gate of the market of Naples, which was then closed. And all Naples was armed and ready to fight, and so were the galleys. Seeing this, we formed three pairs and decided that the first who encountered him [Nanni] should kill him. And so it happened. Maso of S. Godenzo and Matteo di Matteo di Messer Luca [da Panzano] met him in the district of the Banchi in Naples. Maso gave him a blow on the head so that he fell unconscious to the ground. Then with knife and dagger, Matteo and Maso gave him five wounds, one in the artery, one in the flank, and three on the head, and they left him there for dead.

The guard arrived on the spot immediately and seized Maso, but Matteo fled. Upon hearing the commotion, we came running and saw them arrest him, so that we had to move away. As we had agreed beforehand, we all gathered in the Seggio di Nidio, in the house of Monna Ciecherella, the mother of Messer Landolfo. We told her what we had done. She received us, and then sent for a knight, who was a cousin of the Grand Seneschal. And he arranged for the release of Maso, who joined us in Monna Ciecherella's house.

On June 17, we six left Naples, disguised as servants sent

by Monna Ciecherella to guard one of her castles. And we
had a safe-conduct pass so that we could get through the
guards. Baldassare, Madonna Ciecherella's son, accompanied
us and put us on the road to Gaeta. . . . And on June 28,
we were all in Florence, safe and sound. On July 6, Mariotto
de' Bardi was here, and he reported that he witnessed the
burial of Nanni di Ciecie, on St. John's day, June 24, in the
church of S. Lorenzo in Naples. So now we have accomp-
lished our vendetta, thanks be to God.

54. The Decline of the Vendetta, 1420*

I record that on December 5, 1420, I went to the court
of the podestà to accuse Simone di Buonarroto di Simone
[Buonarroti]. I initiated this process for this reason. On the
evening of November 1st, at the hour of the Ave Maria, I
was sitting with Rinieri Bagnesi on his bench when Simone
came along . . . and threw a brick at my head. I did not
know how to explain his attack on me. . . .

On December 14, 1420, Vanni di Stefano Castellani,
Buonsignore di Niccolò Spinelli, and Giovanni di Rinieri
Peruzzi wished to settle this quarrel between us in the following manner. [They proposed] that Simone should beg
my pardon in the presence of my relatives and friends. So
we assembled in the church of S. Romeo, and Simone came
and made this statement in the presence of the whole group.
"I have both said and done wrong, and I think that the
devil made me do it. I beg you to pardon me." My relatives

* Source: The diary of Antonio Rustichi; *ASF, Carte Strozziane*, series II,
vol. 11, fol. 26v.

thought that this was a greater revenge than if we had assaulted him. For he was between forty-five and fifty years old, and he had withdrawn the things which he had said, and had given us an explanation. So on the 14th of the month, I withdrew my charges against him. . . .

III. Prepotenza

55. A Despoiler of Property, 1377*

Giovanni di Piero, of the parish of S. Maria da Fugna di Mugello, humbly presents this petition to you, lord priors. In July 1348, Giovanni's grandfather, Giovanni di Baldino, made his will by the hand of a public notary, in which he named his daughter, Monna Giovanna, mother of Giovanni di Piero, as his heiress. In this inheritance was included, among other property, a farm with houses, threshing floor, arable land, and vineyards located in the parish of S. Bartolo a Petroio in the Mugello, with a value of 200 florins or more, with many furnishings in that house as befitted a well-to-do resident of the *contado*. In addition, there was a house located in Scarperia worth some 50 florins or more, and several other pieces of property. Upon the death of Giovanni, the testator, his daughter Monna Giovanna took possession of her father's property and administered it as her own. Then Africhello di Messer Alamanno de' Medici, a man

* Source: *ASF, Deliberazioni dei Signori e Collegi, ordinaria autorità*, 20, fols. 69v–70v.

who has always lived a dishonest life by robbing and preying
upon the poor and the impotent, and exploiting them—as
he has done and as he intends always to do—learned that the
father and the husband of Monna Giovanna were dead and
that she had inherited this property. He thought that she
could live with less expense and that he needed that property
for his purposes, which was to live like a nobleman from the
possessions of the poor. So he planned to do to her what he
had done to other people in the district whom he has driven
from their property. . . . And by these means, he has been
able to double the estate which he inherited from his father,
so that at present he neither pursues a business career nor
any trade and has never earned a penny honestly.

Having previously told Monna Giovanna to accommodate
him by giving him that property, he went to her house and
warned her that she could not resist his will. Replying with
fear, the poor woman . . . pleaded with him to leave her
in peace, saying that her father had bequeathed that property to her. Since he did not normally encounter such resistance from others, he went to her house, and once inside,
without any provocation and without ever having any deal-
ings with her father or husband, seized her by the hair and
with spurs that he had in his hands, [and] beat her unmercifully. . . . And the poor woman, her hands and feet
wounded by the spurs, fled to the house of her in-laws, and
in a short time, she died from her wounds and her
grief. . . .

For God's sake, may it please you, lords . . . that poor
Giovanni [di Piero] should not be the victim of such in-
justice, and that the tyrant Africhello should not continue
to enjoy the fruits of his evil and unjust actions. [Africhello
was proclaimed a magnate, and thus subject to the penalties
attached to that status.]

56. An Assault upon a Peasant Family, 1381*

Lord Executor, I notify you that Bartolomeo di Rinaldo Donati of Florence, one of the magnates and powerful citizens of Florence, in November 1380 perpetrated the following crime. He attempted to rape Monna Jacopa, wife of Antonio di Ser Sandro Biandini, and daughter of Taddeo, a resident of the Florentine *contado*. With malice in his mind, he went to the house of Monna Jacopa located in the parish of S. Giovanni in the *pieve* of Rémole and entered that house with force. With great arrogance and fury, he seized the woman and attempted to seduce her against her will, thus bringing obliquy upon her and dishonor upon her husband Antonio. Unable to obtain his desire with this woman quietly and peacefully, this proud and arrogant man began to beat Monna Jacopa, striking her in the face, throat, and other parts of her body, with some issue of blood from her mouth. As a result of these offenses committed by Bartolomeo, Monna Jacopa fled from the house and began to scream loudly, "Help! Help!" several times. Hearing these shouts, her husband Antonio and several neighbors ran to the house. Thereupon, Bartolomeo left and went to his own house. Shortly afterwards, Antonio also left to work in a field belonging to one of the Benci women. Bartolomeo then saddled his horse and, seizing a spear in his hand, he mounted and rode at full gallop to the field where Antonio was working. He threw the spear at Antonio, recovered it and threw it again. And this he did several times, and if Antonio

---

* Source: *ASF, Atti del Esecutore*, 877, fols. 8v–9v.

had not run away, truly Bartolomeo would have killed him with the spear.

57. The Terror of the Countryside, 1381*

Before you and your court, Lord Executor, I denounce . . . Aghinolfo di Messer Gualterotto dei Bardi, who is a magnate and subject to the Ordinances of Justice. I inform you that in this city there is not a more evil man, of worse reputation or condition, nor one who had done more harm to his Commune or to citizens and residents of the *contado*. Consider the respectable life which he has led and continues to lead.

First, I will tell you what he has done against the Commune. You know that twice he has been expelled from the city by the hostility of the *popolo* and placed under ban and declared a rebel. Once in Pisa, he declared his allegiance to the Ghibelline Party, swearing an oath upon a piece of consecrated bread. And he has committed many other acts harmful and shameful to this Commune, to describe which would require too much time.

Now I will describe one of his quarrels with his neighbors. You should know that Aghinolfo has property in the *contado* at a place called Ponte and in another area called Val di Bisenzio. And in every place where he lives, he has killed several men and has never been placed under ban for his arrogant behavior because he belongs to a great family. Among the other homicides which he has committed is one great crime which he perpetrated against his best friend in

* Source: *ASF, Atti del Esecutore*, 892, fols. 30v–32r.

the Val di Bisenzio. Wishing to assassinate an individual whom he hated, Aghinolfo sent for his dear friend, Nuccio Capoccio della Torre of Pratole in the parish of S. Lorenzo Ansella in the place called Val di Bisenzio. Aghinolfo said to him: "Nuccio, I sent for you because you are my best friend, in whom I place the greatest trust. I am asking a great favor of you, namely, that you find a way to quarrel with X, and then kill him so that it does not appear that I am the murderer." Nuccio replied: "I don't want to do this for I will be called an assassin." Seeing that Nuccio did not wish to help him in his evil enterprise, Aghinolfo was afraid that he might betray him. So he sent a message to Nuccio, inviting him to dine with him on the following Sunday. Being Aghinolfo's dear friend, Nuccio accepted the invitation and on Saturday, he sent some mutton to Aghinolfo's house. Then on Sunday evening, he arrived for dinner at Aghinolfo's house, and was then killed by his host, who carried his body some three miles and buried it in a ditch.

Having done this to his best friend, you may imagine how he behaves toward his enemies. He has treated other neighbors in the Val di Bisenzio in similar fashion, and has never been prosecuted for any of his crimes, because everyone is afraid of him. Anyone who has dared to complain about him to the Signoria has either been murdered or punished. So great is the terror that his neighbors for miles around tremble at the sound of his name, and there is no one in the vicinity whom he has not beaten or robbed. He surrounds himself with a band of three outlaws, and he has forced many peasants to leave the farms which they rented from citizens. . . . Just recently, he has arranged for his two nephews to be banned, as a result of a quarrel which they had with him over their farms, which he had occupied. He ordered his three outlaws to murder his eldest nephew, but Aghinolfo's sister warned him to flee. . . .

If I told you how many men of this area he has assassinated, you would not believe me. But I pray you, Lord Executor, for the love of God and of these poor impotent people who dare not resist such arrogance, that you take a little time and effort to interrogate the witnesses, whose names are recorded below, about Aghinolfo's activities. You will discover that there is no more evil man in this city, and you will be adored in perpetuity as a saint. And if you wish to learn about all of the crimes which he has committed, send a notary to the Val di Bisenzio and instruct him to interrogate whomever he meets, male or female, about Aghinolfo's life. . . . The first man to investigate concerning his crimes is his servant Braccialdino who has often said: "I would like to be arrested by the authorities in Florence, so that I could relate the things which I have seen, which are so horrible that they would obscure the sun. . . ."

58. A Powerful Family: The Strozzi*

[August 10, 1381] Be it known to you, Lord Executor . . . that Nofri di Pagno di Messer Andrea degli Strozzi, a magnate of the city of Florence, is a potent, arrogant, evil, and violent man, who has already killed and wounded many men and women of the city of Florence. . . . On August 9th, he assaulted a *popolano*, Talano di Nasutro Caronasi of the parish of S. Niccolò in Orto of Florence, whom he has wounded on previous occasions, giving him several blows on the head with an oil jar . . . and then wounding him in the

---

* Sources: *ASF, Atti del Esecutore*, 892, fol. 9v, August 10, 1381; *ASF, Carte Strozziane*, series III, vol. 132, fol. 98r.

face with a knife, with a great effusion of blood. And if he
had not been restrained by men who were present, he would
have killed him . . . in defiance of the *popolo* and the
guilds and the guildsmen of the city of Florence who wish
to live in peace.

Every day, he does something similar, or worse, and there
is no one to punish him, or who dares to speak out, for fear
of him and his kinsmen who are powerful citizens . . . and
who terrorize the weak and impotent. . . .

They say, Lord Executor, that you are a valiant man
with popular sympathies. Exercise your office with valor, and
you will be praised by the citizenry. . . . May it please you
to proceed forcefully against this crime, so that the *popolani*
are not offended by great and powerful citizens, nor by their
hirelings. . . .

[Vieri Rondinelli, podestà of Colle, to Leonardo, Piero,
and Matteo Strozzi, 15 January 1425.]

Most honored brothers. With security, faith, and love, I
write to you in fraternity about a very unpleasant incident
which (if I did my duty), I would be forced to report to the
authorities in Florence. But this would be to your dishonor,
and I would rather not do it, since I would not like a similar
situation to befall me. Yesterday a certain monk by the name
of Simone, the parish priest of the church of S. Jacopo di
Colle, was passing the house of your relative, Giacomo
Strozzi. This Giacomo seized the priest roughly and pushed
him several times so that he was about to fall to the ground.
He said, "Oh, priest, if you pass in front of my door again,
I will really fix you, believe me!" And the monk Simone
replied calmly, "Oh, Giacomo, let me speak three words, for
God's sake!" Whereupon, Giacomo rushed into his house
and picked up a sword and approached him and said: "By

God, priest, if you pass in front of my house again, I'll stick this in your belly!"

How little this redounds to your honor and to mine, considering my office, you can readily understand. But to inform anyone except yourselves about this seems to me to take little account of your honor, of which I have always been as solicitous as of my own. So I have decided instead to inform you of this situation rather than do something that would bring dishonor upon your family. You are so prudent that I am certain that you will provide for your honor and mine, and I say this because Giacomo's behavior has caused much hostility and resentment among the people of this community. . . .

59. A Career of Violence: Simone Guicciardini, c. 1395*

[This is a record] of the crimes committed and perpetrated in a very brief span of time by that accursed Simone di Machirone Guicciardini, called Mone.

First, he was employed by Nofri di Ser Parente and Nettolo of Lucca in their silk shop when, as a result of certain troubles and jealousies, he struck Francia, the nephew of Nettolo, several times on the head and back with a bolt of silk cloth, causing blood to pour from his mouth and nose. Francia cried, "Help! Help!" and thus aroused the whole neighborhood, so that many persons came running. For this reason, he [Simone] was discharged by his employers.

Then he was employed in the shop of Andrea del Benino where, one day, he had words with Andrea's son Piero over some matter. He seized Piero's cap from his head and ran

* Source: *ASF, Carte Strozziane*, series I, vol. 16, fols. 5r–5v.

home with it, with Piero chasing him to recover it. Then in the presence of his mother, he attacked Piero and knocked him down and gave him several blows. He seized a kitchen knife and tried to cut his throat, but he was restrained by his mother and by others who had gathered there. He was expelled from the shop.

Later, at the request of Guaspare di Niccolò Cennini, he attacked Marco di Carona behind the guild [headquarters] of Por Santa Maria. He forced him onto a bench and gave him several blows, while holding a knife to his throat. . . . On the day that Tomasello Davizzi was buried, there was a large crowd gathered around his body. . . . The son of Ser Verdiano Arrighi was seated next to the corpse alongside Piero Velluti, and Simone assaulted him . . . so that a great disturbance arose and everywhere in Florence people spoke against him and against us.

Then he assaulted Guaspare di Niccolò Cennini, a mercer, in the house of the Gherardini, in the presence of Luigi di Lottino and Francesco, the goldsmith, who was then a standard-bearer of the companies. He gave him a head wound so that he nearly died, although he promised me that he would not do anything. If it were not for friends, and if we had not made a peace agreement with Guaspare and his spiteful brothers, we would run the risk of ruin, since the offense was committed in the presence of the standard-bearer [of justice].

When ambassadors from Città di Castello came to Florence, one of them had a quarrel with the brother of Malerba of Montespertoli. While accompanied by Malerba, [Simone] encountered this ambassador in the Piazza della Signoria and with clubs they beat him so that he bled and his head was damaged. There were many complaints and accusations made

before the priors who were present. And if it had not been
for our friends, and if Lionello Guicciardini and Niccolò
Ricoveri had not been standard-bearers of the companies,
we would have been in grave peril.

, Then one day at the Toscanelli well, for a single word
that Ceccerello del Bugliafe said, he seized him and tore off
his coat, and he did the same to Bonaiuto Aglione, when they
had a gambling quarrel. In the Piazza of the Mercato
Nuovo, he assaulted Ciari di Sarto of [the parish of] S. Piero
Gattolino and wounded him in the vein so that he nearly
died. And in order to have peace with him, I had to spend.
. . . [No sum is recorded.]

Then he committed an outrage against some of the Machiavelli, by entering one of their houses, while the owner
was absent in the *contado* with his family. With a key, Mone
entered that house night and day, and there he engaged in
his evil activities. One night, Piero di Filippo Machiavelli
complained to Mone that his behavior was so reprehensible
that the women of his household did not dare to show themselves at the windows, whereupon Mone tried to wound him
with a knife and he cursed him so that the whole neighborhood was aroused. . . .

Then he was imprisoned in the Stinche and committed
the following acts. He wounded Marco Piericialdi of Ancisa
in the head with a pair of shears. During the riot of November 1394, he was the first to break out of the Stinche, and the
executor who was then in office wanted to decapitate him, but
I prevented it. Then he fought on several occasions with
Niccolò di Betto and with others, and he was placed in the
dungeon several times. In June 1394, he said that there
should be a revolution and the captain of the *balìa* . . .
condemned him to five years in prison. . . .

IV. Authority and Its Abuse

60. THE OFFENSES OF A MAGISTRATE, 1382*

. . . Behind the palace of the captain [of the *popolo*], Messer Obizzo degli Alidosi . . . was a house inhabited by the family of Ricciardo de' Figliopetri, his wife, and two attractive daughters who were eighteen years old. Since the father, a poor gentleman, was living in exile, he had not arranged marriages for them. Rumors circulated that the captain had fallen in love with one of them, since he could see them through the windows. So he communicated with her, and one night, he sent his notary and several guards to that house, on the pretext of searching to discover whether Ricciardo had violated his sentence of exile and had returned home. The girl was then taken to the captain's house and assaulted. This affair was widely discussed and criticized in the city, but the blame was laid to the notary and to the son [of the captain?]. . . . Finally, the girl was taken to a woman who ran a brothel, who stated that the captain's son had instructed her to keep the girl, and had said that he did not know who she was. Then the girl's brother returned (he had been absent from the city for several days), and learning of this sorry affair, so the story went, he killed his sister and buried her in a secret place. [The captain] committed many illegal and arrogant acts, even sending men into exile who had done no wrong, on the instructions of those who

* Source: *Cronaca fiorentina di Marchionne di Coppo Stefani*, ed. N. Rodolico, *Rerum Italicarum Scriptores*, new ed., XXX, Part I (Città di Castello, 1903–55), rub. 938.

were then in power. And this was apparently true, since he
was accused of receiving bribes and this was proved. . . .

61. THE MALADMINISTRATION OF THE Contado*

[December 10, 1411] Ridolfo Peruzzi said that much has
been spoken about taking measures against our citizens who
hold office [in the Florentine dominion] and who extort
money from our subjects. Anything which can be done about
this would be desirable, for they suffer cruelly from the
depredations [of the officials], which demeans the honor of
the Commune and the city, and harms our subjects.

[July 16, 1414] Giovanni di Andrea Minerbetti said that
a law should be passed so that our subjects are not robbed,
and the method should be that which achieves this most
efficaciously, and so that the violators will be punished and
corrected.

[June 15, 1417] Antonio Alessandri said that the residents of the *contado* do not pay heavy taxes, but their substance is consumed by usurers and by rectors who extort
money from them. . . . Do not remove the rectors for that
would encourage evil men, and it would contribute to the
rise of magnates. . . . So that all will live in peace and
honesty, we must find a way to select honest rectors who will
conserve our subjects and their property, and not the oppo-
site.

Marsilio di Vanni Vecchietti said that the residents of
the *contado* are fleeing [from the territory] daily, and they
leave the land uncultivated. This results from many rectors

* Source: *ASF, Consulte e Pratiche,* 41, fol. 60r; 42, fol. 159r; 43, fol.
152r.

who are sent there who do not govern well, and consequently, those in the *contado* must bear heavy burdens. . . .

62. AN OFFICIAL REPRIMAND, 1418*

To our very dear [citizen, the podestà of Pisa]: From trustworthy sources, we have learned that you, together with Dino di Lapo of Florence, who lives in Pisa, have bought up a large supply of linen. . . . And it was not enough that you purchased the linen at the times and prices that you did, so that many poor men and women who required a small supply for their needs could not obtain it. But you have also seized and detained a number of them, and even condemned some, to prevent them from buying. These methods are abominable, odious, and reprehensible, as anyone can see. They are also in violation of the intent of the Signoria and of our citizens, and they bring disgrace to you personally.

We send rectors and officials [into our territory] to maintain justice among our subjects and to conserve them in peace and unity, and not to engage in violence and extortion under the cover of the offices and dignities which they hold, nor to prevent them from buying and selling the necessities of life. We marvel not a little at your behavior, and we grieve, for it has been difficult for us to believe these things about you. Now we order and command you that in the future you abstain from these and similar practices, and that you permit everyone to buy and sell freely as he desires, observing those regulations which have been promulgated concerning these matters by our illustrious citizens, the Five [Governors] of Pisa. [We order you] to comport yourself in such a manner

* Source: *ASF, Signori e Collegi, Missive*, 29, fol. 112v.

that we will not have similar complaints about you in the future, and to obey our commands so that your obedience will merit commendation and not the contrary.

63. THE MISDEEDS OF A RECTOR, 1461*

Before you, Lord Defenders of the Laws, is brought this accusation against Lorenzo. . . . Altoviti, rector at Barga for thirteen months. . . . On the first day of August last year, Lorenzo was at the fair of S. Pellegrino, pinching the rumps of the Lombard girls in such a fashion that had not the captain of the guard warned him to have some care for the dignity of the Florentine Signoria, there would have been a great scandal. He also told him that it would be better for him to stay at his post and take care of his office, instead of going to foreign fairs and bothering the women. The two men exchanged heated words, and Lorenzo insulted the Marquis of Ferrara, so infuriating the knight that if men of the locality had not come between them, Lorenzo would have been cut to pieces. He went there dressed like a ruffian, so that he was shown little respect. When it was learned that he was the rector at Barga, he received some respect for the honor of the Commune [of Florence].

While he lived in Barga in the palace of justice, he associated day and night with a band of toughs, gambling with cards and dice, shouting and quarreling and cursing, as gamblers do. And when certain older men of the region came to request justice, one for one matter and another for something else, as is the custom of courts, he told them to leave since he didn't want any greybeards coming into his

* Source: *ASF, Giudice degli Appelli,* 85, fols. 112r–114r.

house. And so these men had to leave without settling their affairs, complaining that they could not be heard. . . . Night and day, he went through the region with this gang of armed hoodlums, eating and drinking and carousing in the houses of the citizenry. Once he came to the Porta Reale and closed the gate, then opened and closed it at his pleasure, seizing women and shoving them to the ground, so that there was a great scandal in the town. . . .

When a preacher delivered a sermon on the feast day of S. Colognone, Lorenzo left the church and began to shout loudly that the preacher was mad and did not know what he was saying, and that he should turn to some other profession than preaching. Everyone was scandalized by this behavior, which disturbed the feast and the church services. And people said: "Look at the type of men our rulers send to govern us!" And thereafter, he continually persecuted the preacher whenever he encountered him, and especially at the Mayday feast, where a great throng of people—Lucchese, Lombards, and even Florentines—had assembled on account of the great piety of this area. And while the faithful were listening to the preacher, Lorenzo left the church and spoke to everyone: "You are going to hear a madman preach." Then he began to argue with everyone, so that the celebrations were ruined, and the peasants and foreigners made fun of him and said to the people of Barga: "If this man is your rector, you must truly be malgoverned. Why don't you go to your rulers and ask them to relieve you of his insane activities?"

It also happened during that holiday that he sequestered a knife belonging to a man in the service of the Marquis of Ferrara and refused to return it to him. Consequently, the captain of Castello Nuovo in the Marquis's territory sent four ambassadors to Lorenzo, asking him out of respect for himself and for the Marquis to return the knife. But Lorenzo

refused this petition; he told the ambassadors that he didn't
care a fig for either the captain or the Marquis, saying, "I
am not afraid of your little Marquis!" According to reports,
these statements came to the attention of the Marquis of
Ferrara, who instructed his men to seize Lorenzo if he ventured onto his territory at night (when customarily he went
on his expeditions) and to place a stone round his neck and
drown him.

On the feast day of St. Christopher, the patron saint of
the Commune of Barga, a great crowd of priests and other
clergy, foreigners, and natives, assembled. During high mass,
the preacher was gently reproving Lorenzo for his vices and
bad behavior in the area. Having been informed of this,
Lorenzo—accompanied by his band of armed ruffians—burst
into the church and yelled at the preacher: "Get out, friar!
Go somewhere else for I think you are berserk!" And the
friar interrupted his sermon while Lorenzo continued to
shout in the church, causing a great disturbance. He sent
his ruffians to ring the church bells so that the preacher had
to leave the pulpit; he shouted at him to leave and not to be
so bold as to return. And the friar departed and never returned during Lorenzo's tenure, to the great displeasure and
shame of the community of Barga. This man, Fra Michele,
was a good and valiant preacher, a member of the Observant
Franciscans, respected by the entire region. . . .

Lorenzo became angry with Master Bartolomeo, the Communal physician of Barga, because the doctor had criticized
his behavior on several occasions in a friendly manner. When
Master Bartolomeo was settling the account of his salary
with the Communal treasurer in Lorenzo's presence, the two
men exchanged heated words. Master Bartolomeo complained that he was not treated equitably, whereupon
Lorenzo vilified him and told him that if he didn't leave,

he would order him to be decapitated. Under penalty of death, he ordered him to abandon the territory of Barga, and for some three months, he has been living in exile. And before his departure at the conclusion of his term of office, Lorenzo said to his treasurer, Todi di Testone, at a council session: "I am leaving you 100 lire so that you will cut the doctor to pieces." Everyone marveled at this, knowing the doctor to be a good and worthy person. . . .

Item, this Lorenzo had quarreled with a priest of Barga named Ser Antonio, because the cleric, as his good friend, had reproved him for his behavior, tales of which he had heard throughout the region. Whereupon, Lorenzo seized the priest with his own hands and held him in prison for a day and a night, without any cause. . . . And for this act, Lorenzo was excommunicated by the bishop of Lucca.

Item, he sought to gain some friends when his term of office was ending, and he sent for several men and gave them to understand that they could become rich from Communal property. Having heard this, these men took a certain island and other Communal lands and divided this property among themselves, and placed it upon their tax rolls, in violation of equity and of the statutes. When the rest of the Commune learned of this, a great crowd assembled and came to the city hall to complain to the judge. He told them that he had done this so that they would attack each other and not concern themselves with his affairs. The citizens then dispersed to their houses to seize their arms and then to search for those confederates of the rector who had done this. At this moment, the new rector arrived in Barga to take up his office. He saw men and women running to the gates and the streets through which he was passing, kneeling and raising their hands to heaven and crying, "Mercy!" They thanked God that their rulers had sent a new rector to bring order and peace to Barga, and that his predecessor, who had caused so much trouble and discord, had been forced to depart. [Lorenzo was fined 500 lire.]

64. THE ABUSE OF CLERICAL AUTHORITY, 1415*

We prosecute . . . Father Jacopo di Giachetto Totti, also called Father Coppino of Lucca, [a priest] who lives in the fortress of Picegli in the district of Pistoia, a man of evil character and condition. . . . In April of the present year 1415, Messer Michele di Terrorino of Capognano, a canon of Bologna and rector of the church of S. Maria de Villa Gavinana of the Montanee, on behalf of Father Jacopo, said to Father Antonio di Lando of Siena: "I have met that evil Father Coppino, and he told me that if you didn't give him ten bushels of grain for his children, he would find a way to despoil you of what you have here." To which Father Antonio replied to Messer Michele, "Tell him that before I would give anything to him, I would throw everything I have into the sea."

In July of the present year, Giuliano di Niccolò of Gavinana said to Father Antonio of Siena, that on the feast day of S. Jacopo, he went to have a drink with the vicar of the bishop of Pistoia. There he met Father Jacopo and reproached him for defaming and accusing Father Antonio before the bishop's court in Pistoia. And Father Jacopo said to Giuliano: "If Father Antonio had given me 4 florins as I ordered him to do through Pestello of S. Marcello, he wouldn't have this trouble and I would have cancelled the accusation which I made against him. . . ."

* Source: *ASF, Giudice degli Appelli*, 99, part 3, fols. 17r–18r. The court of Filippo Sacchetti, rector of Montanee, near Pistoia.

In April of the present year, Guaspare di Nenni Francia, also called Pestello of S. Marcello, said to Father Antonio of Siena: "What have you done to Father Coppino that he threatens you with such force?" Father Antonio replied to Guaspare, "I haven't done anything to him, but he is really trying to harass me." Then Guaspare said to Father Antonio, "I begged him, by our friendship, to leave you in peace, and he told me that if you would give him a few bushels of grain, he would leave you alone. . . ."

In the month of April of the current year, Father Jacopo warned Father Antonio di Lando of Siena not to be so daring and presumptious as to celebrate any divine services in the church of Mammiano. If he dared to disobey, he would kill him and would so arrange that the parishioners of Mammiano would not find a priest to serve in their church. . . . In the month of March of the present year, Father Coppino warned Father Antonio di Baldanza of Pisa, presently rector of the *pieve* of Castro S. Marcello, not to celebrate any divine services in the church of Mammiano. Otherwise, he would incur his displeasure and he would kill him. In the month of August of the current year, for the abovementioned crimes, Father Jacopo was seized and committed to the Communal prison of S. Marcello. Together with Antonio di Jacopo of Luzzano, he broke out of prison and fled from the castle of S. Marcello. [Jacopo confessed; he was fined 1,000 lire and ordered to leave Florentine territory. If he ever returned, he would be imprisoned for life.]

PART FIVE

CRIME AND PUNISHMENT

In Florence, criminal procedure in secular cases was based on Roman law, supplemented by the *diritto commune* or common law of Italy and by the statute law of the Commune. Criminal processes in the city originated in the courts of the three foreign judges, in the form of an inquisition or investigation. The inquisition might begin as a result of information collected by the magistrates, or by an accusation presented by an individual. If the accused was in custody, he would be interrogated by officials of the court, who were authorized to use torture in capital cases. The accused was allowed to call witnesses to testify on his behalf; the prosecution could also furnish witnesses who gave testimony under oath. If an accused person failed to respond to the court's summons, and neglected to defend himself, his silence was often construed to signify guilt. Confession, on the other hand, reduced the penalty except in capital cases. On questions of law and of fact, the magistrate was the final authority, although his decisions could be overruled by Communal legislation (no. 73).

From our perspective, the most remarkable feature of Florentine criminal justice was its heavy reliance upon fines, and its limited use of imprisonment as a form of punishment. Judges occasionally sentenced criminals to a period of detention in the Communal prison, the Stinche (no. 73). But most of the inmates were paupers who could not pay their fines, or who were incarcerated for debt or the failure to pay taxes. The penalties imposed by the magistrates indicate how this society regarded various types of crimes; for example, it considered the offenses of an alchemist (no. 72) and a forger (no. 74) to be more serious than those of a robber or an adulteress (no. 80). The large number of cancellations of judicial sentences which are found in the volumes of Communal legislation (nos. 80–81) suggests either that criminal justice was badly administered, or that Florentines were very susceptible to appeals for mercy. Both conclusions may be valid.

I. *Crimes of Gravity*

65. GREED AND UXORICIDE*

. . . We condemn . . . Francesco di Simone Moretti Ruzini, of the parish of S. Simone of Florence, and his sister Monna Tomasia . . . the widow of Giuliano di Andrea Ruchi of Florence. . . . In the present year and the month of September, Francesco and Monna Tomasia agreed to arrange that Lena (the step-daughter of Tomasia), who was gravely ill, would make her will and designate Tomasia as her sole heir. . . . To Lena's home . . . Francesco brought a Florentine notary and certain witnesses. . . . And Lena, a young girl, was persuaded by Tomasia to make her will leaving Tomasia as her heir, even though she had a brother and a sister, Antonio and Piera, the legitimate children of Giuliano. . . .

* Source: *ASF, Atti del Podestà*, 3762, fols. 29r–31v, October 5, 1400.

Motivated by avarice and by a desire to profit fraudulently from Lena's property, Francesco . . . said to his sister Tomasia: "Look, sister, someone has told me that this testament is not valid," and he cited several reasons. "So I want you to use whatever blandishments necessary to persuade Lena to marry me. . . ." And he promised his sister Tomasia that he would divide equally all of the property which would come to him from Lena. . . . Tomasia replied to Francesco, "I will do everything that you have asked. . . ."

In order to bring this about, Francesco brought a notary and certain witnesses to Lena's house while she was lying ill in bed. And after being persuaded by Francesco and by Tomasia, Lena was interrogated by the notary and she consented to have Francesco as her husband, and then in the presence of the notary and the witnesses, the rings were exchanged. On the following evening, Francesco . . . brought several men into a room of that house for a wedding feast, even though Lena was in bed in her room, gravely ill with the plague. . . . Francesco then said to the persons assembled in the room, "Men, be of good cheer, for I want to go sleep with my wife." He left them and entered Lena's room and went to bed with her, a sick woman. . . .

Then two days after the wedding, Francesco had a conversation with certain persons from whom he sought counsel . . . about arranging that Lena would not recover from her illness . . . but instead would die. And since the pestilence was then (and still is) raging, he would never be suspected by anyone. Having received advice on this matter, Francesco went personally to the shop of Leonardo di Betto, a druggist in the Mercato Vecchio, and bought from him eight portions of arsenic . . . and took it home. . . . With Tomasia, he placed that arsenic in a small loaf of bread . . . and gave it to Lena to eat, for the purpose of poisoning and killing her . . . Lena ate that mixture . . . and on the second day she died. [Francesco and Tomasia both confessed to the crime and were sentenced to death. Since Tomasia was pregnant, her execution was postponed until after the birth of her child. However, she later petitioned successfully for the cancellation of her sentence.]

66. Passion and Uxoricide*

. . . We condemn . . . Cristoforo di Giovanni, called Cefo, of Casale in the *contado* of Cortona, Mea di Giovanna of Montegualandi, a resident of Cortona, and her daughter Cristina, the wife of Cristofano, called Cefo. . . . At some time prior to the commission of the crimes described herein, Cefo took for his wife a certain Angela, the daughter of Antonio of Cortona, an honest woman of good condition and reputation . . . and from her he had a male child. Then Cristforo fell in love with Cristina, a nubile girl of some seventeen years, and Cristina returned his love. Desiring very much to sleep with her, Cefo sought on several occasions to persuade her to engage in illicit love. . . . Mea, the mother of Cristina, tried to arrange a marriage for her daughter and discussed this matter with several young men, and particularly Liberatore, called Tori, della Fossa de Lupo, of the *contado* of Cortona, and a certain Giovanni, called Guagni, di Nardo de Pezzola, a weaver of Cortona, and a certain Biagio di Giovanni Guardi. Learning about this, Cefo sought to prevent Cristina's marriage by creating discord and disturbing these negotiations. He urged Mea and Cristina not to contract a marriage with Tori, on the grounds that Cristina was not suited to peasant life and that she could not stand the work. To dissuade Mea and Cristina

* Source: *ASF, Giudice degli Appelli,* 99, fols. 291r–294r, April 1, 1415.

from arranging a marriage with Giovanni, called Guagni, he told them that Giovanni had several children by his first wife who had died, that Cristina would have to take care of those children who were not her own, and that Giovanni had maltreated his dead wife.

On the other hand, he dissuaded those young men from taking her as a wife, and in particular, Biagio di Giovanni, who had agreed to marry Cristina. . . . Burning with love and unable to find peace, Cristoforo did not see how he could prevent that marriage, since previously he had pleaded with Mea and Cristina not to proceed with it but rather to wait. He secretly called Biagio outside of the Porta Picciogrande next to the city walls and said to him: "You know that we are neighbors and that since childhood we have been friends and comrades. I ask you not to marry Cristina because I love her and I want her for myself and for a long time I have kept her and I have slept with her frequently," while in truth he had never cohabited with her. Cefo then added, "I am telling you this because I like you and I don't want a woman to be the cause of our killing each other." Upon hearing this, Biagio immediately promised Cefo that he would not take her, and especially since Cefo asserted that he had been intimate with her, while he had believed her to be a virgin and an honest [woman]. Stating that he wanted a larger dowry, he refused her.

Complaining about her daughter's misfortune, Mea said that she was determined to marry her even if she had to give her to some lowly person. . . . Upon hearing this, Cefo took Mea outside the Porta Colognani next to the fountain by the acqueduct, and with his most persuasive arguments, he urged Mea not to arrange for her daughter's marriage. He had learned from certain soothsayers that his wife was going to die within five years of his marriage to her, and

more than four years had already elapsed. . . . Mea replied that these were fatuous statements, since she did not
believe in soothsayers. But if it were to happen that he no
longer had a wife, then she would gladly give Cristina to
him in the nude, instead of to anyone else clothed, because
she knew that he loved her daughter, and because he was a
neighbor and she knew about him and his condition. Cefo
answered, "I tell you to wait a little while, because if what
was told to me is true (meaning the death of his wife), I
will hasten it along. You can do what you wish with your
daughter, but if you marry her off, you will not be content. . . ."

Cefo told Cristina that he wanted to have her as a wife
and asked her if she loved him, and she replied that she did
love him . . . and willingly would marry him if his wife
should die, but she added that she would grieve over Angela's death since she loved her and was her intimate friend.
Notwithstanding all this, Mea continued to seek a husband
for her daughter and Cefo for his part opposed it. And
among Mea's neighbors the rumor circulated that Cristina
was Cefo's mistress and concubine and that she was pregnant
by him, which was not true. And while Mea tried in every
way to get her married, Cefo opposed it . . . so that she
became ill and stayed in bed. When Mea heard about the
rumor . . . concerning her daughter, she went to Cefo, who
was ill in bed. She found him alone in his house, for his wife
Angela was away, being employed in domestic service. She
told him, "It is not surprising that Biagio didn't want to
marry my daughter, for it is rumored that she is pregnant
by you. I promise you that if she is pregnant, that I will see
to it that she does not bear a child, for I will kill it." Cefo
replied, "This is the first time that you have heard it; I
heard it several days ago, but don't be upset for it isn't true.
. . . I've told you several times: if you wait a little while,

I will remove the scandal, for I will take her for my wife."

Then Mea asked him how he would do this, and they began . . . to arrange for the death of Angela, Cefo's wife, by poison. Cefo said to Mea: "Don't worry about this but leave it to me. Before sixteen days have passed, I will remove this shame from you, and you will see the signs before many days have passed." Hearing this, and filled with anger and grief over those insinuations, Mea realized that her daughter was in such bad repute that she would never find another man. Desiring the death of Angela so that her daughter would marry Cefo, she urged him to commit that [crime]. She said, "How will you do it?" And he replied, "I will hasten her death . . . and if there is no other way, I will give her rat poison." Mea then said to Cefo, "Since it has to be done, do it quickly. . . ." Several days having elapsed, Cefo one night beat and abused Angela and forced her to stay outside of the bed for the greater part of the night, so that she became slightly ill. . . . Then Cefo prepared two dishes . . . and in these he placed some poison . . . so that Angela experienced some pain in her stomach. On the feast day of S. Firenze, which is the first day of June, Cefo, Mea, and Cristina returned from the celebration in the Valle Montimaris and they found that Angela had recovered somewhat from her illness. . . .

On the next day, Cefo bought some poison called *risalgarium* and he took this pulverized poison home and placed a portion in a jar in which he cooked some beans when Angela was out of the house. Then it occurred to him that if Angela ate some of this poison, that it might kill their son whom she was nursing. Moved by penitence, he threw the beans and the poison out and left the pot overturned, thinking that he had emptied it completely. When Angela returned home, she found the pot overturned and wondered what had happened. Cefo said, "It was probably the cat."

Finding a few beans in the pot, Angela mixed them with water and oil and ate them together with the poison. She vomited everything that she had eaten and feeling ill, she lay down in her room. Thereafter, Cefo did not want Angela to nurse his son. . . . On the following day, Cefo bought some quicksilver and placed it in an egg which he prepared . . . and gave it to her. . . . Angela grew worse each day, with grave pains in her stomach and intestines, and vomited almost continually. . . . Mea made a chicken pie and . . . Cefo mixed some poison in it . . . and gave it to Angela, with Mea's knowledge. . . . Then Cefo prepared a confection . . . for Angela and put some poison in it and placed that dish in a separate place, so that no one else would eat it. Then he said to Cristina, "When you go to see Angela, give her some of that food, because it has the stuff in it," meaning the poison. . . .

On several other occasions, Cefo gave poison to Angela . . . from which she died on the sixth day of June. . . . Cefo secretly married Cristina, with her mother's consent, eight days after Angela's death, in the presence of two witnesses. This he did secretly, lest those who heard about it would think about poisoning and homicide. [The three accused confessed to the crime. Cefo and Mea were executed; Cristina was whipped through the streets of Cortona and expelled from the territory.]

67. INFANTICIDE*

. . . We condemn . . . Monna Francesca, the daughter of Cristofano Ciuti of Villa Caso of the district of Pistoia, the wife of Cecco Arrighi of Ponte Boccio of the district of Pistoia . . . a most cruel woman and murderess. . . . During the months of April, May, and June of the past year,

* Source: *ASF, Giudice degli Appelli*, 98, no pagination, March 13, 1407.

Francesca lived at Montemurlo in the Florentine *contado* in a place called Torre al Gravello, on a farm belonging to Buonaccorso Strozzi. There she had conversations with a certain Jacopo of Romagna, Buonaccorso's servant, who told her that he wanted to take her for his wife. So Francesca, persuaded by his words and his arguments, allowed herself to become intimate with him on several occasions . . . so that she became pregnant by Jacopo. . . .

Then Francesca, knowing herself to be pregnant . . . promised to marry . . . Cecco Arrighi of Ponte Boccio . . . in the month of October of last year. . . . They were married according to the rite of Holy Mother Church, and after their wedding they had intercourse together, as is proper between husband and wife. Cecco did not realize that Francesca was pregnant by Jacopo . . . although she had been questioned by Cecco and his brothers about her swollen stomach. But Francesca had insisted that she had a pain in her stomach, and that the swelling resulted from that. . . .

In the month of March of the present year, Francesca was approaching the time of delivery and with God's help, she gave birth to a healthy male child in the house of her husband Cecco. . . . But inspired by an evil spirit and so that no one would know that she had given birth to that child, she threw him in the river which is called Anigne . . . and as a result this son and creature of God was drowned. [Francesca confessed. She was led through the streets of Pistoia on a donkey, with the corpse of her child tied to her neck, and was then burned to death.]

68. FORGERY AND HOMICIDE*

. . . We condemn . . . Stoldo and Papo (or Jacopo), the sons of Annibaldo Strozzi, and Jacopo, called Papo di

* Source: *ASF, Atti del Esecutore,* 1306, fols. 33r–36r, February 27, 1397.

Nero, of Montebuiano of the Florentine *contado*. . . . In
the month of January of this year, Stoldo and Jacopo began
to conspire to commit the crimes described below. . . .
They decided secretly between them to kill . . . Agostino
di Dino Migliorini, called Agostino Cane, of the parish of
S. Felicita of Florence, whom they knew to be wealthy, with
the object of obtaining possession of his inheritance. . . .
They asked Ser Francesco di Ser Puccino of Signa in the
Florentine *contado* to make for them a false testament according to the proper form, promising to pay him adequately
for his efforts. . . . To Stoldo and Papo, Ser Francesco replied that he was prepared to do whatever they required of
him, both for love of them and for the money which they
promised him. . . .

Having arranged these matters, they asked one of their
friends to do something for them, namely, to say that he
was Agostino Cane, and before witnesses to impersonate
Agostino Cane and make his testament and name Papo di
Annibaldo as his heir. Their friend replied that he was ready
to accede to their desire. So having made this agreement, on
a certain day in January, Stoldo and Papa di Annibaldo, Ser
Francesco, and their friend assembled together in the residence of the Friars Minor, or S. Croce of Florence. In a
cell of that place, they assembled seven friars who were foreigners and who, ignorant of this deception, did not know the
true Agostino Cane. . . . In the presence of these friars as
witnesses, [and] the notary Ser Francesco, Stoldo and Papo
di Annibaldo showed them their friend whom they knew
was not Agostino: ". . . This is our friend and he is a worthy
and rich citizen. He wishes to make his will in our presence
and in those terms which you will hear. We beg you . . .
to keep this a secret, so that his relatives will not press him
to change his mind." This having been said, the notary Ser

Francesco, at that day and hour and before those witnesses, read a testament or a document which, among other things, stipulated that in disposing of his property, Agostino Cane named Papo di Annibaldo as his heir. Upon being interrogated by the notary, the friend who was impersonating Agostino Cane stated that he wished to dispose [of his property] as Ser Francesco had indicated.

. . . Knowing that in Agostino's genuine testament, the Commune of Florence was named as a beneficiary, Stoldo and Papo di Annibaldo then proceeded with their intention of defrauding the Commune and Agostino's heirs, by hastening his death. . . . They asked Papo di Nero to commit that homicide, saying to him: "We have a good thing going, and we know that you are poor and have many debts. We want you to kill Agostino Cane. If you will serve us in this matter, we will take care of your debts and lend you 2,000 florins." To these words Papo di Nero replied, "For money I will do anything." And agreeing among themselves to carry out the abovementioned crime, Stoldo and Papo promised to lend Papo di Nero the sum of 2,000 florins, from the money and property of Agostino, if and when he killed Agostino before the revocation of the false testament. . . .

In the present month of February, Papo spoke with Domenico di Domenico Castellani, called Becca, and with Jacopo di Martino, both of the parish of S. Maria della Terra of the Florentine *contado*. He asked them to help him kill Agostino Cane . . . and promised them each 25 florins. . . . On a certain morning, the honorable Florentine citizen, Agostino di Dino Migliorini, called Agostino Cane, left his house, ignorant that the hour of his death was near. Papo di Nero, Domenico, and Jacopo were armed with knives . . . and they assembled near the door of Agostino's house. As Agostino walked a few paces from his doorway, Papo di Nero

said to Domenico and Jacopo, "There he is; get him!" Upon
hearing this . . . Domenico and Jacopo assaulted Agostino, seized him, and struck him with their knives . . . and
from these blows Agostino died. [All of the accused escaped
the authorities and were sentenced to death *in absentia*. In a
separate trial, the notary Ser Francesco was condemned to
death and executed.]

69. INCEST AND SACRILEGE*

. . . We condemn . . . Antonio di Tome of Castro
Tremoleti, a man of low condition, conversation, life, and
family, a blasphemer and offender against the divine majesty, a sacrilegious person, a perpetrator of incest and prostitution, and a violator of virgins. . . . In March 1413, Antonio seized with force and violence Nella Bambolucci of
S. Lucia of this vicariate, who is related to him by blood in
the second degree. . . . Antonio had carnal relations with
Nella, a virgin and a blood relative, to the great harm, opprobrium, and shame of Nella and her family, in violation
of divine law as well as civil and canon law, and also against
the good customs and the statutes of the Communes and
cities of Florence and Pisa. Not content with this but com-
pounding evil . . . at various times and in various places
during that year, Antonio had sexual relations with Nella,
committing with her that horrible and incestuous act . . .
and persevering in that abominable crime until Nella became
pregnant. As a result of that vile relationshp, a girl child
was born in the city of Pisa in the house of Ser Simone de
Farneto. . . .
. . . In May 1406, Antonio went to the city of Pisa for

* Source: *ASF, Giudice degli Appelli,* 99, fols. 161r–163r, September 22,
1413.

certain of his affairs, and began to gamble at dice and lost approximately 3 florins. Thereupon, he left that city to return to his home, then located in the village of Colle Alberti. . . . He entered the house and . . . with the intention of committing sacrilege against the divine majesty of our Lord Jesus Christ and his glorious and immaculate mother, the Virgin Mary, and avenging himself for the loss of the money, he took in his hand a certain tablet upon which was painted the image of the Virgin Mary and her blessed son, our Lord Jesus Christ. And against this image or picture he directed several vituperative, dishonest, and abominable words, saying among other things: "To your shame, Virgin Mary, I will break you into pieces; help yourself if you can!" and other dishonest words against the good customs and the perfect and sincere faith of all Christians, and also against divine and human law. Not content with this . . . but acting even more dishonorably, he took a steel knife which he had in his hands and cut the tablet upon whch was depicted the image—which had been drawn with such solemnity—into four parts. He said: "I can't do anything worse to you; if I were able to do so, I would do it!"

. . . In May 1410 in the village of Cresponi in the above-mentioned vicariate, Antonio was playing dice and lost a certain sum of money. Upon returning to his home in the village of Tremoleti, in an angry mood, he took a silver groat of Pisan coinage, upon which was sculpted and depicted the undamaged and intact image of the Virgin Mary, the mother of our savior. Against that image and representation, he uttered several words saying: "Virgin Mary, I can't do worse to you; if I could, I would, but I will pluck out your eye." And determined to execute this most evil and wicked plan, he seized in his hands a sharp steel knife for use at table, and with this knife he struck that image a blow, in the

face of that unblemished majesty, so that . . . the point of
the knife was broken into four pieces. As a result of a miracle
. . : the point of the knife fell to earth and was never
found, although both Antonio and his wife searched for
it. . . .

In September 1412, Antonio took into his home a young
girl named Margherita, the orphan daughter of Goro di
Andrea Bucachi of Agnano, in the Pisan *contado*, Antonio's
niece and the daughter of his sister. He claimed that he
wished to care for her, as though for the love of God, so that
the girl would not stray from the right path. He was in a
forest, in a place called Castello Vecchio, cutting wood when
this girl brought him bread and wine to eat and drink. . . .
He seized this girl Margherita, a virgin, and threw her on
the ground. When Margherita saw her uncle Antonio preparing to commit this act of Venus, desiring to thwart him
and to resist this iniquitous plan, fearing both God and the
shame of the world, she said to him: "Leave me alone; I
don't want you to touch me! You ought to be ashamed, seeing that I am your niece, that you want to do such things
with me." Whereupon Antonio . . . said to his niece
Margherita: "If you don't shut up, I will kill you!" . . .
Whereupon he deflowered this virgin Margherita and with
force and violence had carnal relations with her. . . . And
while Margherita was staying in his house in October of that
year, he took her forceably and threw her on a bed and
again had relations with her. . . . In April of the present
year, he again took her by violence despite her resistance,
and by threats forced her to accede to his will, and warned
her against informing [the authorities] concerning this
abominable and incestuous crime. . . .

On several occasions during these months, and in various
places, he committed the abominable crime of sodomy with

his niece Margherita, against the instincts and norms of nature, against her will, and to her grave harm, opprobrium, and shame, and against both human and divine law, and in the greatest violation of the divine majesty and human nature. [Antonio confessed and was sentenced to be burned to death in a wooden cage; this punishment was later changed to decapitation. The sentence was executed.]

70. THE CAREER OF A PROFESSIONAL CRIMINAL*

. . . We condemn . . . Bartolomeo di Giovanni, called Griffone, of Poland, a notorious robber of base condition and reputation. . . . In the year 1441 or thereabouts, he was living in the city of Venice with two Polish comrades and thieves called Procopio and Lanslavo. One day they banded together to steal a certain garment . . . from a Greek priest whose name is unknown, who lived in Venice in the church of S. Biagio. . . . They went to that church and Lanslavo entered a room adjacent to the church where the Greek priest stayed . . . and stole that garment . . . which was valued at 13 ducats or thereabouts. One day the Greek priest encountered Bartolomeo when he was wearing that garment. . . . He had him seized and incarcerated in the Venetian prison. . . . But with certain other prisoners, he broke out of jail and escaped. . . .

Item, in August 1444, he was staying in Rome and had a conversation with one Sebastiano, called Belcho, and Michele Obscena, Polish thieves and his companions. One day they went to the church of St. John Lateran . . . adjacent to which was a room in which resided a canon of that church whose name is unknown. And Sebastiano entered that room and stole a garment . . . which he threw from the window

* Source: *ASF, Atti del Podestà*, 4732, fols. 17r–22r, December 19, 1444.

of the room to Bartolomeo and Michele. . . . They seized
it and took it to the district of Trastevere . . . and gave it
for safekeeping to a certain Nardo, an innkeeper and a
Roman citizen. . . . A few days later, Bartolomeo recovered
the garment from Nardo . . . and sold it for 4 florins to
Vincenzo, a German and a cobbler for the archbishop of
Florence. . . .

Item, in August 1444 he was staying with Messer Alberto
of Germany, the penitentiary of our lord pope, and he received there a large silver cup weighing 16 ounces . . .
and worth approximately 18 florins. . . . This cup had been
stolen by Sebastiano and Michele Obscena . . . from a room
belonging to a canon of S. Maria Maggiore. Bartolomeo
buried the cup in Messer Alberto's stable, and a few days
later, Sebastiano entered the house and the stable of Messer
Alberto and . . . took the cup and fled from Rome with
it. . . .

Item, in October of the present year 1444, Bartolomeo
was in Florence with a certain Jacopo called Opella, a Hungarian, and Michele, called Chioschi, a Pole. They knew
about a castle some six miles from Florence called Campi
where a tavernkeeper lived . . . who had a chest where he
customarily kept his money. . . . They went to the village
and all three stayed with Buono di Piero, the innkeeper.
They ate dinner and then Buono gave them a bed. In the
middle of the night, they arose and went to the chest . . .
and with a reed smeared with a sticky substance, they tried
to extract some money from the chest . . . but they only
obtained 7 quattrini. . . . In October of this year, he left
Florence with Michele Chioschi and went to Bologna. . . .
There he entered a shop belonging to a certain Master Andrea, a furrier and a citizen of Bologna . . . and stole a
fur-lined cloak . . . worth 3 ducats. . . . Then he re-

turned to Florence in the company of a Hungarian named Jacopo Buratti with whom he had associated in Bologna. . . . Some twelve miles from Bologna they stayed in a place called Revergiano with an innkeeper named Antonio. . . . After supper they slept in a room with a peasant . . . and a pilgrim going to Rome. In the middle of the night, Bartolomeo and Jacopo arose . . . and stole a ring worth 12 grossi from the clothing of the peasant. . . .

After his return from Bologna, he stayed in Florence in a house rented by Jacopo Buratti. . . . One day he brought to that house Giovanni di Arrigo, a German who lived in Florence. This Giovanni had a private letter bearing the seal of the magnificent Count Francesco Sforza, which he had sent to a stranger and which was written in the hand of Ser Ceccho, his chancellor. When Bartolomeo saw that letter, he realized that with a similar letter, he could travel in every part of the world more freely, and could commit robberies more easily. So he took the letter and, using it as a model, he composed another letter . . . and with horse's urine he separated the seal from the first letter and with hot wax affixed it to the letter which he had written. . . .

One day he told Jacopo that they should go to Siena to prey upon the pilgrims going to Rome via Siena. . . . In November of this year, he and Jacopo traveled to Siena and stayed in a small inn. . . . One evenng, Bartolomeo said to Jacopo, "Wait for me here; I want to go out and try to get some money." He went . . . to the piazza in Siena called Il Campo in the vernacular, and there next to the Fonte Gaia he approached a shop which was open . . . and stole a cape worth 1 florin. [Bartolomeo returned to Florence and was captured by officials of the podestà. He confessed to the crimes and was taken to the place of execution, mitred, and tied to a donkey, and there was hanged.]

II. *Crimes of Subtlety*

71. AN ARTFUL SWINDLER*

. . . We condemn . . . Lorenzo, called Frictella . . . and Picchino. . . . In the month of December of the past year, while in the inn called "The Crown" in Florence, Lorenzo and Picchino . . . met a certain Tommaso di Piero of Hungary, who a few days earlier had come to Florence on his way to Rome. Beginning a conversation with him, Lorenzo stated that he was a great merchant and that he had shops in Rome and Naples and in several other places. He did this to deceive Tommaso, and so that they might take away his horse, which was at the inn, and the money which he had in his possession. With adulatory and deceptive words and with tricks, he persuaded Tommaso, who had been led to trust him, to sell him the horse for 18 florins. He promised to have the money delivered to him by his merchant partners in Rome, and he wrote a false letter of payment and gave it to him in exchange for the horse. . . .

Not content with this but adding evil to evil, Lorenzo and Picchino . . . took Tommaso of Hungary to a tavern to drink. While he was drinking, there came a certain man, pretending to be a merchant, who said that he had some jewels to sell. . . . Lorenzo and Picchino simulated the purchase of the jewels from that false merchant, and they asked Tommaso of Hungary to lend them money, stating that they would make another letter of payment which would include the price of the horse and the jewels. The credulous and trusting Tommaso gave Lorenzo 28 ducats

---

* Source: *ASF, Atti del Podestà,* 3238, no pagination, May 24, 1385.

. . . and Lorenzo pretended to give that money to the fake merchant. Having made this payment, the accused asked Tommaso to go and purchase some wine since they wanted another drink. Unaware of their fraud, Tommaso went to get the wine and upon his return . . . he found no one, for they had fled and have not been found. [Lorenzo and Picchino were sentenced, *in absentia,* to be whipped through the streets of Florence.]

72. THE ALCHEMIST*

. . . We condemn . . . Master Antonio di Luca of Messina in Sicily, a perpetrator of fraud and a man of evil condition. . . . He attempted to defraud the following men: Michele di Messer Vanni Castellani, Otto di Messer Mainardo Cavalcanti, Messer Tommaso of Città di Castello and Ser Francesco of Gubbio. . . . He had a conversation with Michele and Otto . . . and another with Messer Tommaso and Ser Francesco, saying to them: "If you wish, and if you furnish me the means, I will perform . . . an act of alchemy for you, in the following manner. I will transform and reduce copper from its color into a very white color [i.e., like silver]. . . . But to do this, I must have some gold, and the more the better, and we will place it on the fire and liquify it and then reduce it to powder. With this powder, we will be able to transform the copper from its original color and state to a white substance."

Having no doubts about these words of Master Antonio but rather accepting them credulously, Tommaso, Michelino, Otto, and Ser Francesco . . . brought the abovementioned sums of money and hastily prepared the pots in the following manner. Michelino and Otto . . . brought 1,000 gold

* Source, *ASF, Atti del Capitano,* 2177, fols. 13v–16r, June 3, 1402.

florins in an earthern cooking pot, with the intention of placing that pot on the fire to liquify these coins in a kiln which had been built by Master Antonio in his house. . . . When Michelino and Otto brought this pot holding the money to the kiln, Master Antonio instructed them to place the copper in certain receptacles so that they might be placed in the oven. Then, Master Antonio secretly took the pot containing the money and replaced it with another pot, similar in size and appearance. . . . Into that pot Master Antonio placed the following ingredients: sublimate silver, cinnabar, saltpeter, sulphur, and many other things, which he placed . . . upon the fire in the oven. But the pot containing the money he secretly took away . . . and hid it in an underground room of the house. . . .

Item, Tommaso and Ser Francesco brought a pot containing 400 florins to Master Antonio for the purpose of liquifying and pulverizing them . . . in an earthern oven. . . . And on a certain day . . . Master Antonio went to Tommaso's house, pretending to inspect the project and to see how it was progressing. . . . He secretly took the pot and hid it in the sleeves of his jacket, and replaced it in the oven with another pot in which he had put silver, saltpeter, sublimate silver, sulphur, cinnabar, and many other ingredients. . . .

Then, Master Antonio . . . had a conversation with Pierotto and Corsino . . . and said to them: "If you wish, and if you give me the means, I will make you an indigo dye so strong that it can be used a hundred times [for dyeing cloth] and it will be worth 60 florins or more. If we begin [this project], I want to make a large quantity. And so that you don't think that I will trick you, I will invest 200 florins of my own money, and you will invest 1,000 florins. And each of us will share the profit and loss according to his investment. It is necessary to place these florins in a pot on the fire to liquify them. . . . Then we shall mix this molten metal with other ingredients necessary to make the indigo dye." Pierotto and Corsino . . . told Master Antonio that they were willing if he would invest 200 florins. . . . So Master Antonio took some of the money which he had stolen and counted out 200 florins and gave it to Pierotto and Corsino. [Antonio was captured and imprisoned by the captain of the *popolo*.] To avoid paying the penalty for his crimes, he took his belt . . . and made a noose and placed it around his neck. Then he suspended himself from the iron bars of a prison window, and had he not been rescued by a prison guardian, he would have died. [Antonio was condemned to be burned at the stake; the sentence was executed.]

73. EXTORTION*

This petition is presented to you, lord priors, . . . on behalf of Lorenzo, called Nencio, son of Bernardo de' Bardi of Florence, who, with his brother Mainardo . . . was condemned on January 12, 1411 by Alberigo della Bordella de Argenta, count of Mordano, then captain of the *popolo* . . . and fined 2,000 lire. . . . If this sum was not paid within three months of the date of the sentence, he was to be led to the place of justice and there his left hand was to be amputated. . . . And whether or not they paid this fine, Lorenzo and Mainardo were condemned to stay in the Communal prison for two years . . . and also to restore to the heirs of Cione (named in this condemnation) certain pieces of cloth which were mentioned in the condemnation, or else the money obtained when they were pawned. . . . And this resulted . . . from the following events. . . .

* Source: *ASF, Provvisioni*, 109, fols. 61v–62v, June 7, 1419.

In August 1410, Lorenzo and Mainardo discussed how
they might induce Cione di Giorgio da Quarata, of the parish
of S. Lucia de' Magnoli, to come to their house and to extort
from him a certain sum of money and also to obtain the
cancellation of certain debts, of money and cloth, which they
had borrowed from him. Lorenzo said to Mainardo: "This
is what we shall do. I will go to Cione and say, 'Come to
Monna Lisa, our mother, for she wants to speak to you.'
Then he will come, and when he is in the house, we will
make him enter Monna Lisa's room. With threats and
menaces, we will force him to return the cloth which we
have pawned and also to cancel our debts to him which total
290 florins. We will also force him to give us a note for
1,000 florins." On the following day, Lorenzo went to Cione
and said: "Monna Lisa says that she wants to speak to you;
come and see her." Cione replied: "I will come," and Lorenzo returned home and reported this to Mainardo. Mainardo then said: "We will await him but I want to arm
myself," and then Cione appeared at the door of their house
and said to Mainardo: "Where is Monna Lisa?" and he
replied: "She is in her room; come in." Cione entered the
house and the room, although in fact Monna Lisa was not
there. Then Lorenzo closed the door and Mainardo seized
Cione from the rear and they both forced him to sit upon
the bed. All doors and windows being closed, Cione tried to
cry out but he was threatened with arms. They said to Cione:
"We have one debt with you for 25 florins and 30 lire, and
another for 30 florins." They demanded that he write a note
saying that this debt . . . had been satisfied by them,
whereas in fact he had not received any part of that money.
Also, they asked him to write another note saying that he
had received satisfaction in another matter under arbitration . . . in which Cione had demanded some 150 florins

from them. Also, they wanted . . . Cione to write with his own hand a note to his agent in the pawnbroking business, Antonio di Tommaso, instructing him to return a gown of black cloth to Lorenzo which had been pawned for 21 florins, 135 lire and 8 soldi. Also, they demanded that Cione give them a ring which he had on his finger, so that they might show it to the agent Antonio as a sign. . . .

Seeing himself thus confined and threatened with death, Cione said: "Give me pen and paper and I will write whatever you desire." Then Lorenzo gave Cione an account book belonging to himself and Mainardo in which was recorded the debt of 25 florins and 30 lire which Cione was to receive from them. And Cione wrote that he had received the money and cancelled the debt, although he had received nothing. Then, he wrote another note cancelling a debt of 30 florins which Lorenzo, Mainardo, and Paolo . . . owed him although he did not receive it; and in the same manner he wrote another note stating that he had received payment of 78 florins. . . .

Item, he wrote a note to Antonio di Tommaso, stating that he should give Lorenzo the gown of black cloth which had been pawned for 21 florins and 135 lire. . . . And he gave Lorenzo the ring so that he might give it to Antonio and thus more easily receive the pawned item. . . .

Then they told Cione to write two notes, one addressed to Esau Martellini, in which he should instruct Esau to give Lorenzo 500 florins and debit it to Cione's account; the other to Francesco di Angelo Cavalcanti, banker, instructing him to pay Lorenzo a certain sum of money and charge it to Cione's account. . . . Frightened by these threats, Cione said: "I will do what you wish, but I warn you that these bankers will not give you the money, because we don't have any agreement that they should pay you." Then Lorenzo

said: "I will take these notes which you have written to the
agent at the pawnshop and I will tell him: 'Give me the
pawned items.'" He then departed, leaving Cione in the
room with Mainardo to guard him until he returned. And
with these notes he went to Antonio who, recognizing Cione's
ring, delivered the clothing to Lorenzo which he received,
and then gave it to a servant to take home. When Lorenzo
returned to his home, he discovered that Cione had fled
through a window and consequently they were not able to
obtain those notes for 500 florins. . . .

Although there is some truth in this account, Lorenzo was
seized as a suspect in the murder of Cione and was held in
the judge's custody for thirty-two days and was tortured.
But the captain was unable to convict him [of murder] and
so, moved by anger, he concentrated on the other crimes
and forced him to confess to that which is narrated above. But
this was not all true, as became evident later, for he has been
detained in prison for eight years and no evidence of his
guilt has been discovered. And Lorenzo was a young man
of twenty and if anything was in fact committed, [his
penalty] should be lessened on account of his age. He was
committed to the Stinche by order of the captain on January 11, 1411. . . . Again, he was ordered to remain in
prison by order of the Signoria on January 22, 1411.
[Lorenzo's petition for release from prison and for absolution was approved by the councils.]

74. A Forger*

. . . We condemn . . . Lorenzotto di Messer Tome
Soderini of Florence, a citizen and resident of the parish of
S. Frediano of Florence, a forger and a man of evil condi-

* Source: *ASF, Atti del Podestà*, 4038, fols. 57r–62r, August 27, 1405.

tion, life, and reputation. . . . Lorenzotto left the city of Florence and traveled toward the county of Avignon and there, in the month of February of that year [1402], he stayed at the home of Monna Serena Berotti de Cimegne, his mother. . . . He had a conversation with her and complained about the treatment which he had received from his· father, Messer Tome [Soderini]. Among other things, he said that his father wished to exclude him from his inheritance and his property. He said to his mother, "There is a pestilence raging in Tuscany, and if Messer Tome were to die, he would deprive me of his inheritance. We must find a way to thwart him. We need a document written by a notary which will state that you, Donna Serena, are Messer Tome's legitimate wife." To which his mother replied, "I will send for someone immediately." On the following day, Donna Serena sent for her friend, Master Piero Guardi, a cleric of the diocese of Troyes, and at the instigation of Lorenzotto, she asked him to obtain a false marriage contract in the form of a public document. Master Piero promised . . . to serve her well in this matter and to do everything necessary. Lorenzotto thanked him . . . and promised to pay him as much as he could for drawing up this false contract of matrimony. And Master Piero was content.

On the following day, Lorenzotto went with Master Piero, searching through the city of Avignon for contracts and documents drawn up according to the Florentine style. They found the formula of a certain Master Prospero di Ser Lapo of Prato, a notary of the diocese of Pistoia, which was in the possession of one Beraldo Surdi, a cleric of Asti living in Avignon. From that, Lorenzotto and Master Piero copied out [a statement] to the effect that Messer Tome made a certain declaration on August 23, 1361. . . . Then Lorenzo went to one Ser Martino, a Florentine notary living in Avignon, and asked him if he had in his formulas a matrimonial document drawn up according to the Florentine style and custom. Whereupon Ser Martino commissioned his scribe, who was a Florentine, to find a marriage contract and also a dowry agreement, which he copied and gave to Lorenzotto. With this copy, Lorenzotto went to some druggists' shops and found some old sheets of parchment, so that the false document which he intended to draw up would appear to be older.

. . . Then Master Piero wrote out and fabricated two public and solemn documents (although both were totally false), one of matrimony and the other concerning a dowry, in the style used by Florentine notaries according to the formulas which he had obtained from Ser Martino, in which he falsely wrote the day, month, and year, the city, and the names of two Florentine witnesses. . . . One document stated that on August 23, 1361, in the city of Avignon, Messer Tome di Guccio Soderini of Florence . . . took Monna Serena Berotti de Cimegne as his legitimate wife, and that from that union Lorenzotto was born. The other document stated falsely that on September 8 of that year, the marriage having been solemnized in front of the church, and in the presence of one of those witnesses (who is now dead) and others, Monna Serena delivered her dowry of 600 florins to Messer Tome, who increased it by 400 florins, for a total of 1,000 florins. He acknowledged the receipt of that dowry from Monna Serena and he promised . . . to restore it. . . . And for composing those documents . . . Lorenzotto gave Master Piero 25 florins. . . . And at Lorenzotto's request, Master Piero gave those false documents to Monna Serena, who said to her son, "I wish to keep these documents with me until Messer Tome dies, for if he were to learn about them, he would kill me and you."

Lorenzotto was willing to leave them with his mother and he departed from Avignon.

. . . After Lorenzotto returned from Avignon to the city of Florence, it happened that Messer Tome died in the year 1402, leaving several legitimate children born of his union with his wife, Monna Filippa. These included his son Francesco . . . and several daughters, for whom he provided dowries, as is clearly stated in his testament. . . . And knowing that he was not the legitimate son of Messer Tome but a bastard, Lorenzotto . . . went to certain lawyers in Florence with a document of emancipation and legitimization drawn up by . . . Master Piero Guardi . . . and he said that as a legitimate son [of Messer Tome], he intended to demand his share of the inheritance.

Seeing that the document had not been registered at the Merchants' Court, as the statutes of the city of Florence required, the lawyers said to Lorenzotto: "Lorenzotto, you don't have any basis for your claim." Hearing this, Lorenzotto told the lawyers, "Even though this hasn't been successful, I have other ways. Though my father considered me a bastard, the truth is that I am his legitimate son, born of his marriage with my mother who lives in Avignon and who has the official document [of the marriage]." Then the lawyers replied, "If this is true, then bring those documents and we will see what can be done."

. . . In July 1403, during the tenure of the podestà, Messer Apollonio de Viso, Lorenzotto presented through his procurator a document to Messer Andrea, the judge and magistrate of the podestà. . . . He said that he was the legitimate son of Messer Tome, born of his union with Monna Serena, his mother and the legitimate wife of Messer Tome. [He said that] Messer Tome died leaving only Lorenzotto as his legitimate son. . . . And he petitioned

the judge to declare him to be the legitimate heir of Messer
Tome. . . . And although the judge decided against him,
he . . . continued to pursue his nefarious enterprise in several courts of the city of Florence, particularly in the palace
of the Signoria and in the court of the *gabelle* officials. . . .
Even though these documents were declared to be false in
Florence and in Avignon, he never abandoned his evil plan
. . . in vituperation of the memory of his father and to the
harm and detriment of the legitimate sons and daughters of
Messer Tome. [Lorenzotto confessed and was sentenced
to death. He was beheaded.]

III. Prison

75. INMATES OF THE STINCHE*

[September 14, 1459] Bastiano di Spinello Dominici of
the parish of S. Martino a Petroio was delivered to the officials of the Stinche on September 14, 1459, as a result of the
sentence passed against him by . . . the vicar of the Valdarno Superiore, that he should remain in the Stinche in
perpetuity for the many robberies which he committed. . . .

[November 3, 1461] Bartolomeo di Antonio of Piacenza
was consigned to the officials of the Stinche by Ser Michele
di Niccolò of Mantua, the notary of the criminal court of
Certaldo. . . . He was sentenced to remain in prison for
three years, and after his release, he is to leave Florentine
territory within three days or suffer the amputation of his
right foot. . . .

* Source: *ASF, Soprastanti alle Stinche*, 92, no pagination.

[January 26, 1463] Andrea di Antonio, of the parish of S. Margherita in Monte, was consigned to the officials of the Stinche . . . by Ser Giovanni di Angelo, an official of the podestà . . . to remain in prison until he pays his niece Giuliana, the daughter of his dead brother Francesco, the sum of 30 florins for her dowry. . . . He cannot be released from the Stinche until he has made this payment. . . . [He was released on April 28, 1463 after paying the dowry.]

[February 9, 1463] Sandro di Biagio di Giovanni Baldacci was consigned to the officials of the Stinche by order of the magistracy of the Eight on Security . . . and at the request of his father. He is not to be released without the consent of the Eight on Security. . . . [He was released on April 21, 1463.]

[February 14, 1463] Angelo di Francesco Janni, an old-clothes dealer, was consigned to the officials of the Stinche by the notary of the Merchants' Court, at the request of Marchionne di Stefano Bellandrini, for a judgment against him of 53 lire, 6 soldi. . . .

[March 9, 1463] Caterina, the daughter of Domenico Bernardi and the widow of Francesco di Tommaso del Pecora, was fined 375 lire . . . by the podestà of Florence for committing adultery . . . and she was also condemned to death by decapitation for poisoning her husband Francesco. . . . The execution of this sentence against Caterina cannot be carried out on account of her pregnancy, and it must be postponed until after she has given birth. Until the time of her execution, Caterina is to be detained and guarded in the Stinche. [She was executed on June 28, 1463.]

[March 23, 1463] Madelena, the slave of Niccolò di Gentile degli Albizzi, was consigned to the officials of the Stinche by order of the Eight on Security . . . and at the request of Niccolò. She is not to be released until the Eight so decree. . . . [She was released on May 16, 1463.]

[April 15, 1463] Adimari di Scolaio Spini was consigned to the officials of the Stinche by Ser Giovanni Marini, the notary of the Merchants' Court, at the request of Amerigo di Niccolò Frescobaldi, a banker, for a debt of 36 florins. [He was released on July 6, 1463.]

[August 18, 1463] Messer Piero di Ser Paolo de Mondola [a cleric] was consigned to the officials of the Stinche by Ser Antonio Spani, an official of the podestà, by virtue of this bulletin: "Giovanni . . . archbishop of Florence . . . orders you, the officials of the Stinche . . . to detain Messer Piero di Ser Paolo de Mondola and to guard him well, by day . . . and by night in the prison, and he is not to be released without our express consent. . . .

[August 18, 1463] Nora, the wife of Tommaso di Lorenzo, a weaver of linen cloth, is consigned to the officials of the Stinche by order of the Eight on Security . . . and at the request of her husband Tommaso.

IV. Diminished Responsibility: Insanity

76. A DEMENTED WOMAN*

. . . We condemn . . . Margherita, the wife of Lotto, who lives in Porta Fugia in the territory of Prato, an insane woman of lowly reputation and condition. . . . In October [1406], with her customary madness, she went during the night with a lamp in her hand to the house of Monna Mea,

* Source: *ASF, Giudice degli Appelli,* 97, part 2, fols. 15r–16r, January 20, 1407.

the wife of Stefano of Prato. She asked Monna Mea for a light, and Monna Mea opened the door to her and gave her a light, saying to her: "What are you doing at this time of night? Why don't you send Lotto for a light instead of coming yourself?" And then Margherita replied: "He didn't want to come because he was afraid of the servant," and she asked Monna Mea: "What time is it?" And she replied: "It is almost daylight," and she added: "Go home carefully, because they say that last year you set fire to the house and the stable of Leonardo, called "El Begolla," and also they say that you ruined that good man Cecco di Simone, the blacksmith, when you went to his shop for a light. And there have been other times when you were put into jail and Lotto beat you." And Margherita, frenzied and insane, said: "I won't do anything! I won't do anything! I won't give you any trouble, for I am going home to my Lotto who wants to go to work."

On her way home, Margherita came to the house of Stefano Tomasini, a baker, of the parish of S. Niccolò of Prato in that place which is called "the bakery of the nuns of S. Niccolò" and she saw the yard open where the firewood was stored. She entered that yard to take some wood and straw for fire, to take home to warm herself. She began to feel cold, and since she had taken that wood for the above-mentioned purpose, and had the lighted lamp in her hand, she lit the straw, on account of her insane condition. Then, unable to put out the fire, she ran out into the street and began to cry: "Fire! Fire!" But the fire had progressed so far that the bakery . . . and two other houses were burned. . . .

In that same month and year, Margherita in her insane and frenzied state left the territory of Prato and came to the village of Tizzano in the *contado* of Pistoia. During the night, she approached the house of Andrea di Tommaso of Tizzano in a place called "Le Piastre," and begged him to allow her to spend the night in his house. But Andrea's wife said: "I don't want to open [the door], for you are the mad Pierazza of Florence." And Margherita replied in a furious voice: "I am not the mad Pierazza. I am Margherita of Prato, mother of Ciuta who lives in the house of Monna Ciosa. Let me in for I wish to warm myself." Andrea's wife replied: "There is a fire in the bakery and you can go there to get warm. I don't want to let you in for you are a crazy woman and I don't want to let insane people into the house." Then Margherita went to the bakery and she found it as the other had said, and at the foot of the oven she made a fire . . . and warmed herself. During that same night she built another fire next to a strawstack and this spread so rapidly that the stack was burned. [Margherita confessed and was fined 150 lire, "her penalty mitigated on account of her confession and her insanity." In addition to the monetary fine, she was committed to the city prison for one year, "so that her insanity will not harm others." If she did not pay the fine within ten days, she was to be whipped through the streets of Pistoia "as is the custom."]

77. A Plea of Insanity*

. . . We condemn . . . Anastasio di Ser Domenico di Ser Salvi Gai of the parish of S. Reparata. . . . Armed with a stick of wood which he carried in his hand, he insulted Monna Novella, his mother and the wife of Ser Domenico . . . to whose property he and his brothers could succeed either by testament or intestate. . . . With this stick, he

* Sources: *ASF, Atti del Capitano,* 2605, fols. 5v–6r, February 11, 1415; *ASF, Provvisioni,* 119, fols. 100r–100v, June 21, 1428.

struck Monna Novella, his mother, on the head, with a heavy effusion of blood, from which wound she died. . . .

It is clear, notorious, and manifest to the court that at the time of this homicide or parricide—as well as before and after—Anastasio was and is mad and insane, and therefore according to law his penalty should be mitigated. However, so that no similar crime may occur, and so that upon his body some punishment may be inflicted, we sentence him to perpetual imprisonment in the Stinche. . . .

On behalf of Anastasio di Ser Domenico di Ser Salvi, of the parish of S. Reparata, this petition is presented with all due reverence, to your magnificent lordships, the priors . . . of the Commune of Florence. . . . He was sentenced by . . . the captain of the *popolo* to perpetual imprisonment. . . . [The text of Anastasio's condemnation is then recorded.] The truth is that Anastasio had been having quarrels with his brothers, and was so exhausted with anger and bitterness, that he actually became demented and was totally insane. Before this crime, he had thrown himself into the well of his house and had committed several other acts by which anyone of proper judgment would have realized that he was insane. And he has been detained in the Stinche, and has been so completely cured of his disease that he has done nothing reprehensible to this day.

Wherefore on his behalf, your lordships are petitioned to order that on the feast day of the Blessed John the Baptist, which is on the 24th day of the present month of June, he should present himself before the church of St. John the Baptist in the accustomed manner with head bare and with a torch in his hands, and at the proper time and preceded by trumpets, to participate in this oblation. . . . Thus, by means of this ceremony, he will be fully released from this condemnation and will receive full absolution . . . and will thereby gain release from prison. [The petition was approved.]

78. A SACRILEGIOUS ACT*

This petition is presented with all due reverence to you, lord priors . . . on behalf of Bartolomeo Magi di Galatrona, of the Florentine *contado*. On August 16, 1421 he was condemned by Angelo di Giovanni da Uzzano, then vicar of the Upper Valdarno. He was fined 100 lire as a subsidy to the church of S. Lorenzo de Caposelvi (to be spent on a missal for that church), and was also sentenced to ten years in prison. . . . Thereafter, he could not be released while he was afflicted by madness, not without the deliberation and consent of the Signoria and the colleges. . . . This condemnation resulted from the fact that . . . on August 10, 1420, on the feast day of S. Lorenzo in the village of Caposelvi, Ser Battista di Domenico di Giovanni of Siena, the rector of the church of S. Crestina of Radda, was at the altar saying mass in a devout and solemn manner. The body of our Lord Jesus Christ had already been sacrificed, and in the holy chalice there was his most holy and precious blood. According to the customs and rites of the Holy Roman Church, these sacraments were celebrated at the altar by the aforementioned priest. . . . He then spoke the commemoration for the dead which begins: "Remember, O Lord, thy servants, etc." Bartolomeo, that son of Babylon, motivated by a diabolical spirit . . . went to the altar and with force and violence irreverently committed and perpetrated this horrible crime. He took from the altar the Eucharist and the

* Source: *ASF, Provvisioni*, 112, fols. 238r–238v, December 23, 1422.

body of our Lord Jesus Christ and placed it into his mouth
and swallowed it, in violation of the honor of the Holy
Mother Church and the devotion of the Catholic faith. . . .

The truth is that he did in fact commit this act; that is,
he took the body of our Lord Jesus Christ without permission. This was the reason [for his behavior]. He had heard
that when he was plagued by evil spirits, he would be cured
from this torment if he could share the body of our Lord
Jesus Christ. On several occasions, he had asked priests to
show the Eucharist to him, and because they did not believe
him to be either sane or spiritually pure, he was never able
to obtain his wish. And so motivated by this impulse, and
for this purpose, he committed this grave crime, for which
he was apprehended and committed to the Stinche on August 17, 1421. . . .

He is a very poor man and has suffered many persecutions,
and on May 29, 1422, someone on his behalf gave 100 lire
to Ser Giovanni Buonaccorsi, the rector of the church of
S. Lorenzo de Caposelvi. Moreover, he has entered into a
peace agreement with the priest Battista di Domenico on
May 30, 1422. . . . In addition to this, he was absolved
from this crime by license of the lord bishop of Arezzo, on
condition that he visit the shrine of S. Antonio of Vienna.
And since his confinement in prison, he has led a miserable
existence. Not only does his detention harm himself, but it
deprives his children of their bread and guidance. And
thanks to God, he has been freed of those evil spirits and
hopes to live as a faithful Christian if he receives grace from
your benign authority. . . .

Therefore, your lordships are petitioned to permit this
Bartolomeo, on the birthday of our Lord Jesus Christ . . .
to go to the church of St. John the Baptist . . . and in the
accustomed manner to be led with uncovered head and with

torch in hand . . . to receive this oblation and . . . thus
to be pardoned. [The petition was approved.]

V. Mercy and Its Rationale

79. RELIGIOUS ENTHUSIASM AND THE RELEASE
OF PRISONERS*

. . . In these extraordinary times, it appears that nearly
all of the citizens of Florence, as well as those subject to the
city and residents of surrounding cities and regions, have put
on white linen garments, and after making confession and
receiving the sacraments, have joined in processions. They
have gone outside of the city to various places, piously singing lauds, engaging in acts of penitence, abstaining from
meat for nine consecutive days, and from wine for another
day, not sleeping in beds. The air vibrating with their voices,
they have petitioned the Almighty for peace and mercy. . . .
The lord priors are firmly convinced that all of this has proceeded from divine inspiration, since where and when the
spirit wishes, it animates many to give alms in bread and wine
to the multitude, and the penitents who have come to Florence . . . have been warmly received.

Among the works of mercy, [the priors] have considered
one, namely, the visitation and subsidizing of prisoners in
the Stinche . . . who have been incarcerated for debts . . .
and who may be treated with mercy and liberated from the
misery of imprisonment. They realized, however, that this
cannot be done without suspending those laws which prohibit

* Source: *ASF, Provvisioni,* 88, fols. 147v–148v, September 10, 1399.

this, and so desiring to open the way to this pious and holy
objective, they have decided on the following measures.
. . . [The provision suspends, until October 15, those laws
which limit the authority of the priors and their colleges to
release prisoners from jail.]

80. THE PLEA OF AN ADULTERESS*

This petition is presented with reverence to you, lord
priors . . . on behalf of Monna Bartolomea, wife of Cecco
di Matteo, of the parish of S. Lucia Ogni Santi of Florence,
who on June 16, 1386 was condemned, together with Lorenzo di Niccolò . . . by the podestà . . . to pay a fine of
2,000 lire for robbery and, in addition, a fine of 500 lire each
for adultery. . . . If this fine was not paid within ten days,
and if either or both of them were to fall into the hands of
the podestà or his successors, they were to be taken to the
place of justice and there hanged on the gallows until dead.
. . . This judgment was made because Monna Bartolomea
had committed adultery with Lorenzo, and because they
went to Cecco's house and stole property valued at 60 florins.

The truth of this matter is that Cecco and Bartolomea
were deceived by Lorenzo, who said that he wished to be
Cecco's intimate friend. And under this bond of friendship,
Cecco and Lorenzo had a very close relationship. With false
and deceptive words, Lorenzo intimated to Cecco that someone wished to offend him, so that Cecco . . . carried a
knife hidden on his person. Then Lorenzo went to the authorities and Cecco was apprehended with the knife and
jailed. Lorenzo visited him and told him that he was willing
to spend 6 florins to obtain his release from prison. He then
went to Monna Bartolomea and told her that it would be

* Source: *ASF, Provvisioni*, 82, fols. 57r–58r, May 23, 1393.

necessary to sell or pawn some of the furnishings in order to obtain the money necessary for Cecco's release. So she gave him some clothes and other things and with the money which he received for them, he seduced her so that she went away with him outside of Florentine territory.

Meanwhile, Cecco became aware of Lorenzo's malice and of Monna Bartolomea's simplicity, and he made peace with her by means of a public document . . . dated April 27, 1387, and since that time they have lived together in harmony, without fearing condemnation. But a certain Communal official, desiring to obtain some money from Cecco, had words with Monna Bartolomea, and he had her seized by an official of the podestà . . . and then imprisoned on May 27, 1393. [Her petition for absolution was approved by the councils.]

81. The Excuse of Poverty*

On behalf of Angelo di Taddeo Gaddi, a painter, of the parish of S. Piero Maggiore of Florence, this petition is presented to you, lord priors. . . . On October 7, 1392, Angelo was fined 600 lire . . . by Jacopo, count of Fulgineo and podestà of the city of Florence. . . . This proceeded from the fact that Angelo, who was holding a piece of wood in his hand, insulted and attacked Miniato Tuti of the parish of S. Frediano of Florence, a servant and messenger of the officials of the Monte of this Commune. With this club he struck Miniato several blows on his shoulder and kidneys, and on his left arm, without any shedding of blood. . . .

What actually happened was much less serious than was described in the condemnation. Angelo attacked Miniato

---

* Source: *ASF, Provvisioni*, 81, fols. 268r–268v, December 20, 1392.

because he had been most grievously injured by him. To force Angelo to pay the sum of 40 soldi which he owed the Commune, Miniato broke down the door of his house and, not content with this, he spoke disrespectful words to Angelo's wife. . . . Moreover, Angelo is a pauper and cannot pay that fine. . . . [The petition was approved.]

82. A Juvenile Delinquent*

. . . This petition is reverently presented to you, lord priors, on behalf of the father, mother, and kinsmen of Chiovo di Gherardino Machiavelli of Florence, against whom a criminal process has been instituted . . . by the podestà. . . . In the month of October of the current year, Chiovo . . . went to a house or shop owned by the heirs of Messer Vieri de' Medici, which is rented by Tasso, a carpenter, and his brother . . . in the parish of S. Tommaso. . . . He took a wooden ladder which was in that house and placed it against the adjacent house. . . . With an iron hammer which he carried with him, he smashed a window which had been walled in, and then with a rope . . . he entered that building where wine is sold at retail. . . . In that house or cellar was a chest . . . and with his hammer he broke into that chest and stole 4 gold florins, 105 lire in quattrini . . . and 33 lire in grossi . . . which belonged to Agnosino Cursini of the parish of S. Felice in Piazza. . . .

Chiovo confessed to the facts . . . contained in that process. . . . Although he was described as a notorious public thief in that document, in fact he has never committed any other robbery or similar crime. He is a youth of twenty-four years or thereabouts, and he was forced by necessity to commit that theft. For he and his parents and sisters were not

* Source: *ASF, Provvisioni*, 88, fols. 224r–225r, November 10, 1399.

only poor but destitute, and they had no property and were heavily burdened with debts. This resulted from the fact that Gherardino had been recently taken prisoner in the war with the enemies of the Commune. . . . And so moved by the misery of his father Gherardino and his family, he committed that crime . . . for which every honest man should grieve, and his father and family deserve sympathy. . . . Moreover, Chiovo should receive some consideration for the many worthy deeds which his Machiavelli ancestors have performed on behalf of the Commune. . . . [The petitioners requested that Chiovo be fined for this crime, and not sentenced to death or mutilation. The petition was approved.]

PART SIX

PUBLIC MORES

A complex pattern of motives and impulses inspired Communal efforts to control public mores. There was, first, the recognition that some vices, like prostitution and gambling, could not be eliminated but only regulated to minimize their nuisance value (no. 88). The efforts to limit expenditure on clothing and jewels were prompted by fiscal and social motives (nos. 83, 84). Sodomy and the violation of convents were more serious matters, for these vices were believed to be so abhorrent to God that their existence could bring disaster to the city. In periods of tension and anxiety, the authorities were more concerned about these activities and they took stronger measures to suppress them. It is no accident that decrees concerning the extravagance of women (no. 84), the vice of sodomy (no. 95) and the sanctity of convents (no. 97) were all promulgated in the crisis years of the 1430s.

I. Sumptuary Legislation

83. THE FISCAL RATIONALE, 1373*

It is well known to all that the worthy men, Benozzo di Francesco di Andrea . . . [and fifteen others] . . . have

* Source: *I Capitoli del Comune di Firenze*, ed. C. Guasti and A. Gherardi (Florence, 1866–93), II, 173–74.

been selected to discover ways and means by which money will accrue to the Commune. . . . Considering the Commune's need for revenue to pay current expenses . . . they have enacted . . . the following:

First, all women and girls, whether married or not, whether betrothed or not, of whatever age, rank, and condition . . . who wear—or who wear in future—any gold, silver, pearls, precious stones, bells, ribbons of gold or silver, or cloth of silk brocade on their bodies or heads . . . for the ornamentation of their bodies . . . will be required to pay each year . . . the sum of 50 florins . . . to the treasurer of the gabelle on contracts. . . . [The exceptions to this prohibition are] that every married woman may wear on her hand or hands as many as two rings. . . . And every married woman or girl who is betrothed may wear . . . a silver belt which does not exceed fourteen ounces in weight. . . .

So that the gabelle is not defrauded, and so that citizens— on account of clothing already made—are not forced to bear new expenditures, [the officials] have decreed that all dresses, gowns, coats, capes, and other items of clothing belonging to any women or girls above the age of ten years, which were made up to the present day and which are decorated in whatever manner, may be worn for ten years in the future without the payment of any *gabelle*. . . .

84. THE SOCIAL RATIONALE, 1433*

. . . After diligent examination and mature deliberation, the lord priors have seen, heard, and considered certain regulations issued in the current year in the month of August

* Source: *ASF, Deliberazioni dei Signori e Collegi, ordinaria autorità,* 42, fols. 5v–6r.

by Francesco di Andrea da Quarata and other officials who are called "the officials to restrain female ornaments and dress." They are aware of the authority granted to the lord priors and the officials responsible for ornaments by a provision passed in July of the current year. . . . They realize the great desire of these officials to restrain the barbarous and irrepressible bestiality of women, who, not considering the fragility of their nature, but rather with that reprobate and diabolical nature, they force their men, with their honeyed poison, to submit to them. But it is not in accordance with nature for women to be burdened by so many expensive ornaments, and on account of these unbearable expenses, men are avoiding matrimony. . . . But women were created to replenish this free city, and to live chastely in matrimony, and not to spend gold and silver on clothing and jewelry. For did not God himself say: "Increase and multiply and replenish the earth"? The lord priors, having diligently considered the regulations recorded below . . . and in order that the city be reformed with good customs, and so that the bestial audacity of these women be restrained, approve and confirm the following regulations. . . .

85. PROSECUTIONS AND PENALTIES, 1378–97*

[June 10, 1378] We prosecute Nicolosa, daughter of Niccolò Soderini, of the parish of S. Frediano, aged ten years. Nicolosa was discovered wearing a dress made of two pieces of silk, with tassels and bound with various pieces of black leather, in violation of the Communal statutes. [She confessed through her procurator and paid a fine of 14 lire.]

* Source: *ASF, Giudice degli Appelli,* 59, no pagination.

[November 12, 1378] We prosecute Nanna, the daughter of Master Guido, physician, of the parish of S. Firenze. . . . She was discovered wearing a gown of black cloth with silver ornaments in front, in violation of the Communal statutes. [She confessed and paid a fine of 28 lire.]

[November 12, 1378] We prosecute Flora, a servant of Messer Jacopo Sacchetti. . . . Flora was discovered wearing a knitted gown and also a cap of samite and slippers on her feet in violation of the Communal statutes. [She confessed and was fined 22½ lire.]

[June 8, 1380] We prosecute Monna Bice, daughter of Simone di Giorgio, and husband of Benedetto di Uberto Benvenuti, parish of S. Felice in Piazza. Bice was found going through the city of Florence wearing five rings on the fingers of her hands, that is, four with pearls and one with a stone, of which three were in violation of the Communal statutes. [She confessed and was fined 37 lire, 10 soldi.]

[June 19, 1397] We prosecute Monna Bartolomea, wife of Meo di Puccio Orlandi, parish of S. Piero Scheraggio, who is older than ten years. . . . Bartolomea was discovered walking through the city of Florence wearing a cloak of black cloth with sleeves wider than one yard in circumference, in violation of the Communal statutes. [She confessed and paid a fine of 28 lire.]

[June 27, 1397] We prosecute Monna Agnella, wife of Giovanni di Messer Michele de'Medici, parish of S. Lorenzo. . . . Agnella was found wearing a prohibited gown, one part of sky blue cloth and another part of velvet with sleeves wider than one yard in circumference, in violation of the Communal statutes. [She confessed and paid a fine of 28 lire.]

[August 16, 1397] We prosecute Biagio di Pace, tailor, parish of S. Piero Gattolino. . . . In the month of July of the current year, Ser Guaspare, notary and official of the appellate judge, found in Biagio's shop a woman's cloak of red cloth with sleeves wider than one yard in circumference and with a leather belt, in violation of the Communal statutes. . . .

Bartolo di Giminiano, of the parish of S. Piero Maggiore, a witness called by Biagio di Pace, examined by the judge concerning the inquisition of Biagio, testified that he possessed information concerning this process. . . . He said that the cloak had been cut in accordance with the instructions of a foreigner named Cenni di Venture da Baburaccio for a girl who lived in Foligno, and who intended to wear that cloak in that city. . . .

Marco di Piero, of the parish of S. Michele Bertelde, a witness called by Biagio di Pace, examined by the judge concerning this inquisition against Biagio, testified that he possessed information concerning this process. . . . He said that when the cloth for this cloak was brought by Cenni, he told Biagio to make a cloak with wide sleeves and with slashes. The accused replied that he could not make a cloak in that style, for he would incur a penalty of ten ducats for each violation. Then Cenni said that this was not true, since the cloak was ordered for a girl living in Foligno. [Biagio was absolved of the charge.]

II. Gambling

86. THE CLIENTELE*

[March 12, 1433] You are hereby notified, Defenders of the Laws, that on January 4, there occurred a big gambling

* Source: *ASF, Giudice degli Appelli*, 77, part 2, fols. 155r, 238r; 79, fol. 21r; 81, no pagination; 82, fols. 275r–275v.

session in the piazza of S. Andrea where wine is sold. The gamblers were the following: Prospero di Goro, a retail cloth merchant from Pisa; Lottieri di Piccino, a woolen cloth manufacturer; Moro, who is employed by the *Prestanze* [the Communal bureau which collected forced loans]; and Matteo di Domenico, a belt-maker. Concio, the cook at the neighboring tavern, loans the dice to them and he obtains money by cheating, and he does this every evening to whoever wishes to gamble. [Concio was absolved of the charge.]

[June 10, 1433] In the Via de' Servi on May 17, 1433, Giovanni di Pasquale, a moneychanger in the Mercato Vecchio, and Matteo di Luca of Ancisa . . . were gambling with cards. The man who organizes the gambling and lends the dice in the Via de' Servi is Federico d'Angino, a horse-dealer. . . . Among those who were gambling on that day in the Loggia de' Canigiani were Bernardo del Siepe Peruzzi, Pippo, a yarn-broker, and the brother of Manno, the barber [whose shop is in the palace of] the Parte Guelfa. In that same place, Meo di Cercina and Ceccho di Ser Giunta . . . were organizing the gambling and lending the dice. In the Corso dei Tintori, Accerito di Stefano Ciucci, the painter Piero di Donnino, and Giovanni, the barber [in the palace of] the Alberti, were gambling with cards. [Giovanni di Pasquale and Matteo di Luca were each fined 10 lire, 19 soldi. The others were absolved.]

[December 2, 1435] With reverence, Defenders of the Laws, we inform you that there regularly assembles in the porch of S. Piero Gattolino the following: Antonio di Paolo, used-clothes dealer; Nenni di Gherardo, cloth-stretcher; Stefano di Nanni, called Fortino; Antonio, called El Zio, a weaver (all of the parish of S. Piero Gattolino); Ceccho di Nanni Giubetti, an oil vendor; Ridolfo, a stocking-maker;

Piero di Zanobi of S. Gaggio (all of whom live in the district outside the gate of S. Piero Gattolino); and Mariano di Nanni, called Lombardo, who lives outside [the gate of] S. Giorgio. The abovementioned men gamble with cards . . . and they attract swindlers and others who play with loaded dice, and they curse God and the celestial court [of paradise], and whoever does the worst, he is considered the best. And we are amazed that the omnipotent God does not send the pestilence and other evils to this city which permits this nest of thieves. . . . We pray your lordships to take action against the gamblers and blasphemers named above. [Antonio, called El Zio, was fined 25 lire; the others were fined 10 lire.]

Today, November 13, 1445, I notify you . . . that Domenico, called Schartera, who lives in the Via S. Gallo, operates a gambling place in the Canto di Doni, across from S. Maria Novella, and there he keeps a band of thieves who play with loaded dice and who rob poor men. . . . It would redound to your honor to drive out this band of robbers, and to do the same to Schartera as you did to Mostaccio and to Mango who used to be in the Loggia dei Buondelmonti. . . . Schartera is a fine, healthy man; he is neither sick nor crippled, and he is able to do something other than gamble with dice. [Schartera was fined 50 lire.]

[January 2, 1448] We notify you, Defenders [of the Laws], concerning a certain Francesco di Gaddo who, when he wants to work, is a first-rate shoemaker, and is strong and healthy. But he is a miserable poltroon, so given to evil that he runs a gambling den and lends dice, which is an infamous thing in this city. For the past three years, this Francesco di Gaddo has gambled in the Via de' Servi in the house of the Macigni. . . . And this would not be such a scandalous matter if it were not that so many foreigners come to Florence, and they all want to visit the [church of the] Annunziata, and on their way they see this throng of men who assemble there to gamble. [Francesco was fined 50 lire.]

87. A COMPULSIVE GAMBLER*

. . . We condemn . . . Francesco di Niccolò, also called Franceschino, of the parish of S. Ambrogio of Florence, and Giovanni di Donato, also called Giovanni Cattivello, of the parish of S. Frediano of Florence, infamous, villainous, and lawless men of evil habits and reputation. . . . In the month of October of the present year, at a place called the Loggia dei Castellani, Francesco saw Messer Niccolò di Antonio of Florence, the abbot of S. Tommaso in Foglia, dressed in the garb of a priest or monk with a priest's black cap on his head, and a cloak of Romagna cloth over his priest's gown. Stopping to watch, he saw Messer Niccolò engaged in gambling, and he asked him: "Are you a priest?" And Messer Niccolò replied that he was a priest. Then Francesco said: "If you are a priest and you are gambling, you must come to the office of the Eight on Security." To which Messer Niccolò replied: "I would risk my life to gamble." And so Francesco, without having obtained a license from the podestà or the Eight on Security or from any other office, by his own authority seized Messer Niccolò and escorted him to the palace of the Signoria where the office of the Eight on Security is located. As they walked through the streets, Messer

* Source: *ASF, Atti del Podestà*, 4703, no pagination, December 10, 1443.

Niccolò pleaded with Francesco not to arrest him, saying
that he should not humiliate him because he was a priest.
And as they reached . . . the building where money is
coined, which is called the Mint, next to the shops of the
shears-makers, Francesco intended to extort money from
Messer Niccolò, saying to him: "Give me four quattrini and
I won't take you to the Eight, and I'll never say anything
about this." And to avoid being taken to the Eight, Messer
Niccolò gave Francesco . . . four silver quattrini. . . .
And in return for this bribe of four silver quattrini, Fran-
cesco released Messer Niccolò and did not take him to the
Eight.

Then, it occurred to Francesco that if he should seize and
hold the priest, Messer Niccolò, in his house, he would be
able to extort more money from him. After a space of two
days, Francesco saw Messer Niccolò gambling in a place
called Scitorno's corner. He seized the clothing and the
person of Messer Niccolò, who was gambling with money
in hand. . . . He said these words to the priest: "You
must come to the Eight on Security." And several citizens,
in particular a barber, asked Francesco what this priest,
whom he was escorting, had done, and Francesco replied:
"Messer Domenico Martelli told me to take the priest to
him." And as he was escorting the priest through the streets,
Andrea di Giuliano of Florence said to Francesco: "What
has this priest done? Where are you taking him, to the Eight
or to a judge?" And Francesco replied, "He has business
with Piero di Nardo." And Francesco led Messer Niccolò
to the house of Piero di Nardo in the parish of S. Stefano,
for the purpose of holding him and extorting money from
him. . . .

And when Francesco brought Messer Niccolò to the house

of Piero di Nardo, the door of this house was closed, and he banged on the door until Giovanni [di Donato], who was in the house, opened the door. . . . And Francesco forced . . . Messer Niccolò into the house and said to Giovanni: "Take care of this priest." And giving aid and comfort to Francesco, he seized and led the priest, Messer Niccolò, into a small room in the basement of this house, locking him in this room so that he could be kept more easily and more securely in the house. . . .

Then Francesco went to the building which housed the Eight on Security and entered the building. As he was leaving, he said to Andrea [di Giuliano]: "Didn't you hear that priest cursing?" Andrea replied that he had not heard it. And then Francesco said, "I haven't done anything, because this was not the priest that the Eight wanted. So I had to release him." And when Francesco left the building, Andrea said to him, "I saw Bartolo and Giamino standing in the square, and they are officials of the Eight, who will help you if you want to bring the priest here." But Francesco replied, "I had to release him." And when Francesco was coming along the street next to the Mint, he encountered the barber who asked him: "What did you do with that priest?" To which Francesco replied, "Go to the judge if you wish." And as he moved further along the street which runs behind the inn of the Lion, he encountered the abovementioned Andrea, and he told him falsely that Giovanni di Donato had released Messer Niccolò. Andrea then replied, "You have done well." And Francesco then went to the house of Piero di Nardo and upon entering, he called Giovanni di Donato and said: "Where is the priest?" And Giovanni lied and said: "I sent him away," although in fact he had locked him in a room in that house. And Francesco said: "You have acted stupidly, because we could have profited greatly, for he [the priest] had a lot of money that we could have taken." And then Giovanni said: "The priest is in a room."

Francesco said to Giovanni: "Let's take the money which he has on his person and send him away." For he had a large sum of money including the 25 quattrini which Francesco and Giovanni had seen in his hand. . . . Giovanni replied to Francesco: "Very well, but how shall we do it?" And Francesco said: "We'll send him away by the back door, and we'll tell him that I am with the Eight and that he should never return here or he will be arrested." Giovanni said: "Let's do it," and the two were in agreement . . . to steal all of the money which Messer Niccolò possessed on his person.

Then Francesco busied himself with roasting some venison, and went to the kitchen located in the upper storey of the house. . . . And Giovanni entered the room where the priest was held and stayed with him. Suddenly, there arrived Bindo di Ser Battista Bocconti of Pisa, a Florentine citizen, who criticized Francesco and Giovanni for the incarceration [of the priest]. And the priest Niccolò escaped from the room when the owner of the house, Piero di Nardo, arrived. Francesco wished to recapture the priest Niccolò and place him in a study and hide him from Piero di Nardo. But when he asked the priest to enter the study, the priest refused, and seeing Piero di Nardo, placed himself under his protection. Piero di Nardo then released the priest, Messer Niccolò, and sent him away. [Francesco and Giovanni were both captured and confessed to the charges. Francesco was fined 1,500 lire, and Giovanni 750 lire. If the fines were not paid within ten days, Francesco was to be hanged, and Giovanni's right foot was to be amputated.]

III. Prostitution

88. THE ESTABLISHMENT OF COMMUNAL BROTHELS, 1415*

Desiring to eliminate a worse evil by means of a lesser one, the lord priors . . . [and their colleges] have decreed that . . . the priors . . . [and their colleges] may authorize the establishment of two public brothels in the city of Florence, in addition to the one which already exists: one in the quarter of S. Spirito and the other in the quarter of S. Croce. [They are to be located] in suitable places or in places where the exercise of such scandalous activity can best be concealed, for the honor of the city and of those who live in the neighborhood in which these prostitutes must stay to hire their bodies for lucre, as other prostitutes stay in the other brothel. For establishing these places . . . in a proper manner and for their construction, furnishing, and improvement, they may spend up to 1,000 florins. . . .

89. PROFITS OF PROSTITUTION*

[1427] . . . Rosso di Giovanni di Niccolò de' Medici . . . owns a house located at the entrance to the Chiasso Malacucina. . . . [It is rented by Biagio d'Antonio, a pork-butcher, for 12 florins per year.] . . . There are six little shops beneath that house which are rented to prostitutes, who usually pay from 10 to 13 lire per month [for a room], and this rent is never higher. The innkeeper, Giuliano, keeps the keys and he puts whoever he wishes [into the rooms].

* Source: *ASF, Provvisioni*, 105, fols. 248r–248v.
* Source: *ASF, Catasto*, 79, fol. 347r; 498, fol. 531v.

[1433] . . . Piero di Simone Brunelleschi and his mother Antonia . . . own two houses adjacent to each other in the Chiasso Malacucina, with furnishings required by prostitutes. . . . And there are several shops underneath those houses which are also inhabited by prostitutes. . . . They also report that they keep Giovanni di Marco of Venice in these houses . . . so that he, with some boys who stay with him, can collect the rents. They also state that they do not receive more than 4 florins per month from these houses and shops, on account of the depression. . . .

90. PROSTITUTES AND THE COURTS, 1398–1400*

[Angela, wife of Nofri di Francesco, was convicted of plying the prostitute's trade without wearing the required garb, "gloves on her hands and a bell on her head." The following witnesses testified against her.]

Bartolo Gadini . . . stated that he was well informed about the contents of this process, namely that Angela had publicly sold her body for money in the parish of S. Maria a Verzaia, and that it is generally believed in the city of Florence . . . that she was and is a public prostitute. . . . Asked how he knew this, the witness said that he is Angela's neighbor, and that he saw many men openly coming to her house to copulate with her for money. . . . The witness further testified that during the previous November and December, on behalf of all of his neighbors and conforming to their will, he asked Angela to abandon her prostitute's career and live honestly. If she did so, he promised her, on behalf of the neighbors, to furnish her with a basket of bread

* Source: ASF, *Giudice degli Appelli*, 66, no pagination; 67, fols. 14r–18v.

each week for her sustenance. But Angela replied that she did not wish to give up prostitution unless her neighbors first gave her 2 florins. Otherwise she intended to pursue the whore's life since she earned much more money than the amount which her neighbors wished to give her. . . .

Antonio di Zanobi . . . testified that he had information concerning this case. . . . [He stated that] he had copulated with Angela and that for that act, she demanded 19 quattrini. Following the witness, a cloth worker from the parish of S. Frediano, Spina di Alimento, copulated with her and on that occasion he paid her a certain sum of money. . . .

Lorenzo di Riccomano . . . was and is a neighbor of Angela . . . and on several days and nights, he saw and heard men going to have carnal relations with her for money. On several occasions during this time, he reproached Angela for her dishonest and libidinous life. And he saw and heard her . . . say: "I am and I wish to remain a public whore, and I will sell my body to you for money."

This is the inquisition carried out by the excellent and honorable doctor of law, Messer Giovanni of Montepulciano, the appellate judge . . . of the city of Florence . . . against Salvaza, wife of Seze, parish of S. Lucia Ogni Santi. . . . It has come to the attention of the abovementioned judge and his court . . . that this Salvaza, wife of Seze . . . has publicly committed adultery with several persons and has sold her body for money. . . . With respect to all of these charges, the judge intends to discover the truth; and if she is found guilty of walking without gloves and bells on her head or with high-heeled slippers, to punish her according to the Communal statutes; and if innocent, to absolve her from this accusation.

This inquisition was begun by the judge against Salvaza on November 16, 1400. Sitting in tribunal in the accustomed seat of his office, the judge ordered . . . Bartolo di Bartolo, a public messenger of the Commune of Florence, to go to the home of Salvaza and order her to appear before the judge to clear herself of this accusation and to defend herself. . . .

November 16. The messenger has informed the judge and myself, the notary, that he went to the house of Salvaza and finding her there, informed her of everything herein inscribed and personally left a copy of this inquisition. . . .

November 19, 1400. Salvaza appeared personally at the residence of the judge, and since according to the statutes, no woman is allowed to enter there, the judge . . . ordered me, Jacopo de Silis, his notary, to descend to her near the entrance door . . . to hear and receive her reply, defense, and excuse. Before me, the notary, Salvaza replied to this accusation by stating that it was not true. . . . [She was then informed that she had eight days in which to furnish evidence of her innocence.]

November 24, 1400. Bartolo di Bartolo informed me, Jacopo de Silis, that he had personally informed the witnesses, identified below, from the parish of S. Lucia Ogni Santi, to appear on that same day before him at his accustomed residence to swear to tell the truth . . . concerning the statements in this accusation. . . .

The following witnesses against Salvaza were sworn in and examined by the judge and myself, the notary, on November 24, 1400.

Antonio di Ugo, parish of S. Lucia Ogni Santi . . . stated that everything in the accusation was true. When asked how he knew this, the witness replied that on numerous occasions, he had seen Salvaza enter the houses of many men—both natives and foreigners—by day and night. They played and danced with her, and did many illicit and indecent things with her, touching her and fondling her with their hands, as is done by public prostitutes. Asked whom he had seen touching and fondling her, and in whose houses, he replied that Salvaza went to the house of a certain Mancino, a Florentine citizen, and stayed with him for several days; also a certain pimp named Nanni, Niccolò, a tiler, and many others whose names he did not know. Asked about Salvaza's reputation, he replied that she is commonly regarded as a whore. When asked who voices this opinion, and where he heard it, he replied that it was the general opinion of nearly everyone in the parish. Asked about Salvaza's physical appearance and age, he replied that she is a big woman, about forty-five, quite attractive, with a dark complexion.

Vanni Migliore, parish of S. Lucia, . . . stated that he knew Salvaza, wife of Seze, very well; she lives in the street called the Prato Ogni Santi. He said that the contents of this accusation are true. When asked how he knew, he replied that he had seen many men, both citizens and foreigners, enter her house both day and night, and that she committed adultery with them. He had seen her engaged in indecent acts with them. Asked whom he had seen entering this house and participating in these indecencies, he identified a certain Martino of the parish of S. Paolo, Niccolò, a tiler, and many others whom he did not know. He stated that one night his door was closed and he was told that Niccolò had closed it. Thereupon, the witness encountered Niccolò and quarreled with him and told him that he was doing wrong. And Niccolò replied: "And I will fornicate wherever I please," and he held a key in his hands, and Salvaza was mouthing obscenities at him. Asked about Salvaza's reputation, he replied that among all of the residents of the parish, she had a bad reputation as a prostitute. Asked about her physical appearance and age, he replied that she was a large, dark woman of about forty years of age. . . .

Monna Leonarda, widow of Damello, parish of S. Lucia, . . . said that the contents of this accusation were true. Asked how she knew, she replied that she had seen many men entering Salvaza's house . . . both day and night when her husband was absent, and that men were said to have committed adultery with Salvaza. Asked whom she had seen entering the house, she replied that she had seen a certain Mancino and many others. Asked about Salvaza's reputation, she replied that she had a bad reputation and was considered a whore by nearly everyone in the parish.

Paula, wife of Lorenzo of the parish of S. Lucia, asserted that the contents of the inquisition were true. Asked how she knew this, the witness replied that she was Salvaza's neighbor and that she had often seen men enter her house, and had often heard her playing and joking with them. She also stated that on one occasion, a foreigner wished to go to Salvaza and the witness was standing on her doorstep. Feeling ashamed, the foreigner said to her: "You should go inside to your house," and then the witness went inside and the foreigner entered Salvaza's house. . . .

Margherita, widow of Ugo . . . stated that the contents of the accusation were true. When asked how she knew this, she replied that she is a near neighbor of Salvaza, and that she had often seen men enter her house. . . . The witness said that she had frequently looked through a window of Salvaza's house and had seen her nude in bed with men, engaging in those indecent acts which are practiced by prostitutes. [Salvaza was declared to be a public prostitute, and was required to wear gloves, bells, and high-heeled slippers.]

91. THE RECRUITMENT OF PROSTITUTES, 1379*

. . . We condemn . . . Niccolò di Giunta, called Bocco, formerly of Prato and now living in the parish of S. Lorenzo, a man of low condition, life, and reputation, a kidnapper of women, violator of virgins and widows, and a panderer who persuades honest women to lead a life of sin and corruption. This Niccolò went to a house owned by Landino di Martino, in the *pieve* of S. Severi de Legravallis Marine, where there lived Meo di Venture and his wife Riguardata, an honest couple of good reputation. He had several secret conversations with Riguardata, and with cunning and deceptive words, he tried to persuade her to commit adultery. These were his words: "Monna Riguardata, I have great sympathy for your youth, since you are a very beautiful girl and you have not married well, in terms of the person and the property of your husband. You know that Meo is crippled in one arm and one leg so that he is not really a man. Of the things of this world, he has none. You know this very well, for you are poorly dressed and badly shod, and you possess nothing in this world. You have little bread and wine, and there is neither meat nor oil in your house. I have never seen such a pretty girl living in this poverty and misery. I have the greatest compassion for you, particularly since your husband is the ugliest and most wretched man in the world, and you are so beautiful. So I have decided to take you away from this misery and arrange matters so that you will lack for nothing, and you will be well clothed, as your youth and beauty require. . . ." But Riguardata did not consent to

---

* Source: *ASF, Atti del Capitano*, 1198, fols. 70r–72r.

these appeals but said: "I want to stay with my husband."
However, Niccolò was not satisfied with this reply but said
to Riguardata: "Please don't make this your final response,
but think about it. If you will do as I ask, I will make you
the happiest girl in the world."

And with these and similar words, Niccolò persuaded
Riguardata to commit sin. . . . In the present month of
November, he went to the home of Meo and Riguardata
. . . and took that woman of good condition, behavior, and
reputation with him and brought her to a place called Trespiano. There, in the inn of Ceccarello of Trespiano, he kept
her one day and two nights and committed adultery with
her on several occasions. Then he decided to take her to the
city of Bologna and place her in the public brothel of that
city so that she might earn money. . . . And he would have
done so if he and Riguardata had not been captured in Ceccarello's inn by one of our officials and the husband of Riguardata.

Item, this Niccolò with bland and false words persuaded
Bona, the daughter of Clari and wife of Janni of Florence,
who now is called Caterina, to commit sin. These were his
words: "Bona, if you wish to stay with me, I will clothe you
and provide you with your living expenses, if you will sell
wine in my tavern. And I will pay you for your work [as a
prostitute] and you may keep two-thirds and I will take
one-third, and we will sell more of our wine." With these
words and others, he induced her to sin and she had relations
with several men. From this adultery, Bona earned money
for Niccolò, against the wishes of her husband and her father
Clari, and to their shame and disgrace.

Item, in the current year and the month of January, Giovanna of Borgo Citramontina was staying in Niccolò's hostel. He saw this pretty girl, poor and badly dressed. He

said to her: "How do you manage alone in your wanderings? You are young, and restless feet do not gain much. I beg you to stay with me and work in my hostel and I promise never to leave you and I will clothe you very handsomely. And with these false and deceptive words, he induced Giovanna to sin . . . and kept her in the hostel. She dined with the guests and other men, so that they would pay to commit adultery with her. The money which she received from this adultery was turned over to Niccolò for his use. Then, persuaded by Niccolò, Giovanna entered the public brothel of the city of Florence. . . .

Item, when Monna Margherita of Reggio, who today lives in the house of Niccolò di Cristoforo, came to Florence with Antonio di Masso of Reggio, she stayed in the house of the above-mentioned Niccolò [di Cristoforo]. And Niccolò [di Giunta] persuaded her to commit sin. . . . And so that he might gain his evil objective more easily, he arranged with an official of the city of Florence to seize, torture, and expel Antonio [di Masso] from the city of Florence. Then he spoke to Margherita: "You have been left here alone. How are you doing? I want you to stay with me, and I promise not to bother you. And I will arrange for you to earn a lot of money, and I will provide you with fine clothes and shoes." And with these words, he persuaded her to commit sin . . . and on several occasions he committed adultery with her.

Item . . . this Niccolò, a notorious pimp, with bland and deceptive phrases has induced several married women and widows of Florence to lead a life of sin and to commit adultery with various men, with officials and nobles of Florence, and also with foreigners, in his house. [Niccolò di Giunta confessed to these crimes; he was executed.]

92. A PANDERER'S CAREER*

. . . We condemn . . . Bartolomeo di Lorenzo, of the
parish of S. Piero Gattolino of Florence, a pimp and a vendor of his own flesh, a man of evil condition, life, and reputation; Stella, called Pellegrina, the daughter of Master
Pace, a painter of Faenza, and wife of Bartolomeo, an adul-
terous woman and a violator of holy matrimony; and Jacopo
di Lorenzo, called El Padovano, of Padua, an exploiter of
women. . . .

Forgetting his own honor and the spiritual nature of the
matrimony which he had contracted with . . . Stella on
the feast day of S. Bartolomeo in August 1416, Bartolomeo
had a conversation with a certain Checco of Florence, who
lives in Lucca and is the operator of a brothel there. Bartolomeo said, "You know that I have a wife, Stella, and you
will recall that a few days ago, we agreed that you would
employ her in your brothel in Lucca. Now if you will give
me 30 florins, I will consent to your keeping her in your
bordello. . . ." Checco then replied to Bartolomeo, "I will
give you 12 florins, or 16 at the most, and no more. For she
is poorly clothed and I will have to furnish her with a new
wardrobe." After this conversation, Checco departed from
Pisa . . . and Bartolomeo was not able to put his iniquitous
plan into effect. . . .

Item, in the present year and the month of August, Bartolomeo . . . on various days and at various times . . .
sold his wife to Ser Jacopo de Interanne, to Piero of Villa
Tartagli in the Florentine *contado*, and to Ser Jacopo di

---

* Source: *ASF, Giudice degli Appelli*, 82, part 2, fols. 412r–414v, November 13, 1417. The court of Gherardo Machiavelli, podestà of Pisa.

Simone of Prato. He brought them at night to his house . . .
and permitted them to have carnal relations with his wife
Stella, to the shame and opprobrium of Bartolomeo himself
and of his wife. . . .

Item, in September of this year, he sold his wife Stella to
a Florentine notary whose name he does not remember. . . .
He received a wine flask full of oil as the price for this
prostitution. . . .

Item, persevering in this iniquitous course, Bartolomeo
took Stella with him . . . to the house of Corrado di Jacopo, a hosier, in the district of S. Martino in Chinocha of
Pisa, with whom Bartolomeo and Stella dined. After dinner,
all three went into the same bed, and the next morning,
Corrado had carnal relations with Stella with Bartolomeo's
knowledge and consent. After this intercourse, Corrado gave
Stella a Florentine silver quattrino and a silk jacket with a
belt as the price for her labor. Stella gave the coin to her
husband Bartolomeo. . . .

Item, in his house Bartolomeo sold Stella to Antonio
Biffoli of Florence, for which he received some money and
a doublet. . . .

Item, he sold his wife to Nanni di Duccio, a Pisan druggist
. . . who gave Stella ten Bologna pennies and a quattrino.

Item, Bartolomeo forced his wife Stella to have carnal
relations on various occasions with different men for certain
sums of money. . . .

Item, in the current month and year, Jacopo di Lorenzo,
called El Padovano, went to Bartolomeo's house in Pisa in
the Campo S. Cristoforo and abducted Stella, Bartolomeo's
wife, knowing and believing that she was a woman of good
condition and honest life, and with force took her outside
the city of Pisa, against her will and Bartolomeo's. [All
three of the accused confessed to their crimes. Bartolomeo

was sentenced to be whipped through the streets of Pisa and fined 1,000 lire. After paying the fine, he was to remain in prison for two years. Stella was to be whipped through the streets and remain in prison for the month of November. Jacopo was to be whipped, and required to leave Pisa by November 15.]

IV. Sodomy

93. CIVIC OPINION, 1415*

Paolo di Bernardo Bordoni, speaking for the Sixteen standard-bearers, said that those clerics who write concerning the vice of sodomy are to be commended, for the city is excessively corrupted [by it]. Since there are laws pertaining to this, the Signoria should summon the magistrates who should be encouraged to prosecute those corrupted persons. . . . The Signoria should also summon [for consultation] some members of the colleges and two citizens from each quarter who are sober and honest and who are not stained by this vice. . . .

Antonio di Niccolò, speaking for the Twelve, recalled how abominable are [these acts] in the sight of God, and how [their suppression] will redound to the honor and the reputation of the Signoria and the city. They commended the clerics. . . . There exist laws [against sodomy], although they are flawed in their implementation. The Signoria should provide for their execution. . . .

* Source: *ASF, Consulte e Pratiche*, 43, fol. 76v.

94. Legislation Against the Vice, 1418*

Desiring to extirpate that vice of Sodom and Gomorrah, so contrary to nature that the anger of the omnipotent God is incited not only against the sons of men but also against the community and even inanimate objects, the lord priors . . . have deliberated that . . . at least once per month in perpetuity . . . they should call together . . . the principal foreign magistrates of the city of Florence . . . and urge them to enforce the laws which denounce sodomy and those who are polluted by that nefarious vice, and to investigate, prosecute, and punish those who perpetrate that crime. . . .

Item, the lord priors . . . are prohibited from instructing any magistrate, who is . . . investigating or prosecuting anyone who committed or attempted to commit the vice of sodomy, not to proceed in such investigation or process . . . under penalty of 500 lire for each prior. . . .

Item, the lord priors . . . are authorized during the next three years . . . to reward any of the three foreign magistrates of the city of Florence, if it appears to them that he has labored to extirpate that vice, either with money . . . or with any other object which will bear the insignia of the Florentine *popolo*. . . . And for this purpose . . . they may spend up to 100 florins for honoring each magistrate. . . .

Item, whenever any scrutiny is to be held for any office of the Commune . . . both internal and external, and including those of the Merchants' Court . . . as well as those of

* Source: *ASF, Provvisioni*, 108, fols. 2v–3r.

any guild, the notary is required . . . to warn the electors . . . that they should not cast their votes for anyone who has been suspected of that crime, or whom they believe to be polluted by that vice. . . .

Item, the lord priors currently in office . . . together with their colleges . . . shall elect eight citizens, Guelf and *popolani*, whom they consider to be virtuous and worthy and who are free of this vice . . . for a term of one year . . . to consider ways and means by which this vice may be eradicated from the city and *contado* of Florence. . . .

95. ESTABLISHMENT OF A MAGISTRACY TO EXTIRPATE SODOMY, 1432*

[The provision authorized the election of a magistracy called the Officials of the Curfew and the Convents for a term of one year.] Item, these Officials of the Curfew . . . are to investigate diligently and to discover—whether by means of secret denunciation, accusations, notifications, or any other method—who commits the vice of sodomy, whether actively or passively . . . and those whom they find to have committed that crime after the passage of this provision shall be declared to have erred and to have committed that vice. As precisely as possible, the officials should make note of the time and of those involved, and then each of them . . . shall be fined 50 gold florins. . . .

Item, whoever thus designated . . . again commits or perpetrates the vice of sodomy . . . is to be declared a debtor of the Commune of Florence for 100 gold florins . . .

Item, whoever thus designated [as having committed

* Source: *ASF, Provvisioni*, 123, fols. 31v–35r.

sodomy twice] . . . again commits . . . the crime of sodomy . . . is to be fined 200 florins and in addition, the
officials shall declare him to be ineligible for all offices of the
Commune . . . for two years. . . .

Item, whoever thus designated . . . again commits the
crime . . . is to be . . . fined 500 gold florins and perpetu-
ally excluded from all offices. . . .

Item, whoever thus designated . . . again commits the
crime . . . is to be led through the customary public squares
to the place of justice and there to be burned so that he dies
and his soul is separated from his body. . . .

Item, the Officials of the Curfew, by virtue of this provision, cannot declare anyone to have erred nor can they condemn anyone save by the confession or admission of those
who were accused . . . or unless [guilt is] proved by the
testimony of two witnesses who observed [the crime], or by
four witnesses testifying concerning public knowledge. . . .

96. Convictions and Penalties*

. . . We condemn . . . Jacopo di Cristofano, formerly
of Arezzo and now living in the parish of S. Maria Maggiore, a nefarious sodomite and a man of base condition and
reputation. . . . In May 1425, while Jacopo was in his
house, he called to a boy who was standing next to the house,
whose name he does not remember. He coaxed the boy into
his house and then fed him a meal. Afterwards he committed
the unnatural act of sodomy on the table where they had
previously eaten. Then he allowed the boy to leave the
house. . . .

Not content with this but persevering in his wicked and

* Source: *ASF, Atti del Esecutore,* 2059, fols. 23r–24r, June 16, 1425;
2145, fols. 21r–22r, October 1, 1429.

abominable vice, in that same month . . . Jacopo was seated on a wall adjacent to his house and called to Berto, the son of Jacopo di Salvestro of Florence, who was then crossing the street in front of his house. He persuaded him to come into his house by saying to him: "Come here, boy. Would you like a ball?" And Berto replied, "Yes, I would." Then they entered Jacopo's house and first he gave Berto some bread and cheese and then he took him to a bed located in the upper floor of the house and there he wished to commit the vice of sodomy with him. However, he was not able to put his plan into effect because Berto began to cry loudly. Fearing that his abominable vice would be discovered, he led him to the lower floor of the house. With many pleas, suggestions, and blandishments, he promised to give Berto an orange if he would consent to his desire and this abominable vice. Having done this, he placed Berto upon a bench . . . and committed the vice of sodomy with him. [Jacopo confessed to the crimes. He was fined 750 lire; a mitre was placed on his head and he was whipped through the streets of Florence. If the house where the crimes were committed was owned by Jacopo, it was to be burned down. If owned by others, Jacopo and his family were to be driven from the premises.]

. . . We condemn . . . Piero di Jacopo, a coppersmith from Bologna, now living in Florence in the parish of S. Lorenzo, a notorious sodomite, a man of lowly condition, life, and reputation. . . . In the month of August of the current year, a ten-year-old boy, Baldassare di Angelo of the parish of S. Lorenzo, was crossing the street in front of Piero's house, and he [Piero] asked him to come into his home. After he had him in the house, he closed the door, threw Baldassare on a bed and placed a gag in his mouth so that he could not cry out. Then with force and violence, he committed the act of sodomy with him. And so that Baldassare would not cry as he left the house, Piero gave him 2 quattrini. As a result of the commission of this detestable crime . . . Baldassare was gravely ill for several days and was in a physician's care. . . . And this was committed by Piero . . . in violation of the statutes and ordinances of the Commune of Florence, and in violation of good customs, and divine, human, and natural law. [Piero confessed to the crime; he was sentenced to be burned at the stake. The sentence was executed.]

V. The Surveillance of the Convents

97. CIVIC RESPONSIBILITY FOR CONVENTUAL PURITY*

In the name of Christ our Savior, amen. The trumpet of the Lord and the voice of the Highest shall call out on the day of judgment: "You who are worthy, come, O blessed of my Father; and you who are unworthy, O accursed ones, go into the eternal fire. . . ." For above there will be the angry judge, and below will be chaos; on the right will be those accused of sin, and on the left, an infinite number of demons. Without and within the earth burns . . . All of this was described by Augustine, the doctor of the church.

Furthermore, natural law has ordained that the human species should multiply and that man and woman be joined together by holy matrimony, and that this [institution] is

* Source: *ASF, Giudice degli Appelli,* 79, part 2, fols. 68r–69r. From the deliberations of the Officials of the Curfew and the Convents, 1435.

and should be of such gravity and dignity that it should be respected by everyone. Nothing is more pleasing to God than the preservation of matrimony; nothing is more displeasing to him than its violation. And if a mortal being is angered by this violation, how much more outraged ought to be the Creator, the Father of every living creature. There are many nuns, brides of God and dedicated to Him, who are enclosed in convents in order to serve him with their virginity, but who through carnal desire have failed in their reverence to Him. As a result of this, divine providence is perturbed and has afflicted the world with the evils of wars, disorders, epidemics, and other calamities and troubles. In order to avoid these, the severity of the Florentine people has decreed that no one is permitted to enter any convent, and that a heavy penalty be meted out to delinquents. Not only carnal relations with nuns but also access to the convents are prohibited, so that these nuns, whose sex is weak and fragile . . . will be preserved in security and honor and the convents flourish in liberty. . . . Thus, these nuns will not be transformed, by the audacity of evil men, from virtue into dishonor, from chastity into luxury, and from modesty into shame. . . .

98. A Delinquent Priest*

This is the inquisition formulated by . . . Fra Niccolò de' Boscoli, vicar general of the lord bishop . . . against the priest Bartolo, rector of the church of S. Piero Buonconsigli. . . .

Inspired by lust, the priest Bartolo went on several occasions, both day and night, to visit a certain nun in the convent of Pina in the diocese of Florence. He entered the

* Source: *ASF, Archivio Notarile Antecosimiano,* F 334, vol. 1, fols. 41r–42r, October 17, 1410.

precincts of that convent and stayed there . . . without requesting or obtaining permission from the bishop of Fiesole, the protector of that convent. In December 1408, those residents who lived near the convent gave the order that the priest Bartolo should be seized upon his departure from the convent. As he left during the night, he was captured by the neighbors and detained for several hours, as a result of which a great scandal arose in the convent and its environs.

Item, on several occasions during the month of September in the year 1409, the priest Bartolo entered the precincts of the convent of S. Maria de Prato of Florence and stayed there for a space of three hours, without obtaining the permission of the bishop of Florence or his vicar, and in violation of the episcopal constitution of Florence. . . . And afterwards, he celebrated divine offices on several occasions. [Bartolo confessed to the charges. He was ordered to pay a fine of 30 florins to be distributed to the poor; he was also sentenced to a term of six months in the episcopal prison.]

99. A FOREIGN INTRUDER*

. . . We condemn . . . Ser Niccolò di Ser Matteo, a youth from Narni, a violator and corruptor of convents dedicated to the service of God, a man of evil condition, life, and reputation. . . . [He] went to the convent of S. Salvestro in the parish of S. Lorenzo . . . and there he attempted to corrupt Monna Tita, the daughter of Monna Giovanna of Florence [and] a professed nun of that convent dedicated to God. Seduced by his blandishments and false words, Monna Tita consented to satisfy his lust, saying to him: "Tonight you and . . . the priest of S. Piero Gattolino come to the convent and I will let you in, and I will keep you in my room, and I will find someone to sleep with

* Source: *ASF, Atti del Capitano*, 2523 bis, fols. 9r–11r, August 22, 1423.

the priest. And you can be with me and you may do anything with me that pleases you." Whereupon Ser Niccolò immediately departed and found that priest and after a lengthy conversation, they decided to go that night to the convent to visit the nuns, for the purpose of carrying out their iniquitous plan, which is abominable to both God and man. . . . After nightfall, the accused and his companion, the priest, went to the convent and entered the room of Monna Tita and then the priest left the room. . . . The accused remained alone in the room with the woman with whom he had intercourse . . . in contempt of God and to the shame and disgrace of the woman and the convent. . . .

In the month of July of that year, the accused said to two of his friends: "Come with me, because I want to pursue a certain affair," and his friends said, "Let's go." And the accused with his companions went to the convent and sought to corrupt Monna Tita and to have intercourse with her again. But the nun did not wish to consent, and they exchanged words, whereupon the abbess and other nuns of the convent began to cry out. . . . Seeing that he could not carry out his plan to seduce the nun, and moved by an irate and diabolical spirit, he threw several stones upon the roof of the convent and shouted many vile words. [Ser Niccolò confessed to these crimes. He was sentenced to be whipped through the streets of Florence and then held in the prison until he paid a fine of 500 lire. If he could not pay, his left foot was to be amputated.]

100. TEMPTATION*

. . . [This petition is presented] on behalf of Michele di Piero Mangioni of S. Miniato. On March 8, 1441, he and

* Source: *ASF, Provvisioni*, 132, fols. 109v–111r, June, 1441.

a certain Antonio were fined 50 lire and imprisoned in the Stinche of the Florentine Commune for two years. This sentence proceeded from the fact that . . . on several occasions Michele was working as a mason in a convent in S. Miniato (whose identity shall not be revealed, for decency's sake), and there he became friendly with the nuns, and in particular with a nun named Margherita from Lucca. As a result of this friendship, the nuns sent for Michele to put up some scaffolding. He finished his work at the hour of Ave Maria, and since the weather was dark, cloudy, and rainy, he remained in the convent and slept in a small room with a bed. While he was lying there, that nun came to his bed and when he saw her, he seized her by the hand and pulled her to himself and placed his hand on her breast. But fearing that he would be heard by the other nuns (for she gave him some resistance), he sent her away and in the morning at dawn . . . he departed and went to his home.

. . . When these nuns sent for Michele to repair a door in a stable of the convent, he stayed there until nightfall and slept in a bed . . . and that nun came and put out the light and then Michele seized her and had carnal relations with her on several occasions over a period of several months in that convent, both day and night. In the present year . . . he went to confess his sins to an Augustinian friar and for that confession, he put on the habit of the order and . . . entered that convent alone wearing that habit and spoke to that nun and stayed there the entire day. When he wished to leave, he saw several men in the road next to the convent, and so he realized that he must remain in the convent . . . and he slept there and several times he had carnal relations with that nun. . . .

Now the truth is that when he first went to work at that convent, he could not leave on account of the rain. . . . He

was persuaded to remain there by the nuns and he was incited to lust by that nun, and moved by his weakness, he had
a relationship with her, and afterwards on several occasions,
but not as many times as was described in his condemnation.
He confessed that he did this when he was tormented by
passion. . . . He now has a peace agreement with the abbess and the nuns of the convent of S. Paolo in S. Miniato.
[After participating in a solemn procession of penance on
the feast day of St. John the Baptist, Michele was to be released from prison.]

101. A Penitent*

The Officials of the Curfew and the Convents have been
notified of a quarrel involving the nuns of the Convent of the
Penitents, and specifically Gianetta di Giovanni of Flanders,
a former prostitute of Giovanni di Gherardo of Flanders,
who recently became a penitent and entered this convent to
serve God and for the salvation of her soul. This Giovanni,
who was formerly Gianetta's pimp, daily molested, and continues to molest, those nuns after Gianetta entered that
convent. . . . He went there to take her away from the convent . . . and to persuade her to return to the life of prostitution. . . . He even sent there some prostitutes and other
women with messages for Gianetta, urging her to leave the
convent and return to that vile profession.

[The Officials] have heard the testimony of Giovanni, the
former pimp (since he does not understand the Florentine
tongue well, Ormanno di Giovanni of Cologne translated for
him . . .), and they have learned that Giovanni complained
of Giovanna's withdrawal, and demanded some objects
and money from her. Finally, they have witnessed an agree-

* Source: *ASF, Giudice degli Appelli*, 80, fols. 151r–152r, June 2, 1439.

ment made between Giovanna and Giovanni . . . to the effect that if Giovanna pays him 15 florins, he agreed to absolve her of everything he might demand or receive from her . . . and also that he will leave the city of Florence by the 8th day of the present month of June . . . and will not return for three years. . . . [The Officials] have decreed that, upon the payment of 15 florins to Giovanni by Gianetta and the return of a book in which is written the office of the Virgin Mary and other offices, that . . . Giovanni di Gherardo must stay outside the city, *contado,* and district of Florence . . . for a period of three years. . . . [He will be fined 500 lire if he returns.]

PART SEVEN

THE *POPOLO MINUTO*

The *popolo minuto* or "little people" of Florence comprised more than one-half of the city's population. They were poor, impotent, and illiterate; they eked out a marginal subsistence in living conditions of misery and squalor. Many obtained employment in Florence's cloth industry, and they went hungry when, as frequently happened, the shops closed down in times of war, plague, or business depression (no. 111). Others were apprentices and laborers in the craft guilds, or gained a bare livelihood as domestic servants, porters, messengers, and peddlers. Criminals, vagabonds, and beggars formed a substratum in this lowest rank of the social hierarchy. Even slaves, who were employed primarily as domestic servants in wealthy households, enjoyed more security and a higher living standard than many of the *popolo minuto* who were legally free.

The attitude of the Florentine upper classes toward the poor was a complex mixture of distaste, compassion, and fear. To succor the indigent was a Christian duty, and many Florentines left money in their wills for alms, or bequeathed property to benevolent societies like Orsanmichele which distributed money to the poor (no. 112). When unemployment and hunger reached dangerous proportions, the civic authorities were prepared to use public funds to alleviate distress and reduce the threat of disorders (no. 111). The *popolo minuto* had no voice in the Communal government; efforts to organize them were brutally suppressed (no. 115). Only in periods of extreme crisis—for example, during the Ciompi Revolution of 1378—were the voices of the poor heard in Florence (no. 116), and then only briefly and spasmodically.

I. *Tribulations of the Poor*

102. HARASSMENT OF WORKERS
IN THE CLOTH INDUSTRY*

[September 22, 1378] At the request of Nanni di Zuchero, cloth merchant, Dino Romanelli, messenger of the [Lana] guild, acting under the orders of the consuls, reported that he had taken possession of one bed, one pair of shears, one chest with two locks, one cupboard, and one cape, the property of Chimento Noldini, a wool-carder, who owes the above-mentioned Nanni the sum of 26 lire, and these goods have been consigned to Monna Simona di Giovanni and Monna Margherita, wife of Filippo, called Mulino. . . .

[October 16, 1378] At the request of Andrea di Messer Ugo and partners, cloth manufacturers, Dato di Bartolo, called Meza, messenger of the Lana guild, acting under the orders of the consuls, reported that he took possession of one loom for weaving woolen cloth, one bed, one chest with two

* Source: *ASF, Arte della Lana,* 76, fols. 5r, 15r; 85, fols. 7r, 18v; 88, fols. 27r, 63r. Deliberations of the consuls of the Lana guild.

locks, one cupboard, and one mattress, the property of Giusto di Luca Petrini, wool carder, the debtor of Andrea and his partners for the sum of 19 florins, and these items have been consigned to Monna Lucia di Sandro.

September 6, [1389]. At the request of Sandro Mazzetti, Meo, messenger, personally informed Senuccio di Niccolò, cloth manufacturer, that after three days he should not employ Salvatore di Francesco, wool-beater, in his shop unless he reaches a settlement with the above-mentioned Sandro.

September 23, [1389]. Michele di Messer Donato Velluti, cloth manufacturer, appeared before this office [of the consuls of the Lana guild] . . . and stated that Luca di Filippo, wool-carder, owed him 30 lire on account of a loan, and that he had obtained a judgment against him for that sum . . . and that Luca was a person of dubious character, a wanderer and a fugitive. He petitioned this office to seize and detain Luca . . . and force him to pay Michele the sum of 30 lire.

[October 15, 1390] On behalf of Giovanni di Baldo, burler, who was seized at the request of Andrea di Francesco Giovanni, cloth manufacturer, and so that he might be released while still obligated [to pay his debt], Salvestro di Giovanni, groom of the parish of S. Felicita of Florence . . . promised to pay Andrea 4 florins by February 15 next, and with Salvestro's consent, Monna Jacopa, wife of Giovanni di Baldo . . . promised to pay Andrea 8 florins within eight months, and also to pay me [the notary] 4 florins in the event that Salvestro does not pay that sum before the above-mentioned date. As a guarantee of the observance of this [promise], Giovanni pledged himself and all his property to me, the notary, and with his consent, his wife pledged herself and her property, and specifically, a house located in the parish of S. Piero Maggiore in the Via della Pergola. . . .

[October 24, 1390] At the request of Niccolò di Andrea Neri Lippi and his partners, Bartolo di Ghese, messenger of the guild, reported that he had gone to the shop of Marco di Benvenuto and personally informed his partner, Ugolino di Messer Giovanni, that he should not employ Bardo di Piero, wool-carder, unless he pays [Niccolò and his partners] what he owes them. . . .

103. AN IMPRISONED PAUPER*

[This petition] is submitted [to the Signoria] on behalf of Barone di Cose, a Florentine citizen. As a result of forced loans imposed in the city of Florence via the new levy, and which have not been paid by Barone . . . he has been detained in the prison of the Stinche of the Commune of Florence. This is due to the fact that Barone possesses nothing in the world save his own body, his wife, and three small children, another child having died in this prison. He is perishing of hunger in jail, while his family starves outside. This is a consequence of the heavy and insupportable levies of forced loans which were imposed on him. He sold all of the property, both real and moveable, which he owned to pay these forced loans, and he has nothing left. . . . And for these unpaid forced loans, he owes a total of 79 florins, 3 soldi, and 9 denari. While he was detained in prison for these unpaid loans, certain of his creditors, motivated by the love of God, have completely absolved and liberated him [from his obligations to them]. And if your lordships will grant him the customary grace, he has certain friends who, for the love of God and as a gesture of piety, will make the

* Source: *ASF, Provvisioni*, 82, fols. 22r–22v, April 3, 1393.

necessary payments [to obtain his release from prison].
[Barone requested that his debt to the Commune be cancelled; his petition was approved.]

104. A MARGINAL SUBSISTENCE*

[This is the petition of] Niccolò di Salvi, a Florentine
citizen who formerly practiced the cobbler's trade, and who
in the last tax levy was assessed one florin and two soldi. In
order to pay his assessments, Niccolò sold all of the bedding
and the furnishings which he had in his house and his shop.
Then, being unable to pay any more, he went to live in the
contado so that he would not be imprisoned for tax de-
linquency. But while there, Niccolò was captured and imprisoned in the Stinche, and there he stayed for six months.
Then he sold the small cottage which was his last piece of
property in the world, and having paid his taxes with the
proceeds, he was released from prison. But since he was unable to provide for his family, he obtained a position as a
servant in the Stinche, carrying water and other things for
the prisoners, and in that position he remained for three
years, with a salary of 8 lire per month. With this income
he had to sustain himself, his wife, and two sons, for he
possessed nothing else. On account of his poverty and misery,
Niccolò was not registered in the most recent assessment.
However, the tax officials . . . saw that he had been listed
in the old assessment, and so they imposed a levy of one
florin on him. And he was totally unaware of this, but
thought that, as an indigent person, he would not be taxed.
Now unless something is done on his behalf, Niccolò will
be forced to leave Florentine territory, and his family will

* Source: *ASF, Provvisioni*, 85, fols. 243r–243v, December 8, 1396.

be reduced to beggary. [He petitioned to be exempt from all levies; his request was approved.]

105. THE STORY OF THE SERVANT GIRL NENCIA*

On this day, November 17, 1475, I record that on Wednesday, the 25th of the preceding month, . . . my wife told me that from certain signs which she had observed, our servant girl Lorenza, also called Nencia di Lazerino, had missed her period and that she appeared to be pregnant. Having learned about these indications from her, I told her to confront the girl alone and to use threats and persuasions to find out the truth from her. I had to go away, and upon my return in the evening, she told me that she had the girl alone in a room and that, after cajoling and threatening her, she had learned that the girl was pregnant by Niccolò di Alessandro Machiavelli. When asked how this had happened, she said that after we had returned from the country last year, on November 8, she had often gone at night through the window over the roof, and then through the little window next to the kitchen hearth to Niccolò's house to stay with him. This she did most frequently when my wife was pregnant and when she was in labor. During May and June of this past year, when Niccolò's wife was ill, he often entered [the house] through that little window and slept with her on the kitchen hearth.

When I learned all this, I left the house and went to find my wife's brother, Giovanni Nelli. Since his brother Carlo had come to Florence from Pisa, I also met him and told them the story and asked them to come the next morning to have breakfast with me, and to decide on the best course

---

* Source: Bernardo Machiavelli, *Libro di ricordi*, ed. C. Olschki (Florence, 1954), pp. 15–22. Printed by permission of Casa Editrice Felice Le Monnier.

of action. I did this because Giovanni had found the girl for
me and had persuaded her father, who was his friend, to
give her to me. So the next morning, they both came to
breakfast with me, and after we had eaten, we called Nencia
into my room . . . and asked her about this matter described above. She repeated the same story to us, though
Giovanni, Carlo, and I warned her to be careful of what she
said, because it did not seem plausible that Niccolò, who had
a young and beautiful wife, would have paid any attention to
her; [but] she insisted on her story. She also said that when
Niccolò was at the villa (most of the time he stayed at Colom-
baia), he called her through the barred window of her room
from his balcony, and that two or three times a week, they
would stay together. It was true that she was pregnant by
Niccolò and that he had promised to give her a cape and a
gown.

Then, having sent Nencia from the room, Giovanni and
Carlo told me that they would find Niccolò and tell him
about this affair and the girl's story, and they would then
report to me what he said. . . . I told them that I was
content, but that I did not want the girl in my house any
longer and that I thought that the girl's mother—who was
staying with Giovanni—and her father should be informed,
so that they would take her away. They replied that I should
speak first with Niccolò and then what had to be done would
be done. So, on Saturday the 28th, the eve of [the feast of]
S. Simone, the twenty-third hour having already struck, I left
the house and while walking toward the Ponte Vecchio, I
met Niccolò . . . and told him that I wanted to talk to
him. . . . I told him what Nencia had said. He replied
that for six months and longer, he had wanted to tell me
about this, and that he didn't know himself why he hadn't
done so. The story was this. Francesco Renzi, called

"L'Agata," who was the nephew of Master Raffaello of Terranuova, the physician, had told him some six months before that when he had left him in his [Niccolò's] house . . . Nencia had left the house via the roof and had gone into Niccolò's house to stay with him. This had happened on several occasions after I had returned from the villa. The truth was that he, Niccolò, had never had anything to do with her. Francesco had done this, and his only fault had been his failure to tell me.

In reply, I complained bitterly of his injury to me, which would have been grave in any event, but which was even worse, since he was my neighbor . . . and a close blood relation. [I said] that I had never done anything similar to him or his father, and that I did not understand how he could have held me in such low esteem. For both here [in Florence] and at the villa, he was often in my company and had never said anything to me so that I might prevent my house from becoming a bordello. He should also consider the nature of this affair, for this girl was not a slut but came from a good but impoverished family of Pistoia, and her father and brothers were men of some worth. I did not want the girl in my house any longer, and I had no choice but to inform Giovanni Nelli, who had given her to me, or to arrange for her father and mother to come for her. Niccolò replied that he was aware that he had injured me, but that it was Francesco who had harmed the girl, and that his error had been in not telling me. . . .

On Monday, the 30th, I met Giovanni Nelli and told him that I had spoken with Niccolò. . . . Giovanni told me to be patient, since he wished to speak to him too. On the morning of the 31st, I was walking toward the Ponte Vecchio and I met Niccolò . . . and he told me: "Now I want to tell you why I didn't say anything to you about

Nencia and Agata. You know that Francesco Agata is staying
with Master Raffaello, and I beg you not to mention this to
him. He has a beautiful girl in his house whom I wanted,
and Francesco was my liaison, and since he had done me this
favor, I consented to his affair with Nencia. . . . I told
him that this was a fine story, but that the girl . . . said
that it had been himself. . . . [I told him] that I had
spoken about this matter to Giovanni Nelli and asked him to
send for the father and take the girl away, since I didn't
want her any longer, and that Giovanni had said that he
wanted to speak to him [Niccolò] before informing the
father, to see if something could be done to avoid
scandal. . . .

On Friday the 3rd, Giovanni came to dine and spend the
night with me, and he told me that he had been with Niccolò
Machiavelli in the Mercato Nuovo that evening and he had
spoken about this matter. . . . It appeared to him, so he
had told Niccolò, that in order to avoid scandal, which would
arise if the father were informed of this, they should find a
woman to care for the girl until she had been delivered, and
then arrange to give her [a dowry of] 25 florins so that she
could be married and thus save Giovanni's honor, since he
had been responsible for giving her to me. Niccolò replied
that this pleased him, and while insisting strongly that it had
not been himself but rather Francesco Agata, nevertheless he
said that he wished to see if it would be possible to arrange
the matter as Giovanni had suggested. . . .

On the 12th day of the present month, Giovanni Nelli,
Niccolò, and I were together in Giovanni's shop and we
agreed that Niccolò should promise in writing to give Giovanni 100 lire for Nencia's dowry. . . . Last night, Saturday, November 18, 1475, Giovanni Nelli came to stay with
me and told me that on that same evening, he and Niccolò

Machiavelli had been with Monna Lisa, who takes care of
children . . . and they had agreed to take . . . Nencia to
her this morning. She promised to care for her until her delivery, and Niccolò promised to give her 5 lire each month.
. . . This morning, just before the fourteenth hour, Giovanni took Nencia away to the house of Monna Lisa and my
wife gave her all of her shirts and handkerchiefs and other
clothes. . . .

II. Servitude

106. SLAVERY LEGALIZED, 1364*

. . . The lord priors . . . have decreed . . . that
henceforth, anyone from whatever place and of whatever
condition may freely bring into the city, *contado*, and district of Florence those slaves who are not of the Christian
faith . . . and they may possess, hold, and sell them to
whoever they wish. And whoever purchases them may receive, possess, use, and exploit them as his slaves, and do his
will with them. . . .

The lord priors . . . with their colleges . . . may make
whatever provisions and orders they wish concerning the ways
that masters treat their slaves, and concerning the protection
of the masters against the escape, the wrong-doing, or the
disobedience of the slaves, and also concerning those who receive fugitives, and all other things pertaining to these
matters. . . .

* Source: *ASF, Provvisioni*, 51, fols. 115v–116r.

107. The Search for Slaves*

. . . If you haven't written to Spalato [in Dalmatia] to Bartolomeo or to others to send you the two slave girls about whom I wrote you in other letters, I beg you to write him . . . so that he will send you the slaves and the documents of purchase. You can transport them from Venice and send them to me. . . . These slave girls should be between twelve and fiftéen years old, and if there aren't any available at that age, but a little older or younger, don't neglect to send them. I would prefer to have them younger than twelve instead of older than fifteen, as long as they are not under ten. I don't care if they are pretty or ugly, as long as they are healthy and able to do hard work. . . .

108. Christians Forced into Servitude*

. . . We condemn . . . Romeo di Lapo of Florence, a vagabond with no fixed residence . . . a man of base condition, life, and reputation, a thief and a vendor of women and Christians. . . . Romeo went to the suburb of Narente in the city of Ragusa [in Dalmatia] and there . . . with bland and deceptive words he cajoled Ciaola of Albania and Mazia Scosse of Bosnia and her daughter Caterina, all baptized Christians and free, saying to them: "Come with me to Italy and there I will find good husbands for you, and you will remain free." Knowing that they were free and Christian women, Romeo with his associates took Ciaola, Mazia, and Caterina to the city of Lesina in Dalmatia and there he pur-

* Source: Messer Rosso Orlandi in Florence to Piero Davanzati in Venice, February 13, 1392; *ASF, Conventi Soppressi*, 78 (Badia), vol. 315, no. 348.
* Source: *ASF, Atti del Capitano*, 2107, no pagination, September 22, 1399.

sued his evil intention of depriving them of their liberty.
When the women were absent, he had a document drawn up
by a notary who (so he said) was named Ser Domenico di
Cobutio of Viterbo, which stated that Romeo had bought
these women, who were heretics and unbaptized, for the
price of 57 gold florins. . . . Then he took Ciaola, Mazia,
and Caterina to Florence and sold the woman called Ciaola
to Ser Stefano di Rainieri del Forese, of the parish of S.
Trinita of Florence, for 49 florins, asserting that she was a
heretic and unbaptized. [Romeo escaped the authorities; he
was sentenced to death *in absentia* and the three women were
freed.]

109. The Tribulations of a Slave Girl*

This petition is presented to you, lord priors . . . on behalf of Maria, the daughter of Dece de Cigoli of Slavonia,
formerly in bondage and now free, who in Florence is called
Maria di Pippo. On July 17, 1449, she was condemned
(together with a certain Crispino also named in the sentence)
. . . to pay a fine of 150 lire . . . and to restore the items
stolen by Maria, the slave of Bernardo di Berto di Luce,
which items were taken from Bernardo's house at the behest
of Maria di Pippo. She was also sent to the Stinche, to be
detained there until the items stolen from Bernardo's house,
or their monetary equivalent, were restored to him, and until
she paid the fine of 150 lire. . . .

Early in March of the year 1449, when Maria di Pippo
was in the piazza of S. Maria Bertelde, Crispino said to her:
"Maria, go find Maria, the slave girl of Bernardo di Berto,
the silk merchant, and tell her for me that she must come
immediately to my house because I want to speak to her.

* Source: *ASF, Provvisioni*, 141, fols. 112r–114r, June 20, 1450.

After Crispino's departure, Maria di·Pippo went to Maria
the slave in Bernardo's house and told her what Crispino
had instructed her to say. Several days later, the two Marias
were in Bernardo's house and Maria the slave said to Maria
di Pippo: "I went to see Crispino in his house and he told
me that he has made a vow to marry a slave girl and make
her free, and if I wish (since he loves me very much), that
he will marry me in preference to another girl whom he
knows and take me to his house in his native district. However, since the route [to his home] is long, he said that he
doesn't have enough money for the expenses of the journey.
He wants me to take some of my mistress's jewels, a ring
and a necklace and the good pieces in the chest where she
keeps her jewels, and give them to him." Then Maria di
Pippo said to Maria the slave: "Maria, be careful what you
do, because if you are caught, he will be hanged and you will
be in trouble too." Then after several days, Maria the slave
spoke to Maria di Pippo: "I told Crispino what you said
and he told me not to be afraid, and that he will never
leave me." Then Maria di Pippo said to Maria the slave:
"If he wishes to marry you, as he says, and do for you what
he promises, then you can take those things, one at a time,
from the house and give them to him." Maria the slave
replied: ". . . I don't want to do that; instead, I want to
take the jewels and leave the house and go away all at once.
If my mistress discovers that her jewels are missing, she
will beat me, as she has done in the past. . . ."

Item, in the month of April 1449 after Easter, when
Maria di Pippo was in the church of S. Reparata, Crispino
came to her and said: 'Go tell Maria the slave that if she
wants to come with me, she should get ready, since I want
to leave Florence." And Maria di Pippo went to see Maria
the slave in Bernardo's house and told her what Crispino

had said in the church of S. Reparata. . . . And Maria the slave replied to Maria di Pippo: "I don't know what to do for I am terribly afraid to leave." Maria di Pippo said: "Don't be frightened about this; now is the time to go, and what you have to do, you should do quickly." And Maria the slave replied, "I don't trust him, because I fear that he will deceive me." Then Maria di Pippo said: "Don't be afraid; you know that he is a worthy person and that he won't trick you. But you could go away with someone who would sell you."

Maria the slave then said: "I don't know how to open the chest." Maria di Pippo replied, "You should talk to Crispino." So Maria the slave went to Crispino and told him that she had found the key to the chest and showed it to him. And Crispino said to her: "Leave it with me and I will have a copy made by a locksmith. But Maria replied that she didn't want to leave it with him for fear of her mistress. . . . So Crispino gave her some wax to make an imprint of the key . . . which she made and gave to Maria di Pippo to take to Crispino. . . . He went to a locksmith to have a copy made, and took that key to Maria the slave who then tried to open the chest, but she could not open it since the key would not turn.

Then Maria the slave . . . went to the house of Maria di Pippo and told her: "Crispino gave me this key to open the chest; go and tell him that he will have to repair it." Receiving the key, Crispino repaired it and brought it to Maria di Pippo and said: "Take this key to Maria so that she can try to open the chest, and if she cannot, then take a lighted candle and blacken the key so that one can see its flaw. . . ." So both Marias went together to try the key and when they saw that it would not open [the chest], they blackened the key and tried it again. Seeing that they could not open it,

Maria the slave took a bunch of keys . . . and they both began to try them, to see if there was a key which would open the chest. Then Domenico, the son of Bernardo, arrived on horseback and knocked at the door of the house. Maria the slave said to Maria di Pippo: "Go and see who is knocking at the door; I hope it isn't one of my masters." Maria then saw that it was Domenico, and Maria the slave took the bunch of keys and hid them . . . and said to Maria di Pippo: "Go into my room, for if Domenico finds you here, he will beat me to death." So Maria di Pippo hid in the room until Domenico left the house. . . .

Afterwards, in the month of May, Maria di Pippo . . . went to Bernardo's house and said to Maria the slave: "Maria, Crispino says that since you cannot find a way to open the chest, that he will come here into the house . . . and you can carry away the things that are inside and then flee." Maria the slave replied: "I don't want to do this, and you tell him not to come here to ransack the house. If I can find the key to open the chest, I will do it, but I won't do anything else. . . ." Several days later, when a locksmith (whose name they did not know) was passing through the neighborhood and was in front of Bernardo's house, Maria the slave called him and had him make a key, with which she opened the chest. Then she found Maria di Pippo and told her: "I had a key made that opens the chest." Then Maria di Pippo said: "Now that you have the key, what are you going to do? Take those things which you need and then run away." But Maria the slave replied: "I don't trust that man," to which Maria di Pippo replied: "You can really trust him." Several days later, Maria di Pippo went to Bernardo's house and said to Maria the slave: "Crispino tells me that you should give me these things, and if you don't wish to give them to me, then you should tell me what

is in the chest so that he will know what he can carry away."
Maria the slave said: "I don't want to tell you because I
wish to take those things and carry them away myself when
I want to leave. I don't want to give everything to him, because I want to keep some things for myself." Maria di
Pippo replied: "You are acting wisely by not giving him
everything; keep something for yourself in the event of
sickness or some other misfortune. . . .

On the same day, Maria di Pippo went to Bernardo's
house . . . and said to Maria the slave: "Crispino says that
he thinks it is time to go away with those things." And Maria
the slave replied: "It is better to go on a work day after
dinner, because on feast days my mistress and my masters
often come home, but on work days, they go to their shops
and they don't return home so quickly." On Monday, May
19, after dinner, Maria the slave opened the chest with the
key and took from it the following jewels and other objects:
a pair of pearls set in gold, weighing 8 ounces; a pearl necklace, weighing 8 ounces; a diamond ornament; a large
pearl . . . [and other items of jewelry and clothing] . . .
valued at 200 florins or thereabouts. These objects she took
to the Porta al Prato near the wall by the Arno river, where
Crispino had instructed her to meet him, and she gave them
to Crispino. He hid the objects in the saddlebags of his
horse, and after mounting, he said to Maria the slave: "You
go out [of the city] through the Porta a Faenza and I will
leave by this gate. Wait for me there and I will bring another horse for you and we will go away together." When
Crispino went out through the gate with these objects, he
fled and abandoned Maria the slave. [Maria petitioned for
the cancellation of her fine and her release from prison; the
petition was approved.]

III. Succor for the Indigent

110. PENSIONS FOR RETIRED EMPLOYEES*

Moved by compassion for the poor, the lord priors . . .
have been informed that Cristoforo di Ture, Tommaso di Giovanni of Savoy, and Giovanni di Ser Francesco of Ortignano
were formerly employed as servants in the palace of the priors
and worked there, Cristoforo for some ten years, Tommaso
for eighteen years or thereabouts, and Giovanni for more
than twenty-two years. And since they are now old and can
no longer work, they were removed from their posts, and
they have very little with which to sustain themselves. So,
desiring to provide them with some charitable subsidy, [the
priors] . . . have provided . . . that the treasurer of the
Commune . . . shall pay the sum of 5 lire per month to
Cristoforo, Tommaso, and Giovanni for the remainder of
their lives. . . .

111. PLAGUE, FAMINE, AND CIVIL DISORDER*

[June 8, 1383] Uberto di Schiatta Ridolfi, [speaking]
for the [Sixteen] *gonfalonieri*, said that the officials in charge
of the grain supply should be instructed to lend to the poor
up to four *staiora* [three bushels] of . . . grain, according
to the size of their families. Those who receive [the grain]
should be recorded as debtors of the Commune.

Master Giovanni di Master Ambrogio, [speaking] for
the Twelve *buonuomini*, said that the indigent should receive

* Source: *ASF, Provvisioni*, 84, fols. 176v–177r, October 14, 1395.
* Source: *ASF, Consulte e Pratiche*, 22, fols. 60v–61r; 43, fols. 150v–153v.

either bread or flour according to their needs, for the love of God. . . .

[July 1, 1383] Uberto di Schiatta Ridolfi, for the *gonfalonieri,* said that the shortage of grain should be kept secret, and that a plentiful supply of victuals should be made available by every means possible. And if this cannot be arranged quickly, then forced loans should be levied on the citizenry so that money is available. . . . And [the grain officials] should be instructed to obtain grain for the market by breaking into the houses of those [citizens] who are absent. And arrange for the baking of bread marked with a sign, and give that only to the poor.

[June 15, 1417] Messer Lorenzo Ridolfi, speaking for both colleges, said that . . . it is to be feared that the pestilence will become worse. The poor are in a very bad condition, since they earn nothing, and in future they will earn less. . . .

Antonio Alessandri said that on account of the plague which is imminent, it is necessary to provide for the preservation of our regime, keeping in mind the measures which were taken at similar times in the past. First, we should acknowledge our obligation to God, taking into account the poverty of many [citizens], that is, by distributing alms to the needy and indigent persons, appointing [for this task] men who are devoted to God and who lead good lives, and not those who are active in the affairs of state. But since not all are quiet, and in order to instill fear into some, foot soldiers should be hired who are neither citizens nor residents of the *contado,* and who will serve the needs of the Commune and not those of private [citizens]. . . .

Marsilio di Vanni Vecchietti said that nothing will be more pleasing to God than to help the needy and the poor who are dying of hunger. By this means we will placate God so that he will remove this pestilence from us. . . .

Messer Rinaldo Gianfigliazzi said that the poor should be subsidized with public funds since they are dying of hunger. God will be pleased and their evil thoughts will disappear. God should be placated with processions and prayers. . . .

Bartolomeo di Niccolò Valori said that the poor are not earning anything and they are dying like dogs. Many are in prison. . . . The poor who are sick should be helped, and God in his mercy will remove this plague from us.

Paolo di Francesco Biliotti said that up to 20,000 florins should be spent to succor the poor, and this will be most acceptable to God. . . . The rich should be willing to support the burdens of others and especially the poor, since it is not possible for the poor to help themselves. . . .

Buonaccorso di Neri Pitti said that the poor should be assisted so they can feed themselves. Those of our indigent citizens who are capable of doing evil should be hired [as soldiers] and sent to those places where troops are stationed, and their salaries should be increased.

112. The Distribution of Alms*

Alms distributed in the quarter of S. Spirito through the month of October [1356, by the society of Orsanmichele].

To Monna Francesca, who has broken her arm and has four children. She lives near Pino's cell. She had 5 soldi on September 2nd.

To Monna Giovanna, who is pregnant and lives with Madonna Lapa in the Borgo Vecchio of S. Maria Novella.

* Source: *ASF, Orsanmichele,* 254, no pagination.

She received 10 soldi on September 5th. Buoso [a servant] delivered it.

To Monna Caterina, a foreigner who is pregnant. She lives in the parish of S. Frediano in the Via del Fielo. Buoso delivered 10 soldi.

To Monna Fiora, pregnant, whose landlord is the church of S. Apollinare. Buoso gave her 10 soldi.

To Madonna Bella, who lives in the Borgo S. Croce and is very ill, Buoso delivered 10 soldi.

To Nezetta, who is old and sick and lives in the Via S. Gallo. . . . Buoso gave her 20 soldi.

To Madonna Bartolomea di Piero, a widow, with four children; her landlord is the prior of S. Romolo. Francesco brought her 10 soldi. . . .

To Madonna Fiora di Lapo, who is blind and pregnant; she lives in the parish of S. Felice in Piazza. Buoso gave her 10 soldi.

To Madonna Simona di Puccino, pregnant, of the parish of S. Frediano, Buoso delivered 6 soldi.

To Madonna Giovanna, wife of Giovanni, a soldier from Genoa, living in the parish of S. Giorgio, who is ill without her husband, 6 soldi.

To Piera, Elizabeth, Angela, and Caterina, poor women who are cloistered on the Rubaconte bridge, 8 soldi. To Santa, Nucca, and Caterina, also cloistered on that bridge, 6 soldi. To Jacopa and Giovanna, poor recluses on the Rubaconte bridge, 5 soldi.

To Madonna Agnese, a poor and infirm woman who lives in the house of Giovanni di Monna Nella, 5 soldi.

To Monno Bice, whose landlord is Priorazzo in [Via] S. Niccolò, and who is poor, old, and infirm, 3 soldi. . . .

To Monna Dea, who lives with two children in S. Niccolò del Borgo, 4 soldi.

To Caterina, a girl whose host provides for her for the love of God, in S. Niccolò del Borgo, 3 soldi.

To Monna Lippa, a poor and sick market peddler in the parish of S. Ambrogio, 3 soldi.

To Monna Margherita, widow of Giovanni, who lives with two children . . . in the parish of S. Lucia dei Magnoli, 4 soldi.

To Monna Diana di Bartolomeo, a poor woman in the Chiasso of Francesco Forzetti, 2 soldi.

To Stefano, orphaned son of Antonio, whose host provides for him for the love of God, 2 soldi.

To Lisa, widow from Pistoia, who now lives in Florence in the parish of S. Lorenzo with two small children, 2 lire, which the captains [of the society] decided to grant her.

To Monna Isabetta, from the Valdisieve, who is pregnant and in prison, 15 soldi. . . .

To Buona di Rosso, a poor abandoned girl who lives in the Via Ghibellina, 2 lire, which the captains decided to give her.

To Gherardo, a poor sick boy from the Mugello, 12 soldi.

To Monna Dolce, a poor, old, and infirm woman who lives in the Piazza d'Ogni Santi, and who takes care of a girl who was recommended to her by the society, 15 soldi.

IV. Voices of the Poor

113. APPEAL FOR TAX RELIEF*

Lord priors of Florence! You should do something about the taxes which the poor people of Florence must pay, the

* Source: *ASF, Atti del Esecutore,* 575, fol. 48v, June 2, 1369.

forced loans and the extra levies. . . . If you don't do something, you will discover that no one in Florence will be able to save you. There will be an uprising if these forced loans and special levies are not reduced, for there is great privation here. People are living in misery since they earn little and prices have been so high for thirteen months and more. Just think about those who have three or four or five children, and who are assessed two or three florins, and who have to live from the labor of their hands and those of their wives. . . . How can they stay here and live? . . .

114. JUSTICE FOR THE POOR*

Lord executor. Among the priors and the colleges, the rumor circulates that you are here at the behest of the magnates of Florence, and that you will not investigate any case involving them. It would have redounded more to your honor if you had not accepted the office, than to refuse to do what your honor requires. Many secret accusations have been delivered to you and you have done nothing about them. When those who have been offended have no other recourse, they have gone to the palace of the Signoria. . . .

There have been many executors here . . . and they have punished both magnates and *popolani*. There have been executors from Lombardy of the highest rank and they have punished the magnates who committed crimes, and they always favored the *popolani*. But it is widely believed that . . . you call witnesses who don't appear, and that you favor the magnates and the greater citizens. . . . Do your duty, lord exceutor, so that you will gain honor in a Commune such as ours, and so that in the future you will be

* Source: *ASF, Atti del Esecutore*, 530, fols. 68r–68v, May 6, 1367.

acclaimed for the high reputation which you possesss. . . . Do not besmirch your honor by listening to the petitions of private citizens. . . .

115. The Condemnation of a Labor Organizer, 1345*

. . . This is the inquisition which the lord captain [of the *popolo*] and his judge . . . have conducted . . . against Ciuto Brandini, of the parish of S. Piero Maggiore, a man of low condition and evil reputation. . . . Together with many others who were seduced by him, he planned to organize an association . . . of carders, combers, and other laborers in the woolen cloth industry, in the largest number possible. In order that they might have the means to congregate and to elect consuls and leaders of their association . . . he organized meetings on several occasions and on various days of many persons of lowly condition. And among other things done in these meetings, Ciuto ordered that there should be a collection of money from those who attended these assemblies. . . . [This was done] so that they would be stronger and more durable in this wicked organization, and so that they could accomplish the above-mentioned outrages and in order that—with arguments, force, and other means—they could oppose those citizens of good condition who wished to prevent Ciuto and the others in these assemblies from accomplishing those objectives, and their iniquitous thoughts, decisions, and activities.

Moving from bad to worse, he sought . . . to accomplish similar and even worse things, seeking always [to incite] noxious disorders, to the harm, opprobrium, danger, and

* Source: N. Rodolico, *Il popolo minuto* (Bologna, 1899), pp. 157–60.

destruction of the citizens of Florence, their persons and property, and of the stable regime of that city. And the above-mentioned illegal plots planned by him would have taken place, from which there would have arisen tumult, sedition, and disorder among the *popolani* and guildsmen of Florence, except that [Ciuto] was seized and detained by an official of the captain and his court. And the above-mentioned [acts] were committed and perpetrated in the present year and in the month of May in the city of Florence, in the church of S. Croce . . . and in the church of S. Maria de' Servi. [Ciuto confessed and was condemned to death on the gallows; the sentence was executed.]

116. THE DEMANDS OF THE CIOMPI, 1378*

[July 21, 1378] When the *popolo* and the guildsmen had seized the palace [of the podestà], they sent a message to the Signoria . . . that they wished to make certain demands by means of petitions, which were just and reasonable. . . . They said that, for the peace and repose of the city, they wanted certain things which they had decided among themselves . . . and they begged the priors to have them read, and then to deliberate on them, and to present them to their colleges. . . .

The first chapter [of the petition] stated that the Lana guild would no longer have a [police] official of the guild. Another was that the combers, carders, trimmers, washers, and other cloth workers would have their own [guild] consuls, and would no longer be subject to the Lana guild.

* Source: *Cronache e memorie del tumulto dei Ciompi*, ed. G. Scaramella, *Rerum Italicarum Scriptores*, new ed., XVII, part 3 (Città di Castello, 1914), pp. 27–28, 75–78.

Another chapter [stated that] the Commune's funded debt would no longer pay interest, but the capital would be restored [to the shareholders] within twelve years. . . . Another chapter was that all outlaws and those who had been condemned by the Commune . . . except rebels and traitors would be pardoned. Moreover, all penalties involving a loss of a limb would be cancelled, and those who were condemned would pay a money fine. . . . Furthermore, for two years none of the poor people could be prosecuted for debts of 50 florins or less. For a period of six months, no forced loans were to be levied. . . . And within that six months' period, a schedule for levying direct taxes [*estimo*] was to be compiled. . . .

The *popolo* entered the palace and [the podestà] departed, without any harm being done to him. They ascended the bell tower and placed there the emblem of the blacksmiths' guild, that is, the tongs. Then the banners of the other guilds, both great and small, were unfurled from the windows of the [palace of] the podestà, and also the standard of justice, but there was no flag of the Lana guild. Those inside the palace threw out and burned . . . every document which they found. And they remained there, all that day and night, in honor of God. Both rich and poor were there, each one to protect the standard of his guild.

The next morning the *popolo* brought the standard of justice from the palace and they marched, all armed, to the Piazza della Signoria, shouting: "Long live the *popolo minuto!*" . . . Then they began to cry "that the Signoria should leave, and if they didn't wish to depart, they would be taken to their homes." Into the piazza came a certain Michele di Lando, a wool-comber, who was the son of Monna Simona, who sold provisions to the prisoners in the

Stinche . . . and he was seized and the standard of justice placed in his hands. . . . Then the *popolo* ordered the priors to abandon the palace. It was well furnished with supplies necessary [for defense] but they were frightened men and they left [the palace], which was the best course. Then the *popolo* entered, taking with them the standard of justice . . . and they entered all the rooms and they found many ropes which [the authorities] had bought to hang the poor people. . . . Several young men climbed the bell tower and rang the bells to signal the victory which they had won in seizing the palace, in God's honor. Then they decided to do everything necessary to fortify themselves and to liberate the *popolo minuto*. Then they acclaimed the wool-comber, Michele di Lando, as *signore* and standard-bearer of justice, and he was *signore* for two days. . . . Then [the *popolo*] decided to call other priors who would be good comrades and who would fill up the office of those priors who had been expelled. And so by acclamation, they named eight priors and the Twelve and the [Sixteen] standard-bearers. . . .

When they wished to convene a council, these priors called together the colleges and the consuls of the guilds. . . . This council enacted a decree that everyone who had been proscribed as a Ghibelline since 1357 was to be restored to Guelf status. . . . And this was done to give a part to more people, and so that each would be content, and each would have a share of the offices, and so that all of the citizens would be united. Thus poor men would have their due, for they have always borne the expenses [of government], and only the rich have profited.

. . . And they deliberated to expand the lower guilds, and where there had been fourteen, there would now be seventeen, and thus they would be stronger, and this was done. The first new guild comprised those who worked in the woolen industry: factors, brokers in wool and in thread, workers who were employed in the dye shops and the stretching sheds, menders, sorters, shearers, beaters, combers, and weavers. These were all banded together, some nine thousand men. . . . The second new guild was made up of dyers, washers, carders, and makers of combs. . . . In the third guild were menders, trimmers, stretchers, washers, shirtmakers, tailors, stocking-makers, and makers of flags. . . . So all together, the lower guilds increased by some thirteen thousand men.

The lord priors and the colleges decided to burn the old Communal scrutiny lists, and this was done. Then a new scrutiny was held. The Offices were divided as follows: the [seven] greater guilds had three priors; the fourteen [lower] guilds had another three, and the three new guilds had three priors. And so a new scrutiny was completed, which satisfied many who had never before had any share of the offices, and had always borne the expenses.

PART EIGHT

ABERRANTS AND OUTGROUPS

Florence's population included outsiders who were not inte-
grated into the community and whose customs, beliefs, and
values were aberrant. Religious differences were the main
obstacles to assimilation. Jews, heretics, and sorcerers were
pariahs whose rejection of orthodox Christianity subjected
them to surveillance, regulation, and occasional persecution.
Still, by the standards of the age, Florence was a remarkably
tolerant community. Florentines did not indulge in witch-
hunts or massacres of Jews and heretics. A few unfortunate
victims were sacrificed to prejudice and the demands for
conformity (nos. 122, 127), but public sentiment could also
be mobilized to protect the victims of religious persecution
(no. 124).

I. The Jews

117. EARLY COMMUNAL LEGISLATION ON THE JEWS*

Considering that Jews or Hebrews are enemies of the
cross, of our Lord Jesus Christ, and of all Christians, and

* Source: U. Cassuto, *Gli ebrei a Firenze nell'età del Rinascimento* (Florence, 1918), pp. 362–65; provisions of January 24, 1406 and June 12, 1430.

that they engage in usury against the command of Holy Church . . . [the priors] have decreed that no Hebrew or Jew . . . shall be allowed . . . to lend money at usury . . . in the city, *contado*, or district of Florence, or in any city, region, or place under the jurisdiction of the Commune of Florence, under penalty of 1,000 florins. . . .

So that the poor people of Florence are not ruined, particularly in this time of pestilence, by such exorbitant rates as are being charged by those who engage in usury, and so that when necessity impels them, they may provide for their needs with a lighter charge [of interest], and desiring to admit Jews into the city, the lord priors . . . have decreed the following. . . . Until September 15, the lord priors . . . [with their colleges] may authorize any Jew or Jews to engage in usury in the city of Florence . . . with the following limitation, that the Signoria and colleges may not permit . . . any Jew or Hebrew to charge a higher rate of interest than 4 denari per lire per month [i.e., 20 percent per year]. . . .

118. REGULATION OF THE JEWISH COMMUNITY, 1463*

. . . [The priors] have considered that a large number of Jews have come to settle in Florence, and scarcely any of them wear a sign, so that there is considerable confusion, and it is difficult to distinguish between Jews and Christians. There have been numerous errors and mistakes in the past, and it is obvious that there will be others in the future. They are determined to remedy this unsatisfactory situation, which will require some modification of the contract made by the

* Source: Cassuto, *Gli ebrei a Firenze nell'età del Rinascimento*, pp. 372–76.

Commune of Florence, or by those authorized by it to make this agreement, granting permission to these Jews named in the contract to engage in moneylending in Florence for ten years, beginning on June 18, 1459. . . . Having examined this matter with those Jews to whom this permission was granted in the agreement, who also have demonstrated their desire to correct this unfortunate situation, the following provisions have been established.

Every Jew, male or female above the age of twelve, whether or not named in the Florentine agreement, and whether or not a resident of the city of Florence, shall be required to wear a sign of O in the city of Florence. This yellow O shall be worn on the left breast, over the clothing in a visible place; it shall be at least one foot in circumference and as wide as the thickness of a finger. A penalty of 25 lire shall be levied on every occasion that this sign is not worn, with two witnesses required. . . . Outside of the city, those Jews who are not engaged in moneylending operations in the *contado* or district of Florence, and all foreign Jews who are passing through en route to some place, shall not be required to carry this sign in the *contado* or district. And if any Jew arrives in Florence, he shall be permitted to enter the city without any sign, and to go to his house or hotel where he is lodging and there he may deposit his baggage. But thereafter, he may not go in the city without carrying the sign. . . . This provision is not to be construed to mean that the Jews named in the agreement are required to wear the sign in their house, or within ten yards of their house.

To prevent any large concentration of Jews in Florence, or a greater number than is necessary, in future the Jews engaged in moneylending in Florence may not number more than seventy persons in their houses and in their shops, working as factors and apprentices. Included in this number of seventy are Jews of both sexes, masculine and feminine, large and small. And if this number be exceeded, and those additional Jews remain in Florence for more than five days, the community will be fined 50 florins for each person and for each violation. And all other Jews not included in this community of seventy may not stay in the city of Florence or its suburbs for more than five days in any single visit. . . and having left the city, they cannot return again . . . before one month. . . .

The present addition to the agreement . . . has been drawn up with the consent of the abovenamed Jews and in particular, in accordance with the wishes of the heads of the community, who have desired [to make] their future life and business activity more honest, less dangerous, and less subject to opprobrium. . . . This clause is added, namely, that all Hebrew books which pertain to the faith, law, or church of these Jews, and also all scholarly books of whatever discipline, may be possessed, read, studied, and copied by the Jews of this community. . . . This is not to include the possession, reading, and study of any book like those which have brought infamy and opprobrium to the Jews living in Cortona, or any similar book against the Christian faith which may appear in future. The community, and each abovenamed Jew, is to be permitted—without penalty or prejudice—to perform and recite the ceremonies and offices in the synagogues and houses in which they live . . . according to the mode and customs which is practiced by the Italian Jews. . . .

119. The Condemnation of a Jewish Physician*

. . . We condemn . . . Master Jacob Astrughi de Arillo, of the province of Provence, a physician and a Jew . . . of

* Source: *ASF, Atti del Podestà*, 3965, fols. 40r–42r, February 26, 1404.

the parish of S. Lorenzo of Florence. . . . He had a discussion with Lagia, daughter of Piero Vulterrani of Lignao, parish of S. Angelo in Monticelli, and the wife of Perracino di Antonio . . . and with Bella, daughter of Bencivenni, parish of S. Ambrogio of Florence (now deceased) and the wife of Falco di Dato, of S. Ambrogio. Lagia went to Bella . . . and told her to ask Master Jacob, a Jew, to give her the means by which she could cause her husband Perracino to sicken and die. This she did because Lagia was very badly treated by her husband. Consenting to Lagia's plan and wish, Bella brought Master Jacob to her house and said to him: "Master Jacob, I have a blood relation who is badly treated by her husband. I want you to prescribe something that will make him become ill and die." But Master Jacob refused, saying that he did not wish to do it, and then left her. Several days later, Lagia and Bella went to Master Jacob's house and again asked him, and with great fervor appealed to him to give them the means by which Perracino would sicken and die, promising to give him 2 florins over the regular price [of the drug]. Then, Master Jacob assented . . . and gave them some powder which was capable of causing Perracino's sickness and death. Lagia then said: "I don't want medicine that causes flatulence." And Master Jacob replied: "Don't have any concern about this." He gave them a powder which he had concocted. . . . This was to be mixed into a cup for Perracino to drink . . . so that Lagia might carry out her iniquitous plan.

For these powders, Lagia gave Master Jacob . . . 33 soldi, and then she returned home . . . and gave her husband Perracino a portion in a cup for him to consume. But seeing that her husband did not sicken rapidly from the consumption of this powder, she went back to Master Jacob and complained to him and quarreled with him. And he advised

her to give her husband all of the remaining powder in one
potion. . . . Having heard this, Lagia gave him the rest
. . . and he consumed it in a cup . . . and died. [Jacob
confessed and was executed. Lagia was sentenced to death
in absentia; her accomplice Bella confessed to the crime and
was executed.]

120. THE TRANSGRESSIONS OF A SEDITIOUS JEW, 1434*

. . . We condemn Guglielmo Dattali of Montefalcone,
a Jew. He planned to have carnal relations with Masina di
Bono of Florence . . . with the assistance of a certain
Michele, a servant in the Crown Inn in Florence. Michele
arranged to meet Masina in a room of the inn next to the
kitchen. . . . And at various times Guglielmo had carnal
relations with Masina, a Christian woman . . . in that inn
and at other times in Masina's house . . . to the shame and
degradation of the Christian religion, in contempt of the
Catholic faith, and against the holy canons and constitutions
and against the statutes and ordinances of the Commune of
Florence, and against good customs and contrary to all
reason. [Guglielmo escaped the authorities and was fined
500 lire *in absentia.*]

The attention of the noble and prudent men, the Eight on
Security, has been called to various enormous and abominable
crimes committed and perpetrated by Guglielmo Dattali of
Montefalcone, a Jew, in the city of Florence, to the dishonor of the most holy Christian faith and our lord [pope]

* Source: *ASF, Atti del Capitano,* 3212, no pagination, November 3 and
December 5, 1434.

Eugenius IV, at present residing in the city of Florence with his court, and also against the honor of the Commune of Florence. His Holiness has stated that he will be very disturbed if he [Guglielmo] is not punished severely. . . . [The Eight have considered] the crimes committed by Guglielmo . . . in vituperation of, and against the honor of, the Commune of Florence. . . . They are aware of the fact that Guglielmo . . . sought to provoke disorders against the present regime of the Commune of Florence, shouting and crying out against the . . . lord priors. . . . This Guglielmo is a seditious and sacrilegious person who continually commits evil and wicked acts against the Catholic faith and the good customs and honor of the Florentine Commune. . . . [Guglielmo was sentenced to death *in absentia*.]

121. Extortion and Betrayal, 1435*

. . . We condemn Joseph Manni, a Jew of Vicenza . . . who eight years ago or thereabouts stole a black cloak valued at approximately 4 florins from Benjamin, a Jew of Vicenza. . . .

Item, some eight years ago, he fled from the Vicenza region with a leather cuirass belonging to a certain Niccolò Ciechini, a citizen of Vicenza. . . .

Item, during the past year—in December, 1434—in the city of Florence, Joseph had custody of a Bible belonging to Guglielmo, a Jew of Montefalcone. This Bible contained parchment pages of great width and ample size, inscribed with ancient Latin characters, and valued at 15 florins or

* Source: *ASF, Atti del Podestà*, 4489, fols. 21r–22v.

more. During this past May, he took this Bible with the intention of stealing and profiting from it, and sold it to Martino Cini, a Florentine moneychanger, for the price of 8 gold ducats. . . .

Item, in August 1435, with the intention of defaming the Jews named below, and extorting money from them, Joseph caused to be drawn up a supplication by Master Giovanni de Gallesio, in which in effect he requested the pope to take action against certain crimes committed—so Joseph asserted —against the Catholic faith by the following Jews: Solomon of Prato, Solomon of Arezzo, Solomon of [Città di] Castello, Isaac of Pisa, and Dactilum of Cortona. So menaced were these Jews by these crimes and the introduction of the supplication concerning them, and inspired by fear, [that] Solomon of [Città di] Castello for himself and on behalf of the other aforementioned Jews promised Joseph that if he would desist from his efforts, he would receive the sum of 200 florins. . . . Then Joseph promised Solomon to cease the actions which he had begun against those Jews. . . . Joseph received 200 gold florins in cash from Solomon of [Città di] Castello . . . and, as he had promised, he desisted from these activities . . . in June 1435.

Item, this Jew Joseph went during the first hour of night to a public brothel in the city of Florence, located in the parish of S. Salvatore, and there he had carnal relations with a Christian prostitute, whose name he does not remember, having carnal knowledge of her against the statutes of this city and in contempt of the Christian faith and the sacred laws and canons. . . . [Joseph confessed and was executed.]

122. ANTI-SEMITISM AND THE COMMUNE, 1488–93*

Today, March 12, 1488, I record the following event. There was a Franciscan preacher by the name of Fra [Bernardino da Feltre] who preached in S. Maria del Fiore. Since he had a reputation as an excellent man, a large crowd gathered to hear him. On several occasions, he had discussed the problem of the Jews, saying that they should not suck the blood of Christians by engaging in usury in this city and *contado*. He repeatedly told his audience that the government should establish a Monte di Pietà [municipal pawnshop] so that poor people in need of cash could borrow money on their property. He urged children and youths to come to his sermons, and this morning when he was preaching on the subject, he appealed to them to serve as his soldiers, in the following manner. Every morning, they should all go to the chapel in the cathedral where the body of Christ is exhibited, to pray that the citizens would remember that they had promised to expel the Jews and to establish the Monte di Pietà. These children should all kneel and recite three Paternosters and three Ave Marias, so that through the prayers which they addressed to our Lord, he hoped—between that day and Sunday—to have them expelled. Many had come [to the sermon], and there was a large crowd—between two thousand and three thousand boys—who came out [of the cathedral], and they ran to the pawnshop in the Vacca and with loud shouts they planned to sack it. The police official came with all of his men, but they weren't sufficient, so that two of the Eight [on Security]

* Source: *Ricordanze di Tribaldo de' Rossi; Delizie degli eruditi toscani,* ed. Ildefonso di San Luigi, XXIII, 238–40, 283–85.

came in person. With the police official, they issued a proclamation that fathers would be banned as outlaws for their sons' crimes.

Finally, after an hour and with great difficulty, they subdued the tumult. They took away a boy who had struck an official in the face with a pipe; but in the square a crowd of factors from the silk guild released him.

The Signoria and the Eight sent for the preacher . . . and held him in the palace and had many discussions with him. Apparently, he demanded complete freedom to preach from the pulpit, and he said that it was necessary for the salvation of souls. So, after a time, he departed and returned to his affairs; and later . . . the Signoria and the Eight sent two or three citizens to his home, accompanied by two servants of the Eight with a torch. And they took him to the city gate and expelled him and forbade him to return again to preach in the city. . . .

I record that on August 15, 1493, one of these Marranos [Spanish Jews] was involved in a quarrel with some boys, and wounded one of them in the throat with a knife. This caused a disturbance, and the boys were going to the police official, when they encountered one of his assistants asleep in the square, and they said: "Arrest that man who wounded one of us." Then they added: "You may be that villain who damaged [the image of] the Virgin. . . ." And the boys, with the assistant, took him to the police . . . and he was tortured eight times with the rope. Then he confessed that he had damaged the marble image of the Virgin at Orsanmichele in the fourth hour of the night. . . . The entire population of Florence ran to see this. With a knife he had struck several blows in the face [of the Virgin] and also in the eye of the Christ child in her arms. A few nights earlier, he had damaged a painting [of the Virgin] in [the church of] S. Maria in Campo. Then, with his own filth he had besmirched the face and body of the Virgin whose image was located on a wall of the hospital of S. Maria Nuova.

The Eight . . . sentenced him to die on August 17. Transported in a cart, he was to have one hand amputated in front of the Virgin at S. Onofrio, and the other outside S. Maria in Campo, and his eyes plucked out at Orsanmichele. But while the cart was moving through the Borgo dei Greci [the officials] decided to shorten the journey, because some boys were planning to seize [the condemned man]. Then in the square in front of S. Croce, a crowd of men and boys threw so many stones that the executioner and his assistants fled. Then the mob stoned him to death . . . and dragged his body through the streets of Florence, beating the corpse with clubs. . . .

II. Heretics

123. LEGISLATION AGAINST THE FRATICELLI, 1382*

On behalf of several Florentine citizens who are motivated by a zeal for the faith and by other reasons, this petition is presented to you, lord priors. For several years now, there have congregated in the city of Florence and its environs certain friars or Fraticelli, some of whom are apostates from the order of the blessed Francis, and who are called by various names: sometimes Minorites, and sometimes Friars of the Poor Life, and sometimes the Poor Preachers. They

* Source: *ASF, Provvisioni*, 71, fols. 175v–176r.

are followers of Michele or Michelino of Cesena of damned
memory, a heretic who was abjectly condemned for heresy,
and a former general of the Franciscan Order. With impious
errors and machinations, these friars or Fraticelli in the city
and its surrounding territory deceive many simple and ignorant laymen, imbuing them with depraved and heretical
opinions, and diverting them from divine services, from the
reception of the sacraments, and from ecclesiastical burial.
They even dare to preach and to celebrate the sacraments in
secular places, without having any commission or authority.
In addition to other errors mentioned below, they contend
that Pope John XXII and other popes who succeeded him
were and are heretics, and that all cardinals who were with
them are heretics, and that no priest can confer the holy
sacraments except themselves, and that they alone can elect
a pope and reform the entire church if they wish. [They
contend that] there is no pope and that they alone are
[members of] the Roman church, and they preach and
affirm other heresies, and they organize secret meetings and
through them spread various scandals, thus offending the
divine majesty and endangering the souls of your subjects.

Unless an opportune remedy is applied to this heresy, it
could grow and spread its roots to such an extent that the
city of Florence could be rent by division, and many evils
could result. So out of reverence for our Lord Jesus Christ,
and for the defense and maintenance of the Catholic faith
and the Holy Roman Church, and for the extirpation of this
heresy and schism (lest your people be infected and corrupted), your lordships are requested to provide and to
solemnly decree that all of the friars or Fraticelli, who believe or affirm in full or in part the above-mentioned errors,
are henceforth forbidden to stay or reside in the city, *contado*,
and district of Florence. Furthermore, everyone on his own

authority is authorized to seize these friars or Fraticelli, and to bring them into the hands of the Inquisitor, for their correction and punishment. . . .

124. FRATICELLI SYMPATHIZERS AND THE INQUISITION, 1383*

. . . Fra Antonio. di Lando of Florence, of the order of St. Francis, commissioner and vicar-general of Reverend Father Fra Galgano of Massa of the Franciscan Order and Inquisitor . . . in the province of Tuscany . . . had learned from many sources worthy of credence about the heretical beliefs and activities of Lorenzo Puccini, of the parish of S. Lorenzo of Florence. Exercising his office of Inquisitor in a laudable manner for the strength and vitality of the Christian faith, he asked for and obtained help from the secular arm to exercise his office and, as was proper, to persecute heretics and heretical depravity. Together with his assistant, Fra Giovanni di Master Guido of Florence, and servants of the lord podestà of Florence (whom he had requested and obtained), he apprehended and led away captive Lorenzo Puccini of the parish of S. Lorenzo, accused on many occasions of heresy and of numerous relations with heretics.

Angelo, the son of Lorenzo . . . resisted Fra Antonio, the vicar and lieutenant of the Inquisitor. . . . He shouted: "Release my father Lorenzo and don't take him away!" Together with others who were with him, he began to create a disorder and to shout: "Stone them!" And they . . . began a riot and started to throw stones at Fra Antonio and

* Source: *ASF, Atti del Podestà,* 3178, fols. 153v–154r.

Fra Giovanni, shouting: "Let us stone those buggering friars and the police!" With stones they struck the two friars and the officials [of the podestà] who . . . fled individually to the shops of the good merchants and artisans of the neighborhood. They closed the doors of those shops so that [they] might evade death and the fury of the mob. [Two men implicated in this riot were fined 300 and 200 lire respectively by the podestà.]

125. THE EXECUTION OF FRA MICHELE OF CALCI, 1389*

[April 30, 1389] This is the condemnation of Giovanni, called Fra Michele di Berti of Calci, in the territory of Pisa, a man of low condition, evil conversation, life, and reputation, and a heretic against the Catholic faith, against whom we have proceeded by means of inquisition. . . . It has come to our attention that this Giovanni . . . with the spirit and intent of being a heretic, had relations with the Fraticelli, called the Little Brothers of Poverty, heretics and schismatics and denounced by the Holy Roman Church, and that he joined that depraved sect in a place called the grotto of the *Dieci Yoffensi,* in which place they congregated and stayed. . . . With the intention of proclaiming this heresy and of contaminating faithful Christians, the accused came to the city of Florence and in public places he did maintain, affirm, and preach the heretical teachings hereby stated:

Item, that Christ, our Redeemer, possessed no property

---

* Sources: Alessandro D'Ancona, *Varietà storiche e letterarie* (Milan, 1883), pp. 345–54; *Storia di Fra Michele Minorita,* in *Scelta di curiosità letterarie inedite o rari dal secolo XIII al XVII,* vol. 50 (Bologna, 1864), pp. 36–37, 43–56.

either individually or in common but divested himself of all things, as the Holy Scripture testifies.

Item, that Christ and his Apostles, according to the Scriptures, denounced the taking, holding, or exchanging of goods as against divine law.

Item, that Pope John XXII [d. 1334] of blessed memory was a heretic and lost all power and ecclesiastical authority as pope and as a heretic had no authority to appoint bishops or prelates, and that all prelates so appointed by him do not legally hold their office and that they sin by pretending to do so.

Item, that all cardinals, prelates, and clerics who accepted the teaching of John XXII on apostolic poverty, and who should resist these teachings and who do not resist, are also heretics and have lost all authority as priests of Christ. . . .

Item, that this Giovanni, a heretic and schismatic, not content with all this mentioned above, but desiring also the damnation of others, in the months of March and April sought to persuade many men and women of the city of Florence, to induce them to believe in and to enter the above-mentioned sect of the Fraticelli. He told them about the above-mentioned sect; with false words and with erroneous reasons he claimed that this sect was the true religion and the true observance of the rule and life of the blessed Francis; and that all those who observe this doctrine and life are in a state of grace, and that all other friars and priests are heretics and schismatics and are damned.

And since this Giovanni appeared before us and our court and confessed to the above-mentioned charges . . . and refused to recant or to reject these teachings, we hereby decree that unless this Giovanni gives up his false teaching and beliefs, that as an example to others, he be taken to the place of justice and there he is to be burned with fire and the flames of fire so that he shall die and his spirit be separated from his body.

Now everything which I here describe, I who write both saw or heard. Fra Michele, having come into the courtyard, waited attentively to hear the condemnation. And the vicar [general of the bishop] spoke: "The bishop and the Inquisitor have sent me here to tell you that if you wish to return to the Holy Church and renounce your errors, then do so, in order that the people may see that the church is merciful." And Fra Michele replied, "I believe in the poor crucified Christ, and I believe that Christ, showing the way to perfection, possessed nothing. . . ." Having read his confession, the judge turned his back upon Fra Michele . . . and the guards seized him and with great force pushed him outside of the gate of the judge's palace. He remained there alone, surrounded by scoundrels, appearing in truth as one of the martyrs. And there was such a great crowd that one could scarcely see. And the throng increased in size, shouting: "You don't want to die!" And Fra Michele replied, "I will die for Christ." And the crowd answered: "Oh! You aren't dying for Christ! You don't believe in God!" And Fra Michele replied: "I believe in God, in the Virgin Mary, and in the Holy Church!" And someone said to him, "You wretch! The devil is pushing you from behind!"

And when he arrived in the district of the Proconsolo, there was a great press of people who came to watch. And one of the faithful cried: "Fra Michele! Pray to God for us. . . ." When he arrived at S. Giovanni, they shouted to him: "Repent, repent! You don't want to die." And he said: "I have repented of my sins. . . ." And at the Mercato Vecchio, they shouted even louder: "Save yourself! Save yourself!" And he replied, "Save yourselves from damnation." And at the Mercato Nuovo, the shouts grew louder: "Repent, repent!" And he replied, "Repent of your sins; repent of your usury and your false merchandising. . . ." And at the Piazza del Grano, there were many women in the windows of the houses who cried to him: "Repent, repent!" And he replied, "Repent of your sins, your usury, your gambling, your fornication. . . ." When he arrived at S. Croce, near the gate of the friars, the image of St. Francis was shown to him and he raised his eyes to heaven and said, "St. Francis, my father, pray to Christ for me. . . ."

And then moving toward the gate of Justice, the crowd cried in unison: "Recant, recant! You don't want to die!" And he replied, "Christ died for us." And some said to him, mocking: "Ho, you're not Christ and you don't have to die for us." And he replied, "I wish to die for Him." And then another shouted, "Ho, you're not among pagans," and he answered, "I wish to die for the truth. . . ."

And when he arrived at the gate near the place of execution, one of the faithful began to cry, "Remain firm, martyr of Christ, for soon you will receive the crown. . . ." And arriving at the place of execution, there was a great turmoil and the crowd urged him to repent and save himself and he refused. . . . And the guards pushed the crowd back and formed a circle of horsemen around the pyre so that no one could enter. I myself did not enter but climbed upon the river bank to see, but I was unable to hear. . . . And he was bound to the stake . . . and the crowd begged him to recant, except one of the faithful, who comforted him. . . . And they set fire to the wood . . . and Fra Michele began to recite the Te Deum. . . . And when he had said, "In your hands, O Lord, I commend my spirit," the fire burned the cords which bound him and he fell dead . . . to the earth.

And many of the onlookers said, "He seems to be a saint."
Even his enemies whispered it . . . and then they slowly
began to return to their homes. They talked about Michele
and the majority said that he was wrong and that no one
should speak such evil of the priests. And some said, "He is
a martyr," and others said, "He is a saint," and still others
denied it. And there was a greater tumult and disturbance
in Florence than there had ever been. . . .

126. THE UNORTHODOX VIEWS OF A PRIEST, 1418*

We, Fra Marco of Assano, of the Franciscan Order . . .
designated as Inquisitor of heresy for Tuscany, make known
to all of Christ's faithful that while we were exercising our
office in the city of Florence, we ordered to appear before us
and our curia Priest Antonio di Stefano of Francavilla in the
Abruzzi, now inhabiting the parish of the abbey of Fiesole
in the Florentine *contado*. Through depositions given to us,
he had been accused by several persons worthy of credence
. . . that in the month of January 1417 . . . and for several months thereafter . . . he had said that St. Peter
Martyr was damned and in hell, and that he had not died
for the love of God but as the result of a vendetta. . . .
Item, that he had taught certain women that it was proper
to sew and weave on feast days. . . .

Therefore, we ordered Priest Antonio to be brought into
our presence by our officials for examination. . . . Seeking
to defend himself against these accusations, he confessed that
he had said that St. Peter Martyr was damned and in hell,
although in fact he did not believe it, even though he had

---

* Source: *ASF, Giudice degli Appelli,* 74, part 2, fol. 139r.

read it in a commentary. He also confessed that he had taught women . . . that it was a lesser sin to work on feast days and to do certain tasks than to remain idle. Nevertheless, Priest Antonio insisted that he had never believed, nor did he now believe, these heretical and profane words, nor did he perceive that they violated the faith, but that he had always been a true Catholic. He had uttered those words through ignorance and not deliberately nor with heretical intent. [While the Inquisitor's court absolved Antonio of the heresy charge, he was ordered to leave Florentine territory. If he returned, he was to be imprisoned until he paid a penalty of 425 florins.]

127. THE PROSECUTION OF GIOVANNI CANI, 1450*

It happened that one Master Giovanni Cani was reputed to hold wrong opinions concerning the Catholic faith . . . and to invoke demons and, with certain followers in his house in the parish of S. Lorenzo in Florence, to adhere to the life, customs, and errors of the Fraticelli. . . . Once when he had gone to a house to visit the sick, he was asked about the faith which he held. . . . Upon being questioned, he replied that Nicholas V, who was then pope, was not the true pope. . . . He stubbornly affirmed that Pope Nicholas could have superiors on earth, and that there were many such . . . and if one could be found who was more worthy, then he should be designated as pope. This is manifestly false, since he appears to believe that this dignity should

---

* Source: Anonymous life of S. Antonino, in R. Morçay, *Saint Antonin fondateur du couvent de Saint-Marc, archevêque de Florence* (1389–1459), (Paris and Tours, 1914), pp. 430–31.

derive, not from the authority of the church, but the merit of the person. He also stated and affirmed that the priests ordained by the archbishop of Florence . . . were not true priests and could not consecrate the body of Christ. . . .

He was asked if he had taken communion of the body of Christ at any time, and he replied affirmatively. Asked in which place, he replied, "In this church." Upon being told that that was a room and not a church, he answered, "In this neighborhood." When asked from whom he had taken communion, he mentioned a priest named Piero, who had since died, and two others whose names he did not wish to reveal. . . . That priest must have been one of the Fraticelli. He was asked if the Gospel of Christ was true or whether it contained some errors; he said that he could not answer. . . . The poor man had become the servant of the devil and had been completely ensnared by him. He was interrogated in his house before the vicar of the archbishop and several masters of theology, who denounced his errors. With respect to medicine, they said that he could believe what he chose, but concerning the Catholic faith, he should obey . . . the teachings of the Gospel, and they expounded the purity of the faith to him lucidly and explicitly. But he was so alien to that faith, and so obdurate, that he refused to confess his error. . . . A platform was constructed before the doors of the cathedral of S. Maria del Fiore, and he was denounced as a heretic and an invocator of demons. Several of his books of necromancy, chiromancy, and demonic incantations were burned, and the archbishop, seated on the platform before a great throng of people . . . released him into the hands of . . . the podestà of Florence, who condemned him to death and ordered him to be burned . . . on May 6, 1450. . . .

III. Sorcerers

128. The Enchantress*

. . . We condemn . . . Monna Caterina di Agostino, who lives in the parish of S. Giorgio of Florence, a woman of the most evil life, condition, and reputation, against whom we have proceeded as a result of an accusation brought before us and our court by Vieri di Michele Rondinelli, of the parish of S. Lorenzo of Florence. . . . Motivated by a diabolical spirit, Caterina committed numerous and various acts of sorcery and magic and also invoked demons, in order that the chaste souls of men, and particularly the soul of Paolo di Michele Rondinelli, of the parish of S. Lorenzo of Florence, an honest and honorable citizen, might engage in libidinous acts with her. In order to attract Paolo to her, and to render him incompetent, and so that she might extort money from him, Caterina placed a wax figure of a man . . . in a bed in her house to which she had led Paolo. . . . Into that figure she had stuck several iron pins. And in that bed to which he was drawn by those acts of magic and sorcery and by numerous other acts and incantations, he had intercourse with her on several occasions. As a result of this, Paolo—an honest and serious man of forty-five years of age and more—deviated and continues to deviate from every right path and left his wife, children, business, and all his affairs to involve himself with that evil woman Caterina.

Caterina also received from Paolo . . . several sums of money totaling more than 400 florins, as well as other items. As a result of this illegal and abominable activity, Paolo has

* Source: *ASF, Atti del Esecutore,* 751, fols. 25r–26r, November 5, 1375.

been nearly reduced to indigence, to the shame and detriment
of himself and his kin. And all this was committed and perpetrated by Caterina . . . against the form of law, the
statutes and ordinances of the Florentine Commune, against
the Catholic faith and freedom of the will, and against good
customs. As a result of these acts committed by Caterina,
disorder, tumult, and scandal have arisen in the city of Florence between the citizens of this city, and particularly
between the relatives of Paolo. [Caterina escaped the authorities, and was sentenced *in absentia* to be burned at the stake.
This sentence was cancelled three years later.]

129. THE PROFESSIONAL SORCERER*

This is a condemnation . . . promulgated and pro-
nounced by the reverend father in Christ, Fra Piero di Ser
Filippo of Florence, of the Order of Friars Minor, most
worthy professor of sacred theology, and specially appointed
by authority of the Holy See as Inquisitor of heresy in the
province of Tuscany, against Niccolò Consigli, of the parish
of S. Maria Maggiore of Florence, for the excesses, crimes,
and illegal acts described below. . . .

In the name of God, amen. We, Fra Piero di Ser Filippo
of Florence . . . make known to all of the faithful that
while we exercised the office of the Inquisition in the city of
Florence . . . it came to our attention, and to the attention of our court, that Niccolò Consigli of the parish of S.
Piero Maggiore of Florence, was endangering his soul and
those of others, that he was offending the divine majesty and
the Catholic faith, and was committing numerous scandals
not only in times past but also in the present. He has prac-

* Source: *ASF, Atti del Podestà*, 3204, fols. 103v–104v, 113r–114v, October 23, 1384.

ticed, and continues to practice daily, various divinations, malefactions, and acts of sorcery which are manifestly heretical. He invokes demons, utters incantations and magical spells, offers sacrifices, and communicates with evil spirits for the purpose of implanting sickness in human bodies, or else to cure them. He predicts the future, finds lost objects, discovers and cures illnesses, investigates and reveals secret and occult matters, and expels demons from bodies which are possessed. He has perpetrated many other similar acts, and continues daily to perpetrate them. For these ends, he has books of necromancy which he uses to deceive and to trap simple and innocent persons and souls. . . .

We have also learned that for several years Niccolò has been, and still is at the present time, insubordinate and rebellious with respect to our office. . . . Not once but several times, we have ordered him to appear personally before us and our court by means of messengers, to answer questions concerning the faith and to respond to an accusation brought against him by one of our predecessors. . . . We then ordered him to be seized and brought to our presence. . . . And having been diligently examined by us for several days and at various times, he frequently suppressed and denied the truth, to the peril of his soul, and in many ways he expounded falsehoods. . . . Then, however, without being . . . molested or tortured, but by his own free will, he confessed that everything contained in the inquisition was true . . . in the presence of several persons both lay and religious. . . .

And specifically, Niccolò admitted that he had confessed (in the court of our predecessor, Master Andrea Ricolgi, Inquisitor) that he had committed an heretical act with respect to the cure of a daughter of Giorgio called Buino, of the parish of S. Remigio of Florence, who was said to be ill

and possessed [of evil spirits]. . . . And for the purgation
and penitence of that [crime], he had promised never to attempt through sorcery to cure souls or to expel demons or
evil spirits or to invoke them. . . . And on oath he promised to obey these terms . . . in the year of our Lord 1376.
And in the months of October and November of that year,
he taught the following formulas and acts of sorcery to a
certain Giovanni, who desired to harm (and even to kill) a
certain Martino and his son, whom he hated. Niccolò instructed Giovanni to leave his house and cross one bridge
and then return via another bridge, and at the exit of that
bridge, he should pick up three round stones in the name
of Lucifer, Satan, and Beelzebub, saying: "I do not collect
stones but the hearts of Martino and his son." And he should
carry these stones to his house, returning by a different
route. . . .

Afterwards, he should buy a small jar, and he should steal
a spindle and six pins, and he should buy a chicken for a
small price. Having done this, he should come to Niccolò's
house. When he entered the house, Niccolò made a certain
sign on the doorpost of his room and spoke certain incantations over the chicken. Then, he instructed Giovanni to open
the fowl with a knife and with his teeth pull out its heart,
saying: "I do not extract the heart of a chicken but the heart
of Martino and his son." Niccolò then stuck the six pins into
the chicken's heart saying, "I do not place these pins in the
heart of a chicken, but in the heart of Martino and his son,
in the name of Lucifer, Satan, and Beelzebub." Afterwards,
Niccolò ordered Giovanni to buy a pound of coarse salt . . .
and told him: "Take a large grain [of salt] and put it into
the fire . . . and say: "I do not put salt in the fire, but the
heart of Martino and his son, so that it will liquefy and be
consumed as is this salt in the fire, in the name of Lucifer,

Satan, and Beelzebub." Later that evening, Niccolò instructed Giovanni to light the fire in the name of Lucifer,
etc., and to place it on the fire, pouring some urine and
vinegar into [the mixture] and to say: "I don't put this, etc.,
into the fire, but the heart of Martino and his son, etc., in
the name of Lucifer, etc. . . ."

When these acts of sorcery and invocations of demons had
not brought about the death or illness of Martino and his
son, Niccolò made Giovanni buy some white wax and from
it, one night in his own home, he made a figure of a man and
stuck six pins into it, while uttering various incantations to
demons. . . . And afterwards . . . he placed some incense
and myrrh upon the figure and suffocated the image in the
name of Lucifer, Satan, and Beelzebub. Then he gave it to
Giovanni so that each night for fifteen days, he would suffocate it in his own house and then bury it in a street through
which Martino customarily passed. When in fact Martino
did not fall ill, and after another fifteen days had elapsed,
Niccolò made another figure of red wax and with even
stronger incantations, he inscribed some . . . characters
upon it and whipped it . . . and placed it in some black
cloth and gave it to Giovanni to suffocate as before. . . .
Then he told him to bury it in a street through which Martino customarily passed. . . . And Giovanni buried the
image between the Via Chiara and the . . . Via dell' Ar-
diglione. . . .

Item, Niccolò confessed . . . that he possessed certain
books or writings on necromancy, with which he made various incantations of demons to inspire hatred or illicit carnal
love between men and women, at the desire of several persons whose names he could not remember. . . . He also confessed . . . that he practiced various divinations by reveal-
ing to relatives hidden secrets concerning human acts and

future events. [He claimed] that he could cure incurable diseases or those unknown to physicians, either immediately or in a very short time, that he could find things which were lost or stolen, that he could expel demons and evil spirits from human bodies, and other similar things that only the knowledge and power of God may control. . . . [He confessed] that he had committed acts of heresy through his consultations with demons and through sorcery . . . and that he had expelled two demons from a girl of ten or eleven years of age in the parish of S. Remigio of Florence, in the house of a certain Bartolo de Volognano. After [performing] other incantations and ceremonies, he took the girl by the hair and laid her on the ground upon a rug and spoke into her ears certain magical words, which could not be heard by others, except a certain diabolical song which began: *"Tanta muructa? tiri?*, etc." Then, placing her upon her feet, he drew out the spirits so that they left her, and during this expulsion, he extinguished a candle . . . which he had caused to be placed at a short distance from the girl. And this was done, and the girl remained free [from spirits], although she was in weak state. . . . And he did this in various places in the city and *contado* of Florence with numerous persons who were similarly afflicted by demons and evil spirits.

. . . Ordered to appear before us and our court, he stubbornly stayed away and refused to appear, and consequently he incurred the sentence of excommunication . . . and for eight years and three months he did not appear before us and our court, until he was finally captured and placed in prison and thus [committed] to judgment. . . . After his seizure he was kept in the custody of the noble knight Messer Jacopo, podestà of the city of Florence, with our knowledge and consent. On several occasions he was interrogated by us concerning several of his excesses . . . and after taking an oath to tell the truth, he suppressed it and spoke falsehoods of various kinds. . . .

Item, it has been established by the testimony of credible witnesses that while he was detained in the palace of the podestà, he remained obstinately impenitent. . . . There without any physical pressure or torment, he was given the opportunity to repent, but on several occasions both day and night, with a loud voice and with his hands joined together and elevated, he recommended himself to the devil, and particularly to those three—Lucifer, Satan, and Beelzebub—whom he customarily invoked to obtain the desires of himself and others. He proclaimed himself to be in their spirit and body, and on no occasion did he ask for a confessor . . . nor did he show any genuine sign of penitence or of true confession. [Judged by the Inquisitor to be a relapsed heretic, Niccolò was turned over to the secular arm, the podestà, and was burned at the stake.]

130. A Sorcerer Manqué*

. . . We condemn . . . Jacopo di Francesco of S. Miniato, in the Florentine district, now living in the parish of S. Benedetto of Florence. . . . For more than a year, Jacopo has been inspired by a diabolical spirit to engage in the incantation of demons and in the black arts . . . to the detriment of human salvation and for the purpose of deflecting chaste spirits toward libidinousness and other enormities. With his own hand he had copied many books of magic and mathematics, containing among other things several prescriptions for persuading chaste men and women to engage in lustful acts, and containing characters of diverse kinds, and

* Source: *ASF, Atti del Esecutore*, 1521, fols. 18r–18v, March 3, 1404.

also incantations and conjurations of demons, and many other prescriptions of evils and philtres against the welfare of all men, and pertaining to this most abominable magical and mathematical art. He then learned the prescriptions, rules, incantations, formulas, and characters in these books and on numerous occasions he began to put them to the test. He was asked by many men (whose names shall not be revealed for the public good) to provide them with counsel so that they could persuade their honest and chaste women to accede to their evil desires. . . . And so that their iniquitous plans could be more easily carried out, he instructed them from these books. . . .

Desiring to practice this illegal art of sorcery and magic according to the instructions in these books, and being importuned by a woman, he inscribed certain characters upon a leaden locket . . . and gave it to the woman, instructing her to carry the locket without her husband's knowledge and thus she would become pregnant. . . .

Jacopo desired to bind to himself his servant, Monna Francesca, with the chains of love, so that she would not love anyone save himself, and so that she would not commit a libidinous act with anyone else. Mixing the brains of a crow with honey, he made an unguent and . . . before engaging in intercourse with that servant girl, he put the unguent on his penis, in accordance with the formulas and instructions in those books. . . .

Jacopo desired to experiment further with the art of sorcery, in the person of an honest and chaste woman, by seducing her. With his own hand, he wrote on a sheet of parchment the Psalm [number 44] which begins, "My heart cries out. . . ." In accordance with the teaching of those books, he planned to place it in a certain place where the woman should cross, so that she would walk over the psalm and thus would be induced to surrender to his evil and lustful will. But since Jacopo did not have the occasion to place that psalm in the above-mentioned location, he was not able to carry out his iniquitous plan. . . . Jacopo then attempted to demonstrate another formula contained in those books, that is, to make a woman go after a man. While seeking to learn if the details of that formula were true, he burned the bones of small birds and after making a powder of them, he applied it to a woman named Maria . . . so that if this experiment should succeed, he could then use it upon more beautiful [women]. Since he found that this experiment did not work, he did not pursue it further. [Jacopo confessed. He was mitred and whipped through the streets and sentenced to one year in the Communal prison. His sorcery books were burned.]

131. A Sorcerer and His Clientele*

. . . We condemn . . . Giovannino di Giovanni of the city of Turin in Piedmont, a man of evil reputation, condition, and life, a robber, murderer, assassin, a sacrilegious practitioner of auguries, a necromancer and highwayman. . . . On several occasions, he practiced the diabolical art of necromancy . . . prohibited and condemned by the Catholic faith. . . . He promised the abbot of Ruota, who resides in the Valdambra, to so operate with necromancy and the diabolical art that the enemies of the lord abbot would not be be able to harm him in anything.

Item, he promised the lord abbot to invoke a diabolical spirit and to place that spirit in a certain ring, at the abbot's request.

* Source: *ASF, Atti del Podestà*, 4261, fols. 38r–39v, June 27, 1412.

Item, he promised the lord abbot to arrange, by means of that art, that he would receive 1,400 florins, which would be brought to him through the air by devils. And for accomplishing this, Giovannino instructed the lord abbot to have made a silver image weighing twenty ounces . . . and for doing this, Giovannino illegally and maliciously extorted 23 florins and 23 silver grossi from the lord abbot.

Item, he received from the lord abbot a gold ring, valued at 1⅓ florins, in which he intended to place that diabolical spirit.

Item, he extorted from the abbot the silver image weighing twenty ounces, valued at 13 ducats. . . .

Item, Giovannino . . . extorted 43 florins and 43 silver grossi from Modesto di Michele of Florence, for the purpose of making an incantation of that diabolical, magical, and mathematical art, by which . . . he promised Modesto that, at his request, demons would be forced by the above-mentioned art to transport a great quantity of money to him by air. . . . Giovannino also extorted 15 florins and 9 silver grossi from Francesco di Giovanni, called Bentoto, of Borgo Sansepolchro, who now resides in Prato. . . . He promised Francesco that he would force demons to bring him money through the air. . . .

Item, he promised an individual (whose name he does not recall) to force a spirit, through the diabolical art, to reveal the location of certain records of dowries and other documents, which this unnamed person had lost. And to accomplish this (for which he received 3 florins), he consulted a certain book in which were recorded certain diabolical designs and images.

[Giovannino confessed to these crimes, and also to several robberies. He was condemned to be led through the streets of Florence on a donkey and wearing a mitre on which were depicted "diabolical designs and images." At the place of justice, his right hand and left ear were to be amputated; his sorcery book was to be burned. His property was confiscated and he was to be expelled from Florentine territory.]

132. A WITCH'S CAREER*

. . . We condemn . . . Giovanna called Caterina, daughter of Francesco called El Toso, a resident of the parish of S. Ambrogio of Florence . . . who is a magician, witch, and sorceress, and a practitioner of the black arts. . . . It happened that Giovanni Ceresani of the parish of S. Jacopo tra le Fosse was passing by her door and stared at her fixedly. She thought that she would draw the chaste spirit of Giovanni to her for carnal purposes by means of the black arts. . . . She went to the shop of Monna Gilia, the druggist, and purchased from her a small amount of lead . . . and then she took a bowl and placed the lead in it and put it on the fire so that the lead would melt. With this melted lead she made a small chain and spoke certain words which have significance for this magical and diabolical art (and which, lest the people learn about them, shall not be recorded). . . . All this which was done and spoken against Giovanni's safety by Giovanna was so powerful that his chaste spirit was deflected to lust after her, so that willynilly he went several times to her house and there he fulfilled her perfidious desire. . . .

With the desire of doing further harm to Giovanni's health through the black arts, and so persisting in what she had begun, she acquired a little gold, frankincense, and

* Source: *ASF, Atti del Esecutore*, 2096, fols. 47r–47v, June 7, 1427.

myrrh, and then took a little bowl with some glowing charcoal inside, and having prepared these ingredients and having
lit the candle which she held in her left hand, she genuflected
before the image and placed the bowl at the foot of the
figure. Calling out the name of Giovanni, she threw the
gold, frankincense, and myrrh upon the charcoal. And when
the smoke from the charcoal covered the whole image, Giovanna spoke certain words, the tenor of which is vile and
detestable, and which should be buried in silence lest the
people be given information for committing sin. . . .

When she realized that what she had done against Giovanni's health was not sufficient to satisfy completely her
insatiable lust, she learned from a certain priest that . . . if
water from the skulls of dead men was distilled and given
with a little wine to any man, that it was a most valid test.
. . . Night and day, that woman thought of nothing but
how she could give that water to Giovanni to drink. . . .
She visited the priest and bought from him a small amount
of that water . . . and that accursed woman gave Giovanni
that water mixed with wine to drink. After he drank it, Giovanni could think of nothing but satisfying his lust with
Giovanna. And his health has been somewhat damaged, in
the opinion of good and worthy [men]. . . .

In the time when Giovanna was menstruating, she took
a little of her menses, that quantity which is required by the
diabolical ceremonies, and placed it in a small beaker . . .
and then poured it into another flask filled-with wine . . .
and gave it to Giovanni to drink. And on account of this and
the other things described above, Giovanni no longer has
time for his affairs as he did in the past, and he has left his
home and his wife and son . . . and does only what pleases
Giovanna. . . .

On several occasions, Giovanna had intercourse with a

certain Jacopo di Andrea, a doublet-maker, of the parish of
S. Niccolò. Desiring to possess his chaste spirit totally for her
lust and against his health, Giovanna . . . thought to give
Jacopo some of her menses; since she knew that it was very
efficacious. . . . Having observed several diabolical rites,
she took the beaker with the menses . . . and gave it to
Jacopo to drink. After he had drunk, she uttered these words
among others: "I will catch you in my net if you don't flee.
. . ." When they were engaged in the act of intercourse,
she placed her hand on her private parts . . . and after
uttering certain diabolical words, she put a finger on Jacopo's
lips. . . . Thereafter, in the opinion of everyone, Jacopo's
health deteriorated and he was forced by necessity to obey
her in everything. . . .

Several years ago, Giovanna was the concubine of Niccolò
di Ser Casciotto of the parish of S. Giorgio, and she had three
children by him. Having a great affection for Niccolò, who
was then in Hungary, she wanted him to return to her in
Florence. . . . So she planned a diabolical experiment by
invoking a demon, to the detriment of Niccolò's health. . . .
She went to someone who shall not be identified . . . and
asked him to go to another diabolical woman, a sorceress
(whose name shall not be publicized, for the public good),
and asked her to make for Giovanna a wax image in the form
of a woman, and also some pins and other items required by
this diabolical experiment. . . . Giovanna took that image
and placed it in a chest in her house. When, a few days later,
she had to leave that house and move to another, she left
the image in the chest. Later it was discovered by the residents of that house, who burned it. . . .

She collected nine beans, a piece of cloth, some charcoal,
several olive leaves which had been blessed and which stood
before the image of the Virgin Mary, a coin with a cross, and

a grain of salt. With these in her hand she genuflected . . . [before the image] and recited three times the Pater Noster and the Ave Maria, spurning the divine prayers composed for the worship of God and his mother the Virgin Mary. Having done this, she placed these items on a piece of linen cloth and slept over them for three nights. And afterwards, she took them in her hand and thrice repeated the Pater Noster and the Ave Maria. . . . And thus Giovanna knew that her future husband would not love her. And so it happened, for after the celebration and the consummation of the marriage, her husband Giovanni stayed with her for a few days, and then left her and has not yet returned. [Giovanna confessed to these crimes and was beheaded.]

SELECTED BIBLIOGRAPHY

Becker, Marvin, *Florence in Transition* (Baltimore, 1967–68), vols. I and II.

———, "Florentine Politics and the Diffusion of Heresy in the Fourteenth Century," *Speculum*, XXXIV (1959), 60–75.

Brucker, Gene, "The Ciompi Revolution," *Florentine Studies*, ed. N. Rubinstein (London, 1969), pp. 314–56.

———, *Florentine Politics and Society, 1343–1378* (Princeton, 1962), ch. 1.

———, "The Florentine *Popolo Minuto* and its Political Role, 1340–1450," *Violence and Civil Disorder in Italian Cities: 1200–1500*, ed. L. Martines (Berkeley and Los Angeles, 1971).

———, "The Medici in the Fourteenth Century," *Speculum*, XXXII (1957), 1–26.

———, *Renaissance Florence* (New York, 1969), chs. 2, 3.

———, "Sorcery in Early Renaissance Florence," *Studies in the Renaissance*, X (1963), 7–24.

Goldthwaite, Richard, *Private Wealth in Renaissance Florence* (Princeton, 1968).

Gutkind, Curt, *Cosimo de' Medici* (New York, 1938).

Herlihy, David, *Medieval and Renaissance Pistoia* (New Haven, 1967).

Jones, Philip, "Florentine Families and Florentine Diaries

in the Fourteenth Century," *Papers of the British School at Rome*, XXIV (1956), 183-205.

Martines, Lauro, *Lawyers and Statecraft in Renaissance Florence* (Princeton, 1968), ch. 3.

——, *The Social World of the Florentine Humanists 1390-1460* (Princeton, 1963), chs. 2, 3.

Origo, Iris, "The Domestic Enemy: Eastern Slaves in Tuscany in the Fourteenth and Fifteenth Centuries," *Speculum*, XXX (1955), 321-66.

——, *The Merchant of Prato* (New York, 1957).

Roover, Raymond de, "Labour Conditions in Florence c. 1400," *Florentine Studies*, ed. Rubinstein, pp. 227-313.

——, *The Rise and Decline of the Medici Bank* (Cambridge, Mass., 1963), ch. 2.

Staley, Edgcombe, *The Guilds of Florence* (London, 1906).

INDEX

Archivio di Stato, vi

Artisans and craftsmen, 182–3, 184, 253
    tax assessments of, 4–5, 12

Artists, 10–2, 176–7

Betrothal, 29, 30, 31, 33, 34, 35, 36

Brothels, 130, 199
    communal brothels, 190, 197, 198, 247

Buonuomini, 229

Burial, 15, 42, 43, 44, 45, 47, 49, 50, 55

Catasto, 1, 6–13

Catholic church, 84, 86, 87, 173, 253, 255, 259
    See also Clergy

Catholic faith, 173, 245, 246, 247, 258, 261, 268

Charity,
    by Commune, 229, 230–1
    by guilds, 92–3
    institutions of, 213, 231–3

Christians,
    and Jews, 245, 247
    as slaves, 222, 223

Churches, 77, 171, 172, 173

Ciompi revolution, 21, 214, 236–9

Civic militia, 96

Clan, the, 70, 113

Clergy, 69, 186–9, 248
    abuse of clerical authority, 137–8, 207–8
    and death, 44, 45, 46, 47, 55
    and feast days, 76
    and heresy, 259
    heretical, 250–8
    insults to, 126, 134–5, 136
    and litigation, 14, 67
    and sacrilege, 172–3

Clothing, 23
    laws regarding, 180–1, 182, 183
    and marriage, 33, 35

Communal bonds, 7, 9, 11, 15, 18, 32

Commune, 1, 21, 43, 123, 241, 242, 246
    administering estates of minors, 60–1
    and Ciompi revolution, 239
    confiscation of property by, 122, 270
    and confraternities, 83–4
    control of public mores, 179–81, 190, 245
    debtors of, 203, 229
    eligibility for office in, 202–4
    and exile, 63

Commune (*Cont.*)

    and the Guelfs, 84, 85, 86, 87, 88

    magistrates of, 96, 112, 139, 202

    petitions to, 17–22, 58–61, 69–70, 120–1, 171–2, 172–4, 176–7, 177–8, 209–11, 216–7, 217–8, 250–2

    and popolo minuto, 214

    power of, 74–5

    property of, 136, 149

    soldiers of, 230

    structure and function of, 3

    subject territories of, 76–7, 131, 133

    and tax assessments, 1, 82–3, 233–4

    and taxes, 25, 36, 179–80, 216–7

    and vendettas, 107

    and wars, 178

Confession,

    in criminal cases, 139, 177, 189, 198, 201, 236, 247

    in Inquisition, 254, 262, 269, 273

    religious, 210

    in violations of public mores, 181–3, 204, 206, 209

Contado (Florentine), 100, 101, 102, 103, 112, 120, 122, 123, 129, 172, 199, 203, 212, 217, 222, 241, 242, 248, 251, 257

    maladministration of, 131–2

Confraternities, 83–4

Convents. *See* Religious orders

Craft guilds. *See* Guilds

Craftsmen. *See* Artisans and craftsmen

Criminal behavior, 98, 99, 101, 103, 150–3, 156–7, 157–9, 172–4, 186–9

    See also Extortion; Forgery; Murder; Rape; Robbery; Sodomy; Vendetta

Criminal procedure, 138–78

    administration of, 140, 203–4

    appeals of sentences, 140, 142, 159–62, 170, 171, 175–6, 177–8, 209–11, 216–7, 224–8

    changes in laws regarding, 237

    executions, 73, 98, 101, 103, 142, 146, 147, 150, 153, 155, 159, 166, 167, 198, 206, 236, 245, 259, 273

    oblation, 171

    origin of, 138

    sentences, 98, 99, 101, 103, 106, 142, 146, 147, 150, 153, 155, 157, 159, 162, 166, 170, 173, 175, 189, 198, 201, 206, 209, 236, 245, 259, 261, 268, 269–70, 273

    suspension of laws regarding, 174–5, 237

    witnesses, 204

    See also Confession; Fines; Torture

Criminals, 95–106, 213

    poor, 95, 176–7, 177–8

    wealthy, 96, 121, 123–7

    young, 177–8

    See also Magnates

Death, 42–9
Debts, 214, 215, 216
    absolvement of, 216–7
    and the poor, 237
    See also Tax assessments; Wills
Documents, forged, 163–6
Dowry, 15, 16, 29–39, 67–9
    mentioned in wills, 43, 50, 51,
        52, 58
    recovery of after widowhood,
        53, 57, 58, 167

Eight on security, 186–9, 245–6,
    248–9, 250
Excommunication, 136, 265
Executor (of Florence), 96, 97,
    122, 123, 125, 126, 129,
    234
Exile, 21, 38, 49, 63, 116, 130,
    136
Extortion, 131, 132, 159–62, 247

Family, 28
    and criminal justice, 96–7,
        123–7, 249
    and death, 42–9
    enemities within, 62–73
    honor of, 26, 95, 126–7
    and marriage, 29–42
    and poverty, 19
    and property and inheritance,
        49
    and tax exemptions, 8, 10, 11,
        12, 13
Farms,
    mentioned in tax assessments,
        6, 7, 20
    mentioned in wills, 53, 54

Fines, 241, 242
    in criminal cases, 138, 175,
        177, 189
    inability to pay, 159, 175, 209
    institution of, 237
    in violations of mores, 181,
        182, 183, 184, 203–4, 209,
        210, 212, 245
Florence,
    civic spirit for, 81
    collectivities in, 74–94
    cost of living in, 2
    criminal procedure in, 139–
        78
    crisis in, 178, 213, 229–31
    in danger of God's wrath, 179,
        201–2
    economic structure of, 1–27
    family in, 27–73
    government of, 3
    money of, 2
    outgroups of, 240–73
    patron saint of, 75
    public mores in, 179–212
    violence in, 95–138
    working and poor classes in, x,
        212–39
    See also Commune
Forced loans, 21, 184, 216, 230,
    234, 237
    See also Taxes; Tax assessment
Forgery, 147–50, 162
Fraticelli, 74, 250–7, 258–9

Gambling, 117, 133, 151, 256
    control of, 178, 183–9
    quarrels over, 111, 129
Ghibellines, 74, 78, 79, 86–7, 88,
    89, 123, 238

Gonfalonieri, 229, 230
Guelfs, 21, 74, 79, 81, 86–9, 203, 238
Guilds, 90–4, 126, 213, 214, 215, 216, 236, 237, 249
  of blacksmiths, 237
  and charity, 92–3
  and Ciompi revolution, 236–9
  of cloth-manufacturers, 17, 235–6
  and confraternities, 84
  and feast days, 76
  and political community, 74, 78–81
  rivalry between, 93–4
  of wine-merchants, 90–2

Heretics, 74, 240, 250–9

Illegitimacy,
  and inheritance, 162–6
  and marriage, 40–2
  See also Legitimacy
Illness, 47–9
Inheritance and property, 49–61
  and legitimacy, 59–60
Inquisition, 252–3, 261–6, 266–73
Insanity, 168–70, 170–2
Investment, 7, 24–5, 67–9

Jews, 240–50
John the Baptist, feast day of, 75–8, 171

Legitimacy, petition for, 59–60
Litigation, 9, 14, 67, 85–6

Machiavelli, family of, 177–8
Magnates, 96, 100, 101, 108, 112, 121, 122, 123, 125, 131, 234
Manufacturing and manufacturers, 15, 184, 213, 214, 215
Marriage, 28, 29–42, 53, 67–70, 141, 142–6, 206–7
  expenses of, 51, 52
  and illegitimacy, 40–2
  negotiations concerning, 32–40, 130
Medici family, 27, 28
Merchants, 4–5, 14–5, 15–7, 22, 23, 90–2, 184, 214, 253
Mobs, 73, 79, 95, 248, 250, 252–3
Monte shares. *See* Communal bonds
Murder, 69–73, 100, 101, 102, 103, 141, 143–6, 170–1, 243–5

Notaries, 21, 203, 215, 224

Officials of the Curfew and the Convents, 203–4, 211
Ordinances of Justice, 96–7, 123

Parish, as social unit, 74
Parte Guelfa, 74, 77, 79, 80, 85–6, 86–7
  decline of, 88–9
Patriotism, 81–2
Peasants, 122–3
Physicians, 135, 182, 243–5
Pilgrims, 155
Plague, 43, 46–7, 95, 141, 230–1, 241

Podestà, 96, 102, 112, 113, 116, 119, 126, 132, 155, 165, 175, 176, 177, 186, 237
and religious persecution, 252–3, 259, 265
Poor and working classes, 24, 78, 229–33
attitudes of upper classes towards, 213
and fines, 177
oppression of, 214–22
organizations of, 74–5, 235
political power of, 214
and prison, 139–40
and taxes, 233
victims of crime, 121, 132
and violence, 95
in wills, 56, 57
See also Criminals, poor; Popolo minuto
Pope, 245, 247, 251, 254, 258–9
Popolani, 97, 108, 113, 125, 126, 203, 234, 236
Popolo, 85, 86, 112, 116, 126
captain of, 96, 107, 130–1, 159, 171, 235
insignia of, 202
Popolo minuto, 24, 213–39
Prepotenza, 120–9
Prison, 71, 78, 139–40, 153, 159, 175, 200, 231, 268
See also Prisoners; Stinche, the
Prisoners, 139, 166–8
release of, 174–5
of war, 178
See also Stinche, the, inmates of
Property, 6–13, 49–61

Prostitution, 179, 190–201, 211
See also Brothels
Public mores, 175
violations of, 150–3, 181–2, 184–6, 191–201, 204–12
See also Sodomy

Rape, 97, 102, 105, 122
Real estate, 7, 9, 10
Rectors, 131–2, 133–7
Religious enthusiasm, 174–5
Religious orders, 16, 42, 50, 55–6, 58–9, 62, 76, 206, 251
violation of convents, 179, 206–12
Religious services, 45, 47, 50, 58–9, 172
Rent, 13, 20, 190–1
Robbery, 97–8, 100, 101, 102, 153–5, 177, 246

Saints, 76, 257–8
Servants, 125, 182, 213, 217, 232
of Commune, 176, 229
in tax assessments, 5
and vendettas, 113–4
Shops, 6, 7, 8, 127
Signoria, 3, 80, 89, 114–5, 116, 124, 132, 133, 162, 166, 172, 201, 236, 237, 249
Slaves, 167, 213, 222–8
Social mobility, 14–22
Sodomy, 179, 201–6
Soldiers, 97–8, 230, 231
Sorcerers, 240, 260–73
Standard-bearers, 111–6, 128, 129, 201, 238

State, honor of, 27, 190

Stinche, the, 129, 139, 162, 171, 173, 210, 216, 217, 224, 238
  inmates of, 166–8

Strozzi family, 28, 37, 111, 125–7

Tax assessments, 4–5, 5–13, 23–4, 25, 36

Taxes, 21, 82–3, 217
  confiscatory taxation, 18–20
  and the poor, 233–4
  See also Tax assessments; Forced loans

Torture, 139, 162, 249

Trade, 9, 15, 66
  See also Merchants

University, 50

Usury, 14, 66, 69, 131, 241, 248, 256

Vendetta, 64–6, 85, 96, 105, 106–20
  authority to pursue, 113, 116
  decline of, 119–20
  and peace agreements, 107

Violence, 95–138
  abuse of authority, 130–58
  crimes, 97–106, 139–57, 159–62, 170–2, 177–8
  prepontenza, 120–9
  vendettas, 106–20

Wealth, attitudes towards, 23–7

Wills, 15, 41, 43, 44, 49–59, 62, 120, 212
  and murders, 140–1
  and vendettas, 109

Widows, 42, 44, 51, 52, 53, 57, 232, 233

Wives, 215–6
  deaths in childbirth, 30, 44–5
  insults to, 176–7
  maltreatment of, 69
  murders of, 140–2, 142–6
  and prostitution, 199
  in wills, 43, 50, 51, 57, 58

Women,
  and clothing, 180, 181, 182, 183
  and concubinage, 59, 218–222
  as criminals, 140–2, 142–6, 146–7, 167, 175–6
  and feast days, 76, 77
  and inheritance, 53
  as insane, 168–70
  insults to, 133
  and marriage arrangements, 33, 34, 35, 37
  as servants, 218–22
  as slaves, 223–8
  as sorcerers, 260–1, 270–3
  and statutes, 193
  and vendettas, 65–6, 109
  See also Prostitution; Rape; Widows; Wives

Working classes. See Poor and working classes; Popolo minuto